SELLING
to
EUROPE

*A Practical Guide to Doing Business
in the Single Market*

ROGER BENNETT

KOGAN
PAGE

First published in 1991

Kogan Page Limited
120 Pentonville Road
London N1 9JN

© Roger Bennett 1991

British Library Cataloguing in Publication Data

A CIP record for this book is available from the British Library.

ISBN 0-7494-0392-6

Typeset by Saxon Printing Ltd, Derby
Printed and bound in Great Britain by
Biddles Ltd, Guildford

Contents

Acknowledgements   8

1. Introduction   9

2. Researching the Single Market   15

3. Advertising in the European Community   45

4. European Direct Marketing, Exhibitions, and Sales
    Promotions   64

5. Getting Goods to the Continent   80

6. Logistics, Agents and Continental Distribution   109

7. Establishing a Permanent Presence in the European
    Community   122

8. Pricing, Insurance and Getting Paid   141

9. The French Connection   164

10. Germany: Powerhouse of the European Community   179

11. Benelux   194

12. Italy   211

13. Doing Business in Spain   218

14. The Smaller EC Markets: Ireland and Denmark   229

15. The Developing Markets: Portugal and Greece   242

Index   252

Acknowledgements

My thanks are due to Rosalind Bailey who word-processed the entire manuscript. I am grateful also to the following organisations for providing valuable help and information during the preparation of the text:

The Advertising Association
BAA Ltd
British Airways Cargo
British Telecom International
Euro Tunnel
The Export Credits Guarantee Department
The Institute of Linguists
The Institute of Practitioners in Advertising
The Institute of Translation and Interpreting
The Market Research Society
P&O Ferrymasters Ltd
Railfreight Distribution
Royal Mail International

Although every effort has been made to ensure the accuracy of the addresses and telephone numbers of the contact points listed in the text, neither the author nor the publisher can guarantee that they have not altered since the book went to press. It is particularly unwise to make international telephone calls without first confirming with International Directory Enquiries that the numbers listed are correct. Moreover, the ranges, costs and contents of the services provided by various organisations described in the text are liable to change periodically.

Chapter 1

Introduction

Large multinational businesses have enormous advantages over small to medium-sized enterprises where preparation for trading in the European Single Market is concerned. They have the resources needed to engage specialist outside consultants; can hire in-house marketing and distribution managers dedicated to European Community work; can employ documentation clerks and accountants familiar with foreign exchange trading, and so on. Big companies, moreover, are far more likely to have experience of selling overseas than smaller firms.

Nevertheless, the creation of the European Single Market will affect – directly or indirectly – *every* business in Britain, regardless of its size. The fundamental frameworks that for generations have regulated UK business activity have changed. Consider, for instance, the facts that:

- UK company law has been and will continue to be altered to correspond to harmonised European Community rules;

- compulsory EC technical product standards (see Chapter 2) will apply to *all* UK firms;

- British laws on competition, mergers and acquisitions, distribution and agency (see Chapter 6) are all subject to EC regulation;

- under the new regime the UK businesses that British firms currently supply may themselves obtain their input requirements from efficient, low price and aggressive Continental companies;

- actual and intended EC Directives on advertising (see Chapter 3), direct marketing and sales promotion (see Chapter 4) are fast redefining the scope and operations of the marketing services industries.

The challenge to small firms

Small businesses have much to contribute to the new Europe. They are flexible, dynamic, innovative; respond quickly to market forces, and represent an important vehicle for increasing employment, output and technological development within the Community. Indeed, firms with fewer than 500 employees account for half of all EC employment, and no less than 80 per cent of total Community GDP. It is essential, therefore, that the managers of small to medium-sized enterprises are as familiar with European trading as their counterparts in larger firms.

Although the full impact of the European Single Market (ESM) on UK businesses is uncertain and will not be realised for several years, certain short-term effects can be easily predicted. The following are worthy of special mention:

(a)   A wider choice of products will be available to your UK customers, who may choose to purchase items supplied from other EC countries.

(b)   Even if you decide not to bother selling to the Single Market, competitors probably will; and the contacts and experience they acquire through doing business in Europe is likely to give them a competitive edge in Britain.

(c)   New Community-wide standards may compel you to alter the sizes, shapes, ingredients, safety features and other characteristics of your products.

(d)   Initially, markets will fragment into many more sub-units than exist at present, and there will be intense competition to rationalise and dominate these smaller market segments, particularly in relation to control over distribution channels and outlets.

(e)   Increased competition will lead to faster environmental change *vis-à-vis* business methods and technological development.

(f)   You can now have your goods delivered to UK destinations using non-UK road haulage firms.

(g)   The business may begin receiving written and telephone enquiries in foreign languages.

(h)   You may need to alter your product packaging to cater for metric measurements and multi-language labelling.

(i)   New approaches to marketing research are needed to investigate foreign EC markets.

(j)   Your traditional suppliers may lose interest in your business as they pursue larger and more lucrative Continental contracts.

(k)   Continental businesses may approach your firm to ask whether you are interested in entering a joint venture.

(l)   Selling to EC customers and allowing them to pay in their own currencies means you have to know about the methods for protecting against the effects of exchange rate fluctuations.

(m)   Existing promotional literature will need translating and modifying to make it suitable for European markets.

(n)   If your firm relies heavily on local authority or other public sector contracts you stand to lose this business to EC rivals. Admittedly, the new rules on public procurement (see Chapter 2) only apply to contracts over a certain value; but the introduction of free competition at the higher level is sure to encourage a new *attitude* towards purchasing by public bodies which will affect all aspects of their buying policies, including their relations with small supplying firms.

(o)   A competitor from another EC country may arrive in Britain and form a restrictive agreement with one or more of your major suppliers in order to block off your input supplies. Thus you need to know whether the arrangement is legal under EC law (see Chapter 6) and, if it is not, how to complain to the authorities.

(p)   Cheaper and higher quality raw materials and other inputs may be available from Continental firms.

(q)   Enhanced business communication between EC countries increases the possibility of your products, ideas or trademarks being pirated and sold by other EC companies. Hence you may need to take extra measures to protect your intellectual property.

(r)   The Single Market has about 320 million consumers. Potential for increasing the scale of operations of a small firm ready, willing and able to participate in EC business is enormous.

Note that under the *Schengen agreement* six EC countries (France, Germany, Benelux and Italy) have agreed to abolish all border controls, making for easier trade and movement of goods within the group but, equally, causing considerable difficulty for outsiders who wish to get in! Spain and Portugal have also applied for membership of the agreement.

What you will learn from reading this book

Whether you are enthralled or horrified by the implications of the European Single Market, you cannot afford to ignore them. Continental European businesses, alas, are generally far better at selling to the UK than are British firms at selling on the Continent. European products have, on the whole, a good reputation in the UK for value, quality, reliability, sound after-sales service, and useful and attractive features. The converse, regrettably, is not always the case.

This book will help you to devise practical policies for advertising, marketing, selling and distributing goods in the Single Market. My objective is to give you the key facts and contacts you need in order to beat the competition in the new regime. You will learn about the ways and means of transporting your output to Continental destinations, the options available, and the criteria to be used in making a choice. Direct marketing to Europe is explained, including the availability of lists for Continental maildrops and the direct marketing rules of various member countries.

After reading the book you will know about EC exclusive distribution agreements, agency laws and franchise arrangements, Continental ware-housing, and if you sell on credit (and you will almost certainly have to do so) how to get paid. You will be told how to research European markets; the essential characteristics of various categories of EC consumers; and the government help and financial assistance available in these respects. Many UK businesses will need to consider the viability and implications of establishing branch offices and subsidiaries in EC states. Accordingly, the procedures for doing this are outlined. Each EC market outside the UK is briefly described, with particular emphasis on Britain's most important Continental markets: Germany and France.

The completion of the Channel Tunnel in 1993 will profoundly affect transportation arrangements between Britain, France and all other Conti-nental destinations. Channel Tunnel freight systems, procedures, cost and delivery implications are discussed, including the consequences of the Tunnel for existing Ro-Ro ferry and airline services.

Coping with the ESM: a strategy checklist

It should be obvious already that every UK business needs a strategic action plan for coping with the threats and opportunities presented by the Single Market. To succeed in Europe you have to discover *where* to do business (see Chapter 2), *how* to attract custom (see Chapters 3 and 4), and the best means for carrying and distributing goods (see Chapters 5 and 6). You need to adopt an *international perspective*; to think and act as a citizen of Europe as well as the UK. This requires your being aware of the main *Euro legislation* affecting business; of the opportunities that a market of 320 million potential customers provides; and the threats of increasing foreign EC competition. You must establish where your firm and its output stand in relation to other businesses and products, and how to position your output relative to that of competing firms.

To test your awareness of the need for a European strategy, ask yourself the following questions:

(a)   What will happen to your company's profits if it does not bother to do business in the new Europe?

(b)   What are the likely consequences of competitor Continental firms expanding their operations here in Britain?

(c)   How will mergers and acquisitions among competitors affect your competitive position?

(d)   How suitable is your product for immediate sale in Continental markets?

(e)   What do you currently know about opportunities for selling the firm's output on the Continent? Do you know what you need to know, and where to find the information you require?

(f) Looking ahead two or three years, and taking into account the fact that EC companies will be attacking your markets on equal terms, how competitive will your products be here in the UK in respect of their:

- price;
- features;
- quality;
- value for money in customers' eyes?

(g) Have you established whether your products will need repackaging to enhance their appeal to Continental customers? If not, do you know how to find out whether this is the case?

(h) Have you predicted Continental competitors' strategies for capturing your current markets? If not, why not? Have you devised an action plan for dealing with possible Continental competition?

(i) How extensive is your present knowledge of Continental advertising media, distribution options, regional consumer tastes and business practices?

(j) Have you considered the methods and problems of distributing goods over a wide geographical area? Would local warehousing be required? Are you aware of how Continental warehousing can be arranged?

(k) How might your cash flow be affected by changes in trading patterns caused by the completion of the Single Market?

(l) Do you currently possess a foreign currency bank account? If not, are you aware of the advantages and drawbacks of having this type of account?

(m) How will your supply costs and profit margins be affected by increases in output resulting from your entry to European markets?

An action plan

Many UK companies, alas, will not survive the enormous changes due to occur in European business. To make sure that yours is not one of the firms that go under, implement immediately (if you have not already done something similar) the following action plan:

(a) Itemise the management skills required for your firm's successful entry to EC markets. These may include language skills, export documentation and administration, trading in foreign currency, familiarity with European advertising media, etc. List the training necessary for the business's staff to become expert in each of these areas.

(b)   Review the firm's product range and, where necessary, redesign products to make them appeal to wider European markets.

(c)   Analyse Continental competitors' marketing strategies.

(d)   Establish an effective information-gathering system to collect new data on EC-related developments affecting the business, eg by subscribing to one of the data-gathering agencies described in Chapter 2 and/or identifying the sources of key items of relevant information. Sources may include trade directories; on-line services provided by Chambers of Commerce or trade associations; government-funded research schemes, etc.

(e)   Analyse current EC product standard legislation (see Chapter 2) affecting your output and amend production processes to ensure your goods comply with Community product standard requirements.

(f)   Identify the market segments in EC countries most likely to buy the firm's products, and assess the best ways of reaching these potential customers.

(g)   Become familiar with the options, procedures and costs of transporting goods to European destinations.

(h)   Redraft existing sales literature to make it suitable for use in other European countries.

(i)   If appropriate, locate the best possible centres for warehousing your goods on the Continent.

(j)   Examine the changes in operating costs likely to result from new transport, distribution and other logistics procedures.

(k)   Identify EC locations suitable for the establishment of local administrative offices, manufacturing, packaging and labelling facilities, etc, and study the regional investment incentives (see Chapters 9–15) available in these areas.

(l)   Redraft your sales and purchasing contracts to ensure they correspond to EC contract law.

(m)   Develop market research facilities (see Chapter 2) for investigating various EC markets.

(n)   Identify new, better and cheaper sources of input supply from Continental Europe.

The book will help you in all these activities.

Chapter 2

Researching the Single Market

Collecting market information on all 11 foreign EC markets is a potentially colossal task that could totally dominate your EC marketing efforts, crowding out other important tasks. Thus, a logical, disciplined and structured approach to market research is required. The first step is to decide *which* European markets to enter. Second, you have to establish *what you need to know* about each market. Third, you must identify the main sources of information on chosen countries, and know where to go for government and other support. The aim is to match the *strengths* of your business with the *opportunities* that exist for selling to the Community.

Choosing markets

There is no way an inexperienced exporter can successfully tackle *all* EC countries simultaneously, so you need a mechanism for screening out 'no hope' markets. Two approaches to the location of suitable countries and/or market segments within countries are available, as follows:

1. Define carefully the characteristics of the European consumers most likely to buy your product and then examine EC countries sequentially, picking out those which contain large numbers of that consumer type.

Alternatively:

2. Determine the EC markets in which it will be easiest to sell the company's product (eg, because a significant proportion of the population speaks English, or since local business methods are essentially similar to those found in the UK) and deliberately adapt the firm's output and advertising messages to make them suitable for these markets.

Adoption of either of these approaches does not necessarily rule out the other, and plain common sense may enable you immediately to select suitable countries and target consumer types. Normally, however, a significant amount of 'desk research' is required.

What you need to know
The following factors may be relevant to your choice of markets, depending
on the nature of the firm's output and the intended scale of your European
operations.

(a)   The sizes of various market segments; their buoyancy and prospects
       for expansion.
(b)   Demographic structures of prospective markets in terms of age, sex
       composition, family structure, geographical spread of the popula-
       tion, and so on.
(c)   Market stability; local rates of inflation and economic growth.
(d)   Whether local cultural norms and values may affect consumer
       perceptions of your product, and if so the implications of this for how
       you need to sell your goods.
(e)   Consumer tastes, lifestyles and spending patterns.
(f)   Average local incomes and the distribution of wealth; living stan-
       dards, housing, education, etc.
(g)   Number of competitors, their strengths and weaknesses and modes
       of response to rival firms' activities.
(h)   Competitor's prices, product quality, credit terms, delivery periods,
       after-sales service, and so on.
(i)   How easily you can monitor competitors' behaviour (price changes,
       product modifications, etc).
(j)   How frequently competitors change their prices. (This is a crude
       indicator of the stability of the local market and the extent to which
       local firms do actually compete.)
(k)   The selling points that competitors stress in their local advertising,
       and why these characteristics are emphasised.
(l)   Technical product standards (see page 36) and labelling
       requirements.
(m)   Local preferences regarding package size, colouring and design;
       weights and volumes, shapes and ease of disposal, etc.
(n)   Local taxation arrangements, investment grants for establishing
       subsidiaries and/or owned distribution outlets (see Chapters 9–15).
(o)   Nature of local distribution channels, especially the number and
       calibre of retail outlets.
(p)   Availability of commercial services (advertising agencies, debt
       collectors, warehousing facilities, and so on).
(q)   Frequency and whereabouts of local trade fairs and exhibitions.
(r)   The geographical locations of the Continental consumers most likely
       to purchase your output.
(s)   The advertising messages and promotional literature to which local
       customers will positively respond.
(t)   Quality of local transport systems.
(u)   Design features of competitors' outputs.

Where to begin

The Department of Trade and Industry (DTI) operates an 'All European Community' desk (tel: 071–215 5549) that may be able to advise on markets especially suitable for your type of product, and a short telephone call to the DTI may be all that is required. Normally, however, some legwork is necessary, beginning perhaps with an assessment of the EC markets within which your type of product is *already* selling well.

A useful starting point is the publication *British Exports* (Kompass Ltd, see page 22) which lists the major products exported from the UK, plus the names and addresses of major exporters in each product category and the overseas areas they serve. You can quickly establish the main markets to which existing exporters are currently sending particular types of goods. If you advertise in the *British Exports* directory your details will also appear on-line through BT's *Telecom Gold, Dialog,* and *Istel* databases, which can reach potential buyers worldwide.

Europ Production is another useful publication. It is a multilingual register of European exports arranged by product, industry, company and country. Subscription details are available from:

Unternehmensgruppe
ABC-Verlagshaus
Postfach 4034
Berliner Allee 8
D–6100 Darmstadt 1

For those who feel comfortable delving into government statistics, a general overview of which UK products are being sold in large quantity in which foreign markets is contained in a monthly HMSO publication, *Overseas Trade Statistics of the United Kingdom,* which you could have a quick look at in order to establish the main countries where products like yours are most likely to succeed. The extent of other nations' exports of these products to these countries can be ascertained from the *Statistics of Foreign Trade,* published by OECD. Only the largest public libraries stock these documents, but all libraries belong to networks that can direct you to where they can be found (a nearby polytechnic library, for instance).

The Export Market Information Library (EMIL)
This houses the most comprehensive collection of foreign economic statistics and market information in the UK. It has up-to-date statistics on foreign markets published by HMSO and UK trade associations, British and foreign trade directories (covering specific European industrial as well as geographical markets), locally published foreign production statistics, demographic information on various EC regions, market reports and

economic forecasts for particular European industries and EC member states.

The library (address below) also holds the complete telephone directories of all EC countries and (most important) many hundreds of publicity catalogues published by European firms. Mail order catalogues of the main EC suppliers are held and may be issued on loan. Trade directories and trade fair catalogues providing the names and addresses of major importers to various countries, important government departments, and details of major purchasing agents in various EC countries may also be available.

EMIL is organised into country sections, and you are expected to look things up for yourself. EMIL staff will direct you towards relevant market research studies and other useful information but cannot undertake statistical research on your behalf. However, the library is prepared to supply a list of independent consultants who may (for a charge) be prepared to undertake research for your firm.

The Product Data Store (PDS)

This contains market information on about 3500 types of product exported from Britain, organised into product categories. The PDS obtains its information from the EC trade press, EC trade association reports, industry surveys conducted by EC banks and from special market reports prepared by British Embassy officials. Use of the PDS may enable you to determine suitable target markets for your output and then to gather important data on the characteristics of competing products already available there. Careful study of competitors' brochures and/or locally produced mail order catalogues helps you to determine differences among competitors' selling points and marketing methods and how you need to adopt your promotional messages to suit local demand.

Product Data Store
Export Market Information Library
1 Victoria Street
(Entrance in Abbey Orchard Street)
London SW1H 0ET
071-215 7877

Customs numbers
Prior to beginning a product search it is useful (sometimes essential) to know the customs categorisation number for your output, since much useful research data is catalogued in this way.

Since 1988 a Harmonised Commodity Coding System (HS) has operated, which contains a special classification scheme (referred to as TARIC) for the new integrated tariff procedures that now apply to the EC. HS numbers are available from a Guide, published annually by HMSO. You may find this in

your local library; otherwise you need to contact the classification office of
HM Customs and Excise, or EMIL.

HM Customs and Excise
Tariff Classification Section
King's Beam House
Mark Lane
London EC3R 1HE
071-620 1313

Further sources of information

Euro information centres
The Community has established a number of *Centres for European Business
Information* in the UK and all other EC countries. These exist to provide
businesses with data and (limited) advice on Community activities including:

- EC grants and other sources of financial assistance;

- new EC legislation;

- updates on product standardisation;

- community industrial research and training facilities.

Centres are not consultancy organisations *per se,* but should be able to direct
enquiring firms towards further sources of help and information.
Britain now has numerous Euro information centres spread around the
country. You can obtain the address of the one nearest you from the DTI's
European 'All Country Desk' or from a DTI regional or satellite office (see
page 28). Centres hold all official EC documents, including the *Official
Journal of the European Community,* which contains full details of every
major public sector contract made available for tender within the EC.
(Tendering procedures are described later in the chapter, page 38.) EC
commissioned industry/sector studies, which frequently contain valuable
material for market research, are also held in these centres.

Services provided by banks
Most UK high street banks have European trade divisions that publish
country profiles, tips to exporters, and (of course) extensive material on
methods of international payment. Banks, moreover, are sometimes
prepared to organise elementary research into intended European markets
on their customers' behalf, eg by having their European branch in a foreign
locality ascertain current prices of competing products, collect the sales

literature of local competing businesses, look up local trade statistics, etc. Also, the bank's European branch will probably be able to introduce you to local business contacts such as advertising agents, distributors, etc, if you decide to visit the market at a later stage.

General

Trade associations and Chambers of Commerce are obviously useful for obtaining information and advice. Even if they do not hold relevant data themselves they will almost certainly be able to refer you to a specialist source. Also, employers' organisations such as the Confederation of British Industries (CBI) (see page 39) and the Institute of Directors offer library facilities which include numerous books, reports and directories on European markets, as do the libraries of the Chartered Institute of Marketing and the British Institute of Management. You must, of course, be a member of such organisations in order to use their facilities.

Institute of Directors
116 Pall Mall
London SW1Y 5ED
071-839 1233

British Institute of Management
Management House
Cottingham Road
Corby
Northamptonshire NN17 7TT
0536 204222

Chartered Institute of Marketing
Moor Hall
Cookham
Berkshire SL6 9QH
06285 24922

Analysis of potential markets

Contact with the DTI, a Chamber of Commerce, a trade association and/or one or more of the previously mentioned organisations should, in conjunction with a preliminary assessment of the available market data, provide you with a rough guide to the countries in which your product is most likely to succeed. Now ask the following questions in relation to each candidate market.

- Will the geographical spread of target customers in that country assist or hinder the distribution of the product?

- Does the firm's output appeal to particular age or income groups and, if so, are there sufficient numbers of these people in the country?

- What is the extent of competition in the market and do local businesses enjoy advantages you will find difficult to overcome (control of local distribution channels, for example)?

- Do any special taxes apply to the sale of your category of product in that country?

- If the product is technically complicated, will you be able to find local representatives who are trained, qualified and capable of understanding the item?

- How easily can you warehouse supplies of your product near to customer outlets?

- What regional development grants (see Chapters 9–15) are available for establishing branches/subsidiaries in that country?

- How similar are market conditions to those prevailing in the UK?

Now select your markets, and then telephone the appropriate DTI 'Country Desks' of the countries concerned and ask for the *Country Guides* for those countries. Tell the DTI about the firm, its products and intentions, and request copies of any further DTI handouts and/or market survey data potentially relevant to your requirements.

All the EC individual country desks are located at the DTI Head Office at 1–9 Victoria Street, London SW1H 0ET. The telephone numbers are as follows.

Belgium and Luxembourg	071-215 5486
Denmark	071-215 5140
France	071-215 4762
Germany	071-215 4796
Greece	071-215 5103
Ireland	071-215 4783
Italy	071-215 5103
The Netherlands	071-215 4790
Portugal	071-215 5307
Spain	071-215 5624
Enquiries concerning more than one EC country (the 'All Country Desk')	071-215 5549

DTI *Country Guides* used to be free but are now chargeable. Currently (1991) they cost about £10.

It is important to identify major consortium buyers (addresses of purchasing offices of chains of department stores for example) of your types of product in target countries. The DTI can usually tell you where to locate lists of these. Additionally, *Kompass* directories, to be found in most main libraries, can be invaluable here. There are *Kompass* directories of firms and products for all EC countries.

Kompass Publishers
Windsor Court
East Grinstead House
East Grinstead
West Sussex RH19 1XA
0342 326692

Dun and Bradstreet also publish directories of companies in several EC states.

Dun and Bradstreet International Ltd
Holmers Farm Way
High Wycombe
Buckinghamshire HP12 4UL
0494 422000

Get hold of catalogues, brochures and other publicity materials issued by local mail order houses and competing firms. This will give you an insight into local consumer perspectives on the item you have to offer and the selling points attached to popular lines. (In a sense, a mail order company has already conducted research into consumer preferences on your behalf!)

It may also be worthwhile looking at some of the guides to 'Doing Business in ...' various EC countries published by the accounting firm Price Waterhouse.

Price Waterhouse
Southwark Towers
32 London Bridge Road
London SE1 9SY
071-407 8989

Private information-gathering agencies

Confronted with the enormity, complexity and diversity of information about European business and changes in EC commercial rules and practices, some firms subscribe to one or more of the private databases currently available to help enterprises cope with the effects and implications of the Single Market. These usually consist of a bank of core information, supplemented by weekly, monthly or quarterly updates on recent developments and how these may affect client firms. This saves having to undertake continuous research in a rapidly changing area, and relevant information is condensed and interpreted by experts in the field.

Data comes either on looseleaf sheets for insertion in binders or through a direct computer link. The best known looseleaf provider is Croner Ltd, which publishes *Croner's Europe*. This has (excellent) summaries of the latest developments on harmonisation of standards; taxation; company, employment and consumer law; and transport. It is available in most libraries or through direct subscription.

Croner Publications Ltd
Croner House
London Road
Kingston upon Thames
Surrey KT2 6SR
081-547 3333

The American division of Croner publishes a first class international directory of directories, entitled *Trade Directories of the World*. It is available from:

Croner USA
211–05 Jamaica Avenue
Queen's Village
New York
NY 11428
010 1 212 464 0866

Other looseleaf information providers advertise in trade journals and (where this is permitted) in publications sponsored by the DTI (*Single Market News,* for example). Subscriptions cost between £100 and £400 per annum at 1991 prices. These publications vary in content, so make sure they meet your specific requirements before placing an order (suppliers are normally willing to send a free sample extract from a recent issue to help you decide whether you wish to subscribe).

The volume of information about the Single Market can be overwhelming. Hence these services are extremely valuable in that they pick out the *important* points about current EC developments: new laws and their implications, tax changes, availability of EC grants and subsidies, information about public procurement contracts available for tender, significant changes in market structures, etc.

Computerised databases
These are more expensive, but update the information available to subscribers immediately it emerges from Brussels and/or government offices in the UK. Additional facilities include:

- complete copies of EC laws, Directives, Regulations and Proposals;

- access to further more specialised databases;

- details of EC contracts available for tender in specialised fields;

- facts and figures on mergers and acquisitions in particular industries;

- up-to-the-minute news on the availability of grants and other invest-ment incentives in EC nations;

- the ability to extract information on a particular topic using just one or two key words. You enter a couple of words relating to the subject, and a list of references about it appears on the screen.

Computerised EC databases are available from commercial companies. To establish which on-line databases may be useful contact:

Aslib Information Resources Centre
26–27 Boswell Street
London WC1N 3JZ
071-430 2671

Also, look for the advertisements of database suppliers in government publications and in trade and Chamber of Commerce magazines. The DTI also has a system, called SPEARHEAD, which is described on page 31.

Segmenting European markets

The European Community has 320 million consumers. Some will be more interested in buying your product than others, so you need to discover the *type* of person most likely to purchase your firm's output in terms of such variables as consumer age, sex, income, family size, living standards, lifestyle, buying habits, attitudes and geographical location.

Market segmentation means breaking down the total market into self-contained and relatively homogeneous sub-groups of consumers, each possessing its own special requirements and characteristics. This enables you to modify your output, advertising messages and promotional methods to correspond to the needs of particular segments.

The aim is to distinguish specific consumer groups (eg high income, middle-aged women with no children living at home, who work in offices, have received a certain level of education, and who cook using electricity) within which potential customers are as homogeneous as possible and then devise advertisements and sales promotions (see Chapters 3 and 4) and select styles, prices, package designs, quantities and quality levels suitable for those markets. Accurate segmentation enables you to pinpoint selling opportunities and to tailor your marketing activities to satisfy consumer needs.

Characteristics of European consumers
Europe contains many cultural, societal, socio-economic and other group-ings, and European consumer behaviour is extremely diverse. Not sur-prisingly therefore, several attempts at analysing EC cultural and attitudinal differences have been made in order to define the precise whereabouts of various target consumer categories. Three questions need to be asked.

1.   What are European consumers like?
2.   Where are the different consumer types located?
3.   What must be done to reach particular segments?

Note immediately that Europeans, on average, are getting older. This results from declining birth rates and increased longevity in most Com-munity states. There are in consequence many more middle-aged people than previously, fewer large families, and a reduced demand for teenage and other young people's products.

Analysis of European consumer lifestyles
Consumers' lifestyles, attitudes, interests, perspectives and opinions fre-quently affect purchasing behaviour. It seems that consumers often buy goods they feel they *ought* to purchase in order to pursue a particular lifestyle, rather than products they objectively need! 'Vicarious participa-tion' in a certain desired way of life (eg healthy, sophisticated, outdoor, 'man-about-town', etc) is sometimes possible via consuming goods mentally associated with the lifestyle to which the individual aspires. Hence, if you can identify the lifestyle characteristics (real or imagined) of consumers likely to buy your goods then you can focus your promotional and general marketing efforts in the most cost-effective manner.

European lifestyles have been analysed and classified into a number of categories. The aim is to identify in consumers certain common characteris-tics, such as:

● whether they are motivated by materialistic or non-materialistic drives;

● the extent to which their main concern is merely to exist and survive rather than engage in luxury and/or conspicuous consumption;

- whether their outlooks are 'conservative and traditional' or whether they are 'innovative and adventurous';

- the degree of logic and rationality they apply to purchasing decisions;

- whether they are 'inner directed' (ie concerned with personal growth, individual freedom and human relations) or 'outer directed' materialists who gain greater satisfaction from physical consumption of goods;

- attitudes towards home, family, security and the propriety of the status quo.

For each of these dimensions a number of sub-categories may be discerned (eg ambitious achievers; the near destitute struggling poor; the materialistic young, etc) within various EC countries. Then the particular characteristics of each group in each market can be described and the geographical whereabouts of such consumers pinpointed. Accordingly, it becomes possible to draw the map of Europe not according to national frontiers, but rather in terms of the locations of specific types of consumer. With European consumers neatly categorised in these ways it may be feasible to launch a variety of pan-European products, each slightly modified to appeal to particular customer categories.

Some of these studies have been published and are available in academic libraries.[1] Others must be (expensively) purchased from commercial market research companies – usually accompanied by detailed consultancy assistance. Note, however, that all these studies and taxonomies rest on the basic assumption that consumers have *consistent* values, beliefs and attitudes that are not subject to sudden and unpredictable change. Casual observation of human behaviour suggests that this is not always true.

Field trips

Field trips enable you to conduct market research *in situ*, to establish direct personal contacts with local people (agents, consular officials, media representatives, etc) who can help you to sell the goods, and generally get the feel of local business conditions. Most important, you can assess the extent of local competition at first hand. Specifically, you will want to assess:

[1.] For a comprehensive survey of these see *Trends and Management Issues in European Retailing* by Steven Burt (MCB University Press, 1989).

- the market impacts of various local competitors;
- brand images of competitors' products;
- the prices, discounts and credit terms that competitors offer;
- competitors' advertising and sales promotion strategies;
- how competitors distribute their goods.

In practice the commonest reasons for field trips are (a) to respond to promising customer enquiries, (b) to visit trade exhibitions (see Chapter 4), or (c) to set up distribution systems and/or local operations via agents, joint ventures, sister companies (see Chapter 7), and so on. Additionally, a field trip gives you an excellent opportunity to visit local retail outlets, and perhaps talk to representatives of other British businesses operating in the area. Details of public holidays, customary business hours, local etiquette, etc for each EC country are contained in booklets, *Hints for Exporters,* available (at £5 each) from the DTI.

A planned itinerary is essential. Arm yourself with a long list of *specific* questions to answer during the visit and with the names and addresses of people you need to see. The DTI will help you to organise the trip, for which financial assistance may be available (see page 30). The DTI will inform the local British Embassy or consulate of your impending visit, and may suggest additions to your programme. It can help you to meet potential agents, representatives of the local Chamber of Commerce, the corresponding branch of your own bank,[2] and other important business contacts.

Research help from the DTI

The DTI provides a range of information and market intelligence services, based mainly on data collected by the commercial sections of UK Diplomatic Posts in foreign countries. The information includes names, addresses and product interests of EC companies, retailers, agents and distributors; directories and trade publications; magazine articles, press cuttings and industry reports; and details of forthcoming trade exhibitions. You can access most of this information through DTI regional and satellite offices, or directly via SPEARHEAD (see page 31) or by a personal visit to the DTI's Export Market Information Centre.

---

[2] UK banks either have their own branches in foreign towns and cities, or enter into arrangements whereby local foreign banks act on their behalf. In return the UK banks provide the latter with comparable services here in Britain.

DTI regional and satellite offices should be given in your local telephone directory. For handy reference their current numbers are listed below.

North East:	Cleveland	0642 232220
	Newcastle upon Tyne	091-232 4722
North West:	Crewe	0270 500706
	Kendal	0539 723067
	Liverpool	051-224 6300
	Manchester	061-838 5000
	Preston	0772 653000
Yorkshire and Humberside:	Hull	0482 465741
	Leeds	0532 443171
	Sheffield	0742 729849
East Midlands:	Chesterfield	0246 239905
	Derby	0332 290487
	Leicester	0533 531245
	Lincoln	0522 512002
	Northampton	0604 21051
	Nottingham	0602 506181
West Midlands:	Birmingham	021-631 6181
	Droitwich	0905 794056
	Stoke on Trent	0782 285171
	Telford	0952 290422
South West:	Bristol	0272 272666
South East:	London	071-215 0574

(This is a satellite office and not the head office in Victoria Street.)

	Chatham	0634 828688
	Margate	0843 290511
	Portsmouth	0705 294111
	Reading	0734 395600
	Reigate	0737 226900
East:	Cambridge	0223 461939
	Chelmsford	0245 492385
	Ipswich	0473 212313
	Norwich	0603 761294
Scotland:	Glasgow	041-242 5495
Wales:	Cardiff	0222 825097
Northern Ireland:	Belfast	0232 233233

The London number for general enquiries is 071-215 5000. The DTI's head office address for EC-related queries is:

DTI Exports to Europe Branch
1–19 Victoria Street
London SW1H 0ET

At the time of writing, the DTI publishes a *Guide to Practical Advice for Business* specifically related to the Single Market. National and regional versions of the booklet are available, which list the names and addresses of Chambers of Commerce, small firms organisations, language advisers, professional bodies, etc with interests in the EC. The services offered by each organisation (eg advice on Community employment law, market research, agency finding facilities) are briefly mentioned. You can obtain these booklets through your local DTI office.

State assistance for foreign marketing research is available via the DTI's *Market Information Enquiry Service,* the *Export Intelligence Service,* the *Export Marketing Research Scheme,* and the *Overseas Status Report* and *New Products from Britain* services. Facilities offered by the *Enterprise Initiative* (see page 41) may also be relevant.

The Market Information Enquiry Service
This uses the services of UK Diplomatic Posts in foreign countries to answer UK exporters' *specific* questions relating to:

- local legislation;
- market prospects for particular products;
- characteristics of relevant local industries;
- economic information.

The service will also provide lists of local buyers, agents and distributors, but will not contact them. You pay (1991 charge) £30 to access the system plus an hourly fee depending on the amount of work involved in assembling the information (eg £60 for up to four hours' work). Answers to queries normally (but not necessarily) arrive within four weeks.

Export market intelligence
The DTI's *Export Intelligence Service (EIS)* gathers, collates and distributes to UK exporters information obtained by the commercial sections of British Diplomatic Service Posts in foreign countries. The service is updated daily. Information provided includes overseas enquiries for various types of product, calls for tender, foreign agents wanting to represent British firms,

background market information, etc. To use EIS you have to subscribe direct, or belong to a trade association or Chamber of Commerce that already has a subscription. Each subscriber submits a 'profile' to the system itemising the sorts of information required (markets, products, etc). The EIS computer then matches its daily information inputs with these profiles and prints out the information relevant to each subscriber. This information is sent out by first class post, fax or E-mail. Direct computer access is available via Profile Information (see page 31). You pay a small fee for each item of intelligence sent to your business.

Export Marketing Research Scheme
The DTI will pay up to half the total cost of commissioning a consultant to undertake overseas market research, plus a third of the cost of purchasing published marketing research data. If you belong to a trade association which does or commissions research on your behalf the DTI will pay up to 75 per cent of the cost. The costs of researching technical standards requirements for certain types of equipment are also repayable.

The scheme offers free professional advice on how to set about conducting in-house research into foreign markets. Certain exceptions apply to the EMRS, namely:

- grant assisted costs in excess of £20,000 (£60,000 for research conducted by a trade association);

- costs of general directories and for updating subscriptions to journals;

- companies with more than 200 workers;

- firms that have already used the scheme more than three times;

- background research that is not part of a specific project;

- sales or promotional visits.

To use EMRS you need to approach the Association of British Chambers of Commerce (ABCC), which manages the scheme on behalf of the DTI.

ABCC
Export Marketing Research Scheme
4 Westwood House
Westwood Business Park
Coventry CV4 8HS
0203 694484

The Active Exporting Scheme
This was launched by the ABCC in collaboration with the DTI in 1990. It

was based on 'Export Development Advisers' attached to local UK Chambers of Commerce and sought (a) to identify firms with the potential to export and (b) to provide them with both short-run practical advice and with long-term assistance. Details are available from the ABCC.

DTI help with finding buyers
The DTI will provide financial assistance to trade associations or Chambers of Commerce that invite foreigners, who are capable of influencing the purchase of UK goods, to visit Britain. The 'Inward Mission' scheme, as it is called, will advise on organisational aspects of the visit and will pay:

- 50 per cent of foreign visitors' travel costs, including relevant travel within the UK;

- 50 per cent of interpreting fees (see Chapter 3);

- visitors' accommodation and meals (up to £50 per night);

- half the costs of a reception, lunch or dinner for briefing or debriefing foreign guests.

For further information contact the DTI's Fairs and Promotions Branch (see Chapter 4).

SPEARHEAD
This is the DTI's on-line database. It provides brief summaries of current and intended Single Market measures, including Directives and Proposals on health and safety at work, employee and consumer protection, social aspects, etc. SPEARHEAD also gives access to the complete texts of all EC legislation. Information is updated weekly.

You can subscribe to SPEARHEAD directly or use it via one of the increasing number of Chambers of Commerce, trade associations and business libraries that already have the system. Direct subscription occurs through Profile Information (a subsidiary of the Financial Times Group) and costs (1991 rate) £150.

Profile Information
Sunbury House
79 Staines Road West
Sunbury-on-Thames
Middlesex TW16 7AN
0932 761444

SPEARHEAD may also be accessed (without further subscription) through BT's Telecom Gold, IRS Dialtech, One-to-One, and Mercury's E-mail service.

The DTI Service Card
DTI services (overseas status reports, market information enquiries, etc) can be obtained using a Service Card which you get from any DTI Regional Office or from:

DTI Service Card Centre
Welbeck House
Bond Street
Bristol BS1 3LB
0272 277442

You are then billed monthly in arrears.

Export Network
This is a private sector on-line computerised export intelligence system with access to the DTI database. It also provides on-line entry to DTI *Hints for Exporters* publications for individual countries. Export Network also handles the marketing and distribution of the DTI's Export Intelligence Service via a subsidiary organisation called Export Opportunities Ltd.

Export Network
(Trade Network International Ltd)
Regency House
1–4 Warwick Street
London W1R 5WA
071-494 4030

Export Opportunities Ltd
Export House
Wembley Hill Road
Wembley
Middlesex HA9 8BU
081-900 1313

Using a research agency

Do as much of your own research as you can, but accept that specialised investigation into (say) customer motivation or qualitative aspects of markets will be beyond your capacity and that outside assistance may be required.

Selecting an agency
A greater volume of marketing research is undertaken in the UK than in any

other EC country, and many more marketing research agencies operate here than abroad. In consequence, the UK market research industry is highly competitive, and fees are considerably lower in Britain.

You can use either a UK based agency with direct contacts in the EC country concerned, or a local researcher in the foreign market. The former option involves fewer control and communication problems and is thus more common, but it could prove expensive and less effective in the long run (local researchers obviously have intimate knowledge of local conditions).

UK based research agencies
Either the agency will do the work itself – sending out its own staff to visit local markets as and when necessary – or will sub-contract to foreign researchers, or place the assignment with its own branch or subsidiary in the country concerned. The advantages of using a UK firm include the following:

1.   'One-stop shopping'. A large UK agency should be capable of supplying all your research needs.
2.   The agency will possess wide-ranging experience of similar assignments already completed for other UK businesses. You benefit indirectly from other companies' efforts in the European market.
3.   When choosing an agent you can conveniently invite proposals from several local UK research firms, compare their costs, personally discuss your requirements with each candidate, and examine examples of past assignments completed for other clients.
4.   You can quickly evaluate the quality of the agency's work.

A UK firm might claim that it is fully competent to operate in all EC markets. However, this need not be the case. And if the agency simply sub-contracts to locally based foreign research firms you not only lose control over the work – your brief to the UK agency may not be comprehensively and accurately transmitted to the agency's contact abroad. Also, there is no easy way for you to establish whether the local sub-contractor is performing satisfactorily.

Local researchers
The problems with using a resident foreign research agency are:

1.   the expensive and time-consuming need to visit the agent;
2.   the fact that (normally) the laws of the other country will apply if you have to sue the agency for incompetence and/or failing to complete the project;
3.   the higher fees typically charged by foreign marketing research companies;

4.   the difficulty of appraising the agent's performance.

However, local representatives are closer (culturally as well as geographically) to local consumers and should be better able to assess local consumer attitudes and tastes.

What research agencies do

Market research companies apply a wide range of investigational devices to their work, including:

- consumer sampling through questionnaires and interviews (undertaken by local employees);

- market surveys;

- test marketing;

- canvassing competent local business people about your product's likely appeal;

- interpreting foreign statistics (eg knowing which products are included in which statistical classification, assessing data reliability, and comparability with UK equivalents, etc);

- estimating the market share of each local competitor;

- obtaining details of the ownership and control of competing firms;

- assessing growth prospects in the local economy;

- establishing *why* competitors choose to distribute their products through certain channels;

- measuring local consumers' reactions to your company's brand name and images;

- providing sales estimates for each of several possible selling prices;

- determining the costs and benefits of various distribution options;

- assessing the cost effectiveness of local advertising media;

- investigating various promotional possibilities.

European retail audits

Research agencies operating in Europe now offer retail audit facilities analogous to those available in Britain. Thus, an agent will select a panel of retail outlets in the country in question and continuously monitor the levels and periodicity of sales of your product through those outlets. This will be done as part of a syndicated effort, with the suppliers of many products in the same area sharing the cost. Similarly, the agent will put together panels of individual local consumers and carefully monitor their purchases of various products over time.

Often the results of such exercises are subsequently sold to other interested parties. Such information can be enormously useful to the small exporting firm.

Interpreting EC demographic data
A market research company should be expert at (a) interpreting European data, (b) reconciling divergences in the data definitions and statistical methods used to collect information in various countries, and (c) choosing which data to believe where there is contradictory evidence from several sources.

A number of difficulties arise in this respect. For example, income data (essential for assessing markets for consumer goods) is collected by government agencies in some EC countries but (less reliably) by private research surveys in the rest. And even when the government is involved, sample sizes may be small and participation voluntary rather than legally required. Other problems are as follows:

1. Educational attainment is frequently used as an index of socio-economic status. Yet the educational systems of the 12 EC member countries are extremely diverse and it is difficult to establish common criteria for defining 'skilled' and/or 'highly educated' consumers. Some national statistics on educational achievement relate to examinations passed, others to the number of years of schooling, some to the number of college graduates, and so on.
2. Marital status is important for defining household characteristics. Yet certain countries do not recognise all possible marital states. The Irish Republic, for instance, will only publish data under three headings: single, married and widowed – completely ignoring people who are separated, co-habiting or divorced.
3. Each country has its own traditional way of measuring social class. Some systems use occupation; others use educational attainment, income, wealth, ethnic origin, etc. Regional surveys of social class are thus hard to compare.

ESOMAR (European Society for Opinion and Marketing Research) publishes booklets on the interpretation of EC survey data, and issues guidelines for the classification of comparative research data.

ESOMAR
J J Viottstraat
1071 JP Amsterdam
The Netherlands

Syndicated research

Trade associations frequently commission research into foreign markets for particular products. The results are then circulated to members either free of charge (as part of the association's overall service) or for a subsidised fee.

Finding an agency

The Market Research Society will advise you of consultancies specialising in areas of particular interest to your firm. Also, the Society publishes an *International Directory of Market Research Organisations* listing over 2000 research organisations worldwide. Entries show each company's turnover, number of employees, data collection and research facilities, international experience and product group expertise. Facilities are cross-indexed by organisations within a particular country. The MRS also publishes a volume of *Country Notes: Western Europe* which provides basic background information on demographics, sampling methods, research procedures and sources of information in West European states. The volume costs (1991 rate) £30 and is available direct from the Society.

> Market Research Society
> 15 Northburgh Street
> London EC1V 0AH
> 071-490 4911

Directories of marketing research organisations and services are carried by EMIL. British research agencies are listed in Yellow Pages under the heading 'Market research and analysis', 'Information services', and 'Marketing and advertising consultants'.

Researching national product standards

A test case (the *Cassis de Dijon* case as it has become known) established the general principle that if a product is lawfully manufactured and approved for sale in one EC country then it *must* be accepted by the governmental standards authorities of other EC states, subject to it satisfying minimum EC harmonised product standards. However, this does not prevent customers insisting that goods be supplied to particular specifications, eg those laid down by a domestic trade association or industry standards body (the German DIN system for instance – see Chapter 10).

Differences in technical standards can seriously disrupt trade between nations, since exporters may be required to modify their outputs to meet the safety, quality and other standards imposed by various governments. Thus, the Community is committed to harmonising standards as quickly as possible. Unfortunately, however, it will be some years before this (enormous) task is completed and until then it continues to be necessary to research the particular standards applicable to a product in each EC country. Government help is available for this purpose via the 'Technical Help for Exporters' (THE) scheme.

Technical Help for Exporters
This is a government subsidised programme, operated by the British Standards Institution, to assist exporters with problems relating to product design and technical standards. THE will advise on foreign safety and environmental requirements, certification practices, industry standards, etc. It will supply, translate and comment on foreign regulations, and assist in obtaining foreign approval for UK products.

Simple enquiries are answered free of charge over the telephone. Otherwise the charge depends on the extent of the research needed to deal with the query. The likely scale of the charge will be advised in advance of the work commencing. On payment of an appropriate fee, a THE engineer will inspect your output to determine whether it meets relevant foreign technical standards and, if it does not, will specify the modifications necessary to ensure technical compliance. THE will also undertake detailed technical research (for which a government grant may be available) on your behalf. Details can be obtained from:

Technical Help for Exporters
British Standards Institution
Linford Wood
Milton Keynes MK14 6LE
0908 220 022

If you wish to contact foreign EC standards authorities directly their names, addresses and telephone numbers are listed in *The Royal Mail Guide to Business Efficiency,* which you can obtain free of charge from the Post Office. This useful booklet also details some of the key trade directories published in major EC markets.

BSI and the 'new approach' to technical standards
BSI is a member of the two major EC standards making bodies: CEN (Comité Européen de Normalisation) and CENELEC (Comité Européen de Normalisation Electro-technique). CEN and CENELEC are based in Brussels and represent, in effect, federations of all the national standards-making institutions of the EC (and also of the European Free Trade Association [EFTA], with which the EC has an agreement in relation to technical standards). New European standards are adopted through weighted majority voting by the national bodies. Eventually these new standards will replace all existing national specifications.

The so-called 'new approach' of the EC to these matters is for the Community to specify the overall level of safety and other 'essential requirements' that a product must satisfy and describe (a) how these requirements can be met, and (b) the evidence ('attestation') needed to prove that requirements have been satisfied for a particular item. Any product that complies is then legally entitled to be sold throughout the Community. Until an EC standard exists for a product, national standards (such as BSI) are deemed acceptable in lieu.

British Standards Institution
2 Park Street
London W1A 2BS
071-629 9000

Researching the European Public Sector

The Community has stated its intention that *all* public sector contracts shall eventually be opened up to competitive EC-wide bidding. At the time of writing, however, certain restrictions continue to apply.

The present system
Currently, there are three types of tendering procedure ('open', 'closed' and 'negotiated') and three categories of contract covered by the system: 'supplies', 'works' and 'excluded sectors'.

Supplies and works contracts
Supplies contracts involve the provision of goods to central, regional and local government and similar bodies such as police forces, local health authorities, etc. The following *exclusions* apply:

1. Contracts with values lower than 200,000 ECU (currently about £140,000) for regional and local government, or 130,000 ECU for central government;
2. 'Excluded sectors' (see below);
3. Nationalised industries;
4. Secret defence contracts.

Works contracts are for building and civil engineering projects for central, regional and local government, and similar bodies. Only contracts worth more than 5 million ECU are covered. The list of excluded sectors (see page 39) does *not* include telecommunications contracts exceeding a threshold of 1 million ECU.

Excluded sectors

Although public purchasing accounts for about 15 per cent of the Community's gross domestic product, legal obligation to tender competitively does not extend to the water, energy, transport and telecommunications sectors, which collectively account for approximately *half* this figure! This is being changed, however, and measures are being implemented (via an EC Directive), to bring excluded sectors (including those recently privatised) under the public procurement rules. Contracts exceeding 200,000 ECU for 'supplies' or 5 million ECU for 'works' will be covered.

The Excluded Sectors Directive

This requires public purchasers in excluded sectors either (a) to adhere to certain detailed rules governing their procurement policies and procedures and then attest that the rules have been implemented; or (b) to devise their own purchasing procedures, and subsequently submit to periodic external audits designed to ensure that their purchasing methods are truly competitive. In practice, it is likely that the audit option will be more popular since it offers greater flexibility when designing purchasing policies. Details of these matters are available from the Confederation of British Industry.

Confederation of British Industry
Centre Point
New Oxford Street
London WC1A 4DD
071-379 7400

Tendering procedures

'Open' tendering means that *any* company may enter a bid. 'Restricted' tendering requires bidding companies to satisfy certain pre-qualifications set by the purchaser (eg providing evidence of their technical expertise and/or financial standing).

'Negotiated' procedures relate to direct discussions between the purchaser and chosen suppliers, without any competition. This may only occur if (a) no tenders have been received using the other procedures; or (b) in consequence of the highly technical nature of the goods (eg the need for compatibility with existing stocks); or (c) for reasons of extreme urgency. Purchasers can be forced to justify a decision to use negotiated procedures to the European Commission.

Purchasers must specify in advance the criteria (price, quality, etc) to be used in awarding contracts. Advance notice of all procurement plans exceeding appropriate thresholds must be advertised in the *Official Journal* of the EC, stating whether the call for tender is open or closed. Results of calls for tenders naming the successful bidders must also be declared in the *OJ*.

Time limits
Under the open procedure, tenders can be accepted for up to 52 days from the despatch of details to the applicant firm. For restricted and negotiated procedures the deadline is 37 days from despatch of details, or 40 days from the issue of a written invitation to bid. Time limits for excluded sectors could differ from the above.

Complaining about unfair policies
If you wish to complain that a public sector's purchasing systems are uncompetitive you may do so formally (and free of charge) via the DTI head office, telephone 071–215 4648/4721. The DTI will advise on how to put your case to the European Commission, which you can do through the Commission's UK office.

The European Commission
(London office)
8 Storey's Gate
London SW1P 3AT
071-222 8122

The Commission will then issue a reasoned opinion, and may take the offending authority before the European Court.

Alternatively, you can pursue the matter through the UK courts, seeking damages and/or an injunction compelling the purchasing authority to alter its procedures.

Locating public sector opportunities
You can subscribe to the *Official Journal* directly or purchase individual copies from:

HMSO Publications Centre
51 Nine Elms Lane
London SW8 5DR
071-873 8409

Otherwise you can visit a European Information Centre (see page 19), all of which stock the *OJ*. Moreover, increasing numbers of Chambers of Commerce and trade associations carry the *Official Journal* for use by their members.

Euro Information Centres also subscribe to 'Tenders Electronic Daily' (TED), the Community's computerised tender information system. Individual subscriptions to TED can be obtained direct via:

Office for Official Publications of the European Community

Sales Department
L–2985 Luxembourg
010 352 499281

Tender opportunities taken from TED feed into the DTI's Export Intelligence Service (see page 29).

Using professional advisers

External consultants can provide practical advice on export strategies and procedures; will 'hand-hold' business owners and managers who feel deluged by the implications of the Single Market; and enable client firms to benefit from other companies' export experiences and mistakes. Specifically, consultants might be able to help with:

- initial feasibility studies for entering particular EC markets (see page 15);

- provision of marketing services such as European sales promotions or public relations (see Chapter 4);

- advertising message strategies for use in various EC countries (see Chapter 3);

- company formations and the establishment of other types of Continental subsidiary (see Chapter 7);

- minimising taxation on European operations;

- location of agents and opportunities for joint ventures (see Chapter 6);

- cross-border staff recruitment.

Finding consultants

Consultancy services are available in the form of private management consultancy businesses and (at the time of writing) through a publicly funded scheme. The latter operates via the DTI's Enterprise Initiative which (currently) will meet half the cost (two-thirds if your business is in an Assisted or Urban Programme Area) of between five and 15 days' consultancy undertaken by a DTI approved consultant – subject to an upper ceiling on the assignment cost. To qualify for assistance you must employ fewer than 500 workers or be a member of a group of companies employing fewer than 500 worldwide.

Access to the scheme in the first instance occurs through your DTI regional office (see page 28). A DTI Enterprise Counsellor (an experienced business person) then visits your firm to discuss your perceived problems and whether the scheme can help. The DTI has appointed certain professional bodies and other organisations to oversee and control the quality of the provision of consultancy services provided through the Initiative. The Chartered Institute of Marketing, for instance, is the 'contractor' for the marketing element of the scheme; the Design Council is the contractor for design. On receipt of an application approved by an Enterprise Counsellor the contractor matches the client with a mutually agreed consultant.

The aim of the Initiative is to provide access to expert consultants who will help you to look at your business at the *strategic* level, rather than actually undertake nitty-gritty work; the scheme does not normally cover particular aspects of functions independent of an overall strategy. Accordingly, EI consultancy is not available solely for such activities as:

- advertising/public relations campaigns;

- market research projects;

- development of pricing, sales and distribution policies;

- redesign of sales literature;

- advice on production inspection methods;

- training of staff;

- assistance with raising finance; and

- software programming or computer systems installation.

However, some of these elements can be covered in projects which take a wider, strategic view of a company's operations.

Help for the small business
Advice on specific European selling issues may be available from the DTI Small Firms Service. You attend 'counselling sessions', the first three of which are free but which thereafter cost (currently) £30 each. To contact SFS you simply telephone operator services and ask for Freefone Enterprise.

Directories
There is a *European Directory of Management Consultants,* published by TFPL, which identifies consultancies possessing particular skills in various Continental countries. It also gives UK based consultancies with European interests. The Directory is divided into country sections within each of which the names, addresses, telephone numbers and business contacts of major local consultancies are listed. Details of parent organisations and the locations of their branch offices are also provided. Consultancies are

indexed three ways: alphabetically; by field of specialisation; and by the industry sectors in which they have expertise. A useful feature of the directory is its listing of the names, addresses and outline information about the national professional bodies representing management consultancies in each of the countries covered. It can be obtained from:

TFPL Publishing
22 Peter's Lane
London EC1M 6DS
071-251 5522

Additionally, TFPL publishes a *Directory of Management Consultants in the UK,* which lists British consultants both by specialism and by the industries in which they operate.

Political/lobbying aspects
Vacher's European Companion and Consultants' Register contains a register of consultants with expertise in the political aspects of the European Community.

Vacher's Publications
113 High Street
Berkhamsted
Hertfordshire HP4 2DJ
0442 876135

Consultancy bodies
There are two main management consultancy bodies in the UK: the Management Consultancies Association (MCA) and the Institute of Management Consultants (IMC). The MCA (currently) comprises 29 large British consultancies which collectively undertake about 65 per cent of all UK consultancy work measured in value terms. At present, 95 per cent of MCA members' work is in the UK, but this proportion is sure to diminish as the Single Market is completed. The Association provides a client information service to advise prospective customers of member firms capable of undertaking various kinds of assignment. MCA members are required to adhere to a code of professional conduct, and to accept the decisions of a complaints and arbitration procedure available to dissatisfied clients. For further information contact:

Management Consultancies Association
11 West Halkin Street
London SW1X 8JL
071-235 3897

The Institute of Management Consultants is a professional body of over 3300 individuals engaged in management consultancy. It offers a free client advisory service, a complaints service and general advice on selecting a consultant.

Institute of Management Consultants
5th Floor
32–33 Hatton Garden
London EC1N 8DL
071-242 2140

Detailed practical advice on the selection, control and evaluation of management consultants is contained in my book *Choosing and Using Management Consultants,* published by Kogan Page.

Chapter 3
Advertising in the European Community

Successful EC advertising requires careful attention to three major tasks: the production of advertisements suitable for Community markets; the location and choice of the best media to carry messages; and (possibly) the selection and control of an advertising agency competent to undertake your European work.

Production of advertising copy

The issue here is whether to standardise advertising messages for common application in all Community countries, or to adapt them to meet the particular requirements of each member state.

Uniformity versus customisation

The advantages of uniformity are that it (a) requires less marketing research than customisation, (b) is convenient and cheap to administer, and (c) demands less creative effort. You (or your agent) need devise just a single message rather than separate advertisements for each EC market.

Standardisation is possible to the extent that consumer lifestyles and perspectives are similar across Community states. You identify comparable consumer groups in various countries, and then hope that each group will respond to the same type of message and see similar media (magazines, posters, local newspapers, and so on) as the rest. Hence you select a single basic image (eg outstanding quality, ruggedness, sensitivity, sophistication, association with a certain lifestyle, or whatever) for promoting the product and then create simple, bland and non-controversial advertisements to reinforce the chosen theme. Customisation, on the other hand, may be essential in consequence of:

- cultural differences between countries and/or market segments within countries;

- language translation difficulties;

- differences in the educational backgrounds of target groups in various countries;

- non-availability of certain media (specialist magazines, for instance) in some regions;
- differences in national attitudes towards advertising.

Alterations may take one or more of the following forms.

(a)   *Different media.* For instance, listeners to commercial radio in one country may typically belong to a different socio-economic group from others.

(b)   *Changes in symbols,* eg using a male rather than a female model as the dominant figure in an advertisement. This may be necessary if males are the primary purchasers of the product in one market and females in another.

(c)   *Changes in advertisement body copy.* This is considered in the section 'Devising messages' below.

(d)   *Changes in the fundamental selling proposition.* An example here is presenting a bicycle as a leisure item in one market, a fashion accessory in another, and a commuting vehicle elsewhere.

Devising messages

Whether you use the same advertisement everywhere or devise separate messages for specific markets, it is essential that the advertisement appeals to consumers in each market. The degree to which the same message can be successfully applied transnationally depends on whether, in various countries, the product:

- is used in the *same way;*
- satisfies the *same consumer needs;*
- appeals to the *same consumer type;*
- can be sold at *similar prices;*
- is purchased in response to the *same consumer motives* (convenience, status, impulse buying, etc);
- evokes mental images that can be manipulated using *pictures rather than words;*
- can be advertised in the *same media;*
- is *perceived* by consumers in similar ways (eg technically complicated electrical equipment may be seen as performing exactly the same function regardless of the customer's location);
- is *evaluated* using similar criteria;
- has just one or two universally intelligible *selling points;*

- is purchased by consumers with *similar income levels;*
- is typically bought by the *same family members* (wives, husbands, parents, etc.);
- is demanded in the *same package sizes and quantities;*
- cannot by *law* be promoted in certain ways;
- is purchased with the *same frequency* (weekly, monthly, irregularly);
- appeals to similar *cultural traditions.*

Translation difficulties

Accurate translation is (obviously) critical, and examples of absurdities arising from bad translation from English into other languages abound. Often, however, it is the implied *concept* underlying a translated message that causes the problem, rather than the translated words themselves. Indeed, literal translations can be worse than useless, because the words transcribed may become totally incomprehensible – even ridiculous – when the *context* in which they are used is changed. Hence, the translation needs to convert the *thoughts* and *ideas* behind sentences as well as the words themselves. Some famous blunders are listed below.[1]

Message in English	*Translated meaning*
Come alive with Pepsi	Rise from the grave (German)
Avoid embarrassment – use Parker Pens	Avoid pregnancy – use Parker pens (Spanish)
Cleans the really dirty parts of your wash	Cleans your private parts (French)
Schweppes tonic water	Schweppes bathroom water (Italian)
Body by Fisher	Corpse by Fisher (Flemish)
Chrysler for power	Chrysler is an aphrodisiac (Spanish)

[1] For further examples, see *Big Business Blunders,* by D Ricks (Irwin, Homewood, Illinois, 1983).

The skill of the translator lies in:

1. understanding the appeal and technical detail of a product and its method of (domestic) presentation;
2. finding equivalent expressions in the foreign language;
3. avoiding errors, approximations, and omissions from the script of domestic promotional literature.

Translators need to think in the appropriate foreign language, since only then can they assess whether translated messages will be received and interpreted in the manner intended.

Translation services
To find a translator you can (a) look in Yellow Pages (under the heading 'Translators and interpreters'), (b) contact the languages department of a local college (which may have teachers or advanced students willing to undertake *ad hoc* assignments for local firms), or (c) use the facilities of a professional institute, British Telecom or a government-sponsored language resource centre.

The Institute of Translation and Interpreting (ITI)
The ITI is not a translation agency as such. Rather, it is a professional body with over 1200 members capable of assisting UK businesses to satisfy their translating needs. ITI publishes an annual index of translators classified by language and subject specialisation and listing their addresses, telephone numbers, and electronic communication and equipment details. Also, the Institute compiles lists of translators in various product/industry/country fields which it will issue to prospective client firms.

ITI recommends that companies requiring *ad hoc* translation services establish ongoing relationships with two or three freelance translators, who will then become familiar with their work and (most important) the technical vocabulary they use. It is essential, the ITI argues, that (a) clients establish personal contact with their translators, (b) the firm's requirements are specified clearly and precisely, (c) queries are discussed at the beginning of the exercise rather than at the end, and (d) adequate time is allowed for research, proof-reading and the production of word processed (or camera ready) text.

Other services provided by the ITI include:

- advice to firms seeking full-time translators on recruitment procedures, qualifications, and appropriate salary levels for linguistic staff;
- lists of reputable large-scale translation companies capable of handling extensive volumes of multi-language work;

- provision of interpreters to enable clients to discuss business face to face with foreign visitors to their premises.

The Institute of Translation and Interpreting
318a Finchley Road
London NW3 5HT
071-794 9931

The Institute of Linguists
This is a professional body comprising more than 6000 members qualified to use their language skills in industry, commerce and related fields. It maintains registers of translators and interpreters and publishes a Directory listing those of its members available for freelance work. The Institute also arranges a professional indemnity insurance scheme for self-employed linguists (who are liable to be sued for damages if they are negligent in their translations and the negligence causes financial loss to employing firms). Details of the Institute's services are available from:

Institute of Linguists
24a Highbury Grove
London N5 2EA
071-359 7445

The British Telecom Translation Bureau
A recent entrant to the translating and interpreting field is the British Telecom Translation Bureau (BTTB), comprising an in-house BT team of native speakers of various foreign languages. The service is willing to translate documents of any size, ranging from a one page letter to a major report. The BTTB will undertake the following:

(a)   printing and foreign distribution via telex, fax or post of documents it has translated on a client's behalf;
(b)   instant voice translations for client companies of incoming telephone calls in foreign languages;
(c)   provision of interpreters at meetings with foreign customers or suppliers, either in the UK or abroad.
(d)   Conducting telephone research into foreign markets.

Moreover, you can use the BTTB's address, fax, telex or telephone number on your European direct mailings (see Chapter 4), and the Bureau will handle all the replies. Details of the service are available from:

British Telecom Translation Bureau
BTI Communications Centre

9 St Botolph Street
London EC3A 7DT
0800 890909

The Association of Language Export Centres (ALEC)
The Department of Education and Science and the Training Agency have
together established an Association of Language Export Centres, primarily
for foreign language training, which also offers interpretation and translation services, cultural briefings and help with export documentation.
Centres compile registers of translators and interpreters and operate in co-
operation with the DTI. The London Centre is located at:

ALEC (London)
72 Great Portland Street
London W1N 5AL
071-323 4977

There are 20 other Centres spread throughout the UK. For their addresses,
contact:

The Centre for Information on Language Training (ALEC)
Regents College
PO Box 1574
London NW1 4NJ
071-224 3748

Further options
Another possibility is to ask your local polytechnic, further education
college or university whether it has a language department and, if so, to
telephone and enquire whether it offers a translation service to local
businesses. If you belong to a Chamber of Commerce it will almost certainly
be competent to help you in these respects.

Fees
Translators usually charge per 1000 words translated (excluding tables,
diagrams, etc). Rates depend on the technical complexity of the subject
matter (and hence the research time required), the total length of the job,
the amount of proof-reading needed, and the commercial reputation of the
translator.

Allowance has to be made for reading and grasping the original material,
for looking up technical terms, resolving ambiguities with the client, and
polishing up the final draft. Expect to pay between £40 and £90 per 1000
words at current prices. The translator will, of course, need to see the job
before giving a firm quotation.

Interpreters engaged in person to person 'on the spot' duties normally charge per day spent with the client. Note that face-to-face interpreting requires intense concentration (it is not possible to look up difficult technical words and phrases in a dictionary) and can involve substantial amounts of stress – especially if hostile negotiations are involved. Thus, two interpreters may be needed for a full day's work, and both must be thoroughly briefed before the meeting.

The specification
Instructions to the translator should include:

- the latest completion date;
- a sample of the material to be translated;
- a statement of the quality of presentation required (typescript, floppy disk, desk top publishing standard, typefaces for headings, etc);
- some background information on the client firm's activities;
- details of the house style used in the client's general promotional literature.

Translation is made easier if your advertisements, sales letters, mail drop leaflets and so on are drafted in simple English. It follows that slang, technical terms and humorous expressions should be avoided at all costs.
On receipt of the finished translation it is a good idea to:

(a)   have the translation itself translated back into English by a completely independent person in order to identify any changes in meaning that may have occurred;
(b)   show the translation to local people living in the area where it is to be used before having it printed, or even have your foreign language literature printed locally on the Continent; ask the printer to inform you of any absurdities that it contains before completing the assignment;
(c)   take advice from your local distribution agent (if you have one) about the quality of the translation.

Using an advertising agency

Confronted with the many vexing problems that European advertising involves, many businesses instinctively turn to an advertising agency for advice and practical help. Large advertising agencies are substantial multinational corporations in their own right, and as such have branch offices throughout Europe. Hence, you could brief one of the leading agencies operating in the UK and then simply leave all your European advertising to that agency. Alternatively, you might look for small local agencies in target markets.

The major criteria to apply when choosing an agency are:

- Does the agency possess an efficient translation service capable of identifying changes in the tone or meaning of an advertisement caused by translation?

- How intimate are the agency's contacts and relations with local media? (Multinationals may be at a disadvantage here.)

- How extensive are the agency's support services, such as advertisement pre-testing or access to mailing lists for direct marketing exercises?

- In the case of a branch of a multinational agency, how do local staff compare with the agency's staff in Britain?

- Is the agency capable of devising an entirely new advertising campaign for your product without having to 'import' ideas about the campaign from the advertisements you use in the UK?

- What is the agency's track record *vis-à-vis* similar products in foreign markets?

- Does the agent offer adequate coverage of target market segments?

UK versus local agents

Using a large UK based agency offers 'one stop shopping' in that it will provide *all* your advertising requirements (creative design of advertisements, production of literature, media relations, public relations, etc) from a single source, and allow you to avoid paying profit margins to the several different links in the advertising process (copywriters, photographers, media space sellers, printers, and so on). Large agencies should already possess extensive stocks of research data on (a) European markets, (b) EC consumer tastes and buying habits, and (c) the sorts of message likely to succeed in various countries. And since the agency is located here in Britain you can liaise with its staff relatively easily.

On the other hand, a large UK agency does not necessarily have better European contacts than you could establish personally; and you could always combine general fact-finding trips to national markets with co-ordination visits to local advertising agents in the field. Other reasons for choosing a local agency might include:

- its ability to give your firm a local image;

- potential for close and effective liaison between the agency and your local distribution agent and/or other representatives;

- possibly a higher level of effort and commitment on the part of a local agency, which needs to offer better service in order to compete with larger and better known multinational rivals;

- flair and creativity that are sometimes absent in big international agencies.

Help with agency selection

For UK based agencies you can look in Yellow Pages, or in the *Advertisers Annual* (see page 54) which carries data on thousands of UK and hundreds of EC based advertising agents. Another useful contact is the Institute of Practitioners in Advertising, which is a trade association representing advertising agencies, consultancies and other marketing services firms. The Institute is prepared to give enquirers a list of three or four agencies seemingly capable of satisfying their needs. Note, however, that the IPA exists primarily to represent its members and that following the disclosure by the Institute of a few names and addresses of appropriate agencies, all further dealings are between you and the firms concerned.

Foreign agencies can be located through the *Advertisers Annual* or from the trade associations representing the advertising industries of various EC member states. The IPA publishes a list of the addresses and telephone numbers of these trade associations which it issues free of charge.

Institute of Practitioners in Advertising
44 Belgrave Square
London SW1X 8QS
071-235 7020

For public relations agencies see *Hollis Europe,* which is a guide to public relations consultancy services throughout the Continent.

Hollis Europe
Contact House
Lower Hampton Road
Sunbury-on-Thames
Middlesex TW16 5HG
0932-784781

Campaign strategy

There is, of course, no immutable law that you must use an advertising agency for European (or indeed any other) work, and you may choose to devise and manage the firm's European advertising yourself. Equally, you could use an agency for just some aspects of a European campaign, while doing the rest personally.

However you do it, the key decisions attached to EC campaign planning concern the following:

(a)   Choice of media;
(b)   Selecting messages (see page 46);
(c)   Deciding how much to spend;
(d)   Organising the advertising;
(e)   Deciding how to evaluate the effectiveness of EC advertising efforts.

Choice of media

Selection of the media most appropriate to carry EC advertisements requires a knowledge of the options available (local newspapers and magazines, radio stations, poster sites, etc) and of their costs, coverages and the markets they serve. Normally, you will need specialist advice on these matters, although an indication of possibilities may be obtained from a number of UK sources. For example, the *Advertisers Annual* has an extensive European section listing EC newspapers, periodicals, radio and television stations, plus:

- EC based advertising agents;

- UK representatives of foreign newspapers and magazines;

- UK consultants undertaking EC media work;

- details of pan-European publications.

Advertisers Annual
Reed Information Services
Windsor Court
East Grinstead House
East Grinstead
West Sussex RH19 1XA
0342-326972.

A useful list of Continental newspapers and periodicals is contained in the European section of the annual *Willings Press Guide,* which is available in most public libraries. This itemises EC publications alphabetically under the countries where they are distributed, giving details of the publisher, subscription or publication price, and a brief description of contents. *Willings* is published by Reed Information Services (see above).

The UK media listing publication *British Rate and Data (BRAD)* contains the names and addresses of comparable publications for Belgium, France, Germany, the Netherlands, Italy and Spain. Subscriptions to these publications are available via *BRAD*.

British Rate and Data
Maclean Hunter House
Chalk Lane
Cockfosters Road
Barnet
Hertfordshire EN4 0BU
081-975 9759

The annual *Benn's Media Directory, International Edition* lists newspapers and magazines in all EC countries, plus UK advertisement representatives for overseas publications and EC media agencies and organisations. Periodicals are categorised according to type of content and country. There is also a list of 'useful contacts' within each EC state.

Benn's Media Directory
Benn Business Information Services Ltd
PO Box 20
Sovereign Way
Tonbridge
Kent TN9 1QR
0732 362666

Another useful contact is the Overseas Press and Media Association, which may be able to point you in the right direction when making your media choice.

Overseas Press and Media Association
16 Bedford Square
London WC1B 3JA
071-323 0886

Factors influencing the selection of media should include:

- the extent and reliability of information regarding circulation, audience characteristics, etc available for each medium;
- the reach of media into various target consumer groups;
- the ease with which media effectiveness can be assessed.

Foreign agents and distributors and the commercial sections of local British Consulates are well placed to advise on the quality and characteristics of the options available.

How much to spend

All the conventional techniques for determining advertising budgets are more difficult to apply to EC than to domestic advertising. The commonest methods are as follows:

(a)   *The operational approach*
A list is prepared of all the tasks necessary to achieve pre-specified advertising goals (eg create brand awareness, penetrate a new market, increase customer loyalty, etc) and the cost of each activity is estimated. Costs are then aggregated under various departmental headings and budgets allocated accordingly. The problems with applying this approach internationally are that:

- objectives are typically less concrete for foreign than for domestic operations (on account of limited experience of local conditions and possibilities);
- the resources necessary to achieve objectives may be uncertain;
- local market conditions may change (thus requiring a revision of advertising objectives) unexpectedly and without your knowledge.

(b)   *The personal responsibility approach.*
Individual managers are asked how much they need to spend in order to complete predetermined advertising tasks (reach a new market segment, persuade customers to accept a big price rise, etc). Resources are then distributed and the managers concerned assume personal responsibility for administering the resulting budgets. This method is harder to apply to European than to UK advertising because:

- the people responsible for actually implementing advertising policies may be based abroad and hence difficult to inspect and appraise;
- a local representative's perception of the resources needed to achieve certain advertising targets may be quite different from your own, yet because the representative is in a foreign country you have no easy way of establishing whether the amounts quoted are reasonable;
- delays in reporting information could make it difficult to establish whether advertising money is being well spent.

(c)   *The 'me too' approach*
Here the firm estimates and duplicates the amounts spent on advertising by major rivals. Unfortunately, monitoring the marketing expenditures of foreign based competitors is far harder than monitoring UK businesses – whose financial accounts (if they are limited companies) are open to public inspection and whose promotional activities are obvious the moment they occur. Also, just because competitors are observed increasing or reducing advertising expenditures does not necessarily mean they are behaving correctly.

Note, moreover, that UK firms sometimes have to spend considerably more on advertising than local rivals in order to gain a foothold in a new and unfamiliar market.

This leaves the 'percentage of sales' method whereby the firm automatically allocates a fixed percentage of the value of its quarterly (say) sales of each of its products to advertising those products. It is assumed that increasing sales require additional advertising to sustain them. There are two major advantages to the method:

1. It guarantees that the firm only spends on advertising as much as it can afford.
2. Advertising effort becomes 'market led' in that resources are channelled only towards products that have genuine market appeal and which therefore are likely to do even better in future. The percentage of sales approach prevents 'good money being thrown after bad'. Each product is given the advertising it deserves.

However, the method ignores the possibility that extra spending on advertising may in fact be necessary when sales are declining, in order to reverse the trend. Other problems are that:

(a) the technique cannot be used to launch new products or to enter fresh markets;
(b) advertising costs can differ significantly from country to country, so that a greater level of expenditure may be needed to achieve a given level of performance in some markets than in others.

Which to select
There are, alas, no simple criteria to apply when choosing a budgeting technique. It may be possible, however, to group together those EC markets which exhibit similar characteristics in relation to advertising (importance of certain media, size of market segments, rules and regulations, media costs, etc) and apply an intuitively appropriate method to each group. If advertising in one group performs better than elsewhere the reasons for this can then be analysed and applied to other markets.

Organising the advertising

The main issue here is whether to take all EC advertising decisions yourself, or rely instead on an advertising agency or on inputs provided by local distributors or other representatives. Your choice should depend on:

- the extent of your familiarity with advertising methods and your knowledge of European markets;

- the availability and quality of advertising agency services in relation to your particular product in EC markets;

- the reliability of advice given by local representatives;

- whether local representatives demand active participation in the formulation of advertising strategies;

- your knowledge of local media (newspapers, magazines, poster site locations, etc);

- your ability to co-ordinate diverse promotional activities and control foreign operations;

- whether your existing administrative system has the capacity to take on additional work;

- how easily you can monitor the consequences of EC advertising campaigns;

- the volume of your European sales.

The problems involved

UK businesses fresh to European marketing frequently fail to realise the substantial differences that exist between British and Continental advertising. The following are especially important:

(a)   To date, there has been significantly more advertising in the UK than elsewhere in Europe (about 2 per cent of UK gross national product is devoted to advertising – more than in any other EC country). Consequently, the UK advertising industry is bigger than in Continental nations, with many more agencies, copywriters, media independents, public relations consultants, and so on. Advertising is completely integrated into UK culture and is accepted by UK consumers as a matter of course. This is not always the case in the rest of the Community.

(b)   Past legislative constraints on media availability (prohibitions on television advertising or commercial radio, for example) in certain EC countries have caused the same product to be advertised in different media in different states – newspapers in one country, trade magazines in another, commercial radio in a third, etc.

(c)   Copywriting, typesetting and printing costs differ markedly across European countries.

(d)   There are (currently) a number of important legal differences between British and Continental advertising.

Legal differences

Each EC country has its own laws on advertising. Superlatives, for instance, are allowable in the UK, Belgium and Italy, but not in Germany or France (at least not on television). In the Netherlands, use of a superlative has to be backed up by factual evidence.

Another sensitive area is the mention of rival firms. This is totally banned in Italy, and severely controlled in Belgium, France and Germany. Rivals may be identified in advertisements in the Netherlands and the UK, but only if comparisons are 'fair' and derogatory statements can be proved.

Numerous restraints apply to the advertising of pharmaceuticals (many EC countries forbid such advertisements completely) and of alcohol and tobacco. Each country's laws are different on these matters. The Netherlands has laws to curb sexism in advertising. In France the use of foreign languages to advertise products is not allowed, and children may not be used to merchandise products. The words applied to the advertisement of foodstuffs in Belgium are subject to stringent control.

EC Directives on advertising

There is an EC Directive to prohibit misleading advertising. The latter is defined as advertising that deceives or is likely to deceive the people it reaches and which, by virtue of its deceptive nature, could affect consumer behaviour or cause damage to a competing firm. The Community insists, moreover, that (a) the burden of proof should lie with the advertiser and not with the consumer, and (b) national courts shall be empowered to halt the publication of misleading advertising.

Satellite broadcasts

The Community cannot, of course, control satellite broadcasts emanating from beyond its frontiers. Accordingly, the European Commission has issued a set of guidelines for advertisements broadcast via satellite, to which it invites advertisers to adhere. These guidelines request that advertisements do not:

- offend religious or political beliefs;

- contain material encouraging racial or sexual discrimination;

- engender fear in those watching the broadcast;

- offend prevailing standards of decency and good taste;

- portray behaviour that is prejudicial to health and safety.

Note the contradiction between the last of these recommendations and tobacco and alcohol advertising.

The Cross-Frontier Broadcasting Directive

Adopted in 1989, this Directive guarantees freedom of transmission in broadcasting across national frontiers and lays down minimum rules on advertising. Responsibility for the control of advertising lies with the authorities of the country in which an advertisement originated. The Directive (a) set limits on the air-time devoted to commercials (no more than 15 per cent of total daily transmissions, with a maximum of 18 per cent during peak hours), (b) banned the TV advertising of tobacco and prescription pharmaceuticals, and (c) introduced guidelines for TV alcohol advertising, for advertising to children and the sponsorship of television programmes.

Proposed legislation

At the time of writing moves are afoot to introduce binding Directives in the following areas:

(a)   Severe restriction on *all* tobacco advertising (not just on TV);

(b)   Restrictions on claims made when advertising food products, notably on assertions that such a product:
- provides nutrition not available in a normal diet
- is 'pure'
- is 'new'
- is free of 'additives'
- is 'natural' or 'farm produced'
- is superior to others;

(c)   Insistence that pharmaceuticals be advertised as medicines and not as foodstuffs or 'health products';

(d)   Prohibitions on commercial sponsors of television programmes influencing editorial content or encouraging viewers to buy particular products;

(e)   Heavy restrictions on all forms of alcohol advertising;

(f)   Banning advertisements aimed at children which exploit (1) their inexperience or credulity, or (2) their trust in teachers or parents;

(g)   Prohibiting motor car advertisements that feature speed and acceleration as primary selling points;

(h)   Controls over the ways in which women are portrayed in advertisements.

The UK Advertising Association has set up a special European issues unit to monitor developments in these areas, as it is anxious to influence all intended legislation. The Association, which is primarily a lobbying organisation for the advertising industry, publishes briefing sheets and booklets on EC advertising legislation and is prepared to advise companies about where to seek specialist help if particular legislative difficulties arise in relation to a specific product. Details are available from:

The Advertising Association
Abford House
15 Wilton Road
London SW1V 1NJ
071-828 2771

Future priorities
The Commission has specified the following as priorities for further EC involvement in consumer affairs:

(a)   Laws to require that guarantees are honoured in EC consumers' countries of residence, regardless of where the product was bought;
(b)   Standardisation of the format in which credit charges are expressed, so that consumers can easily compare competing credit offers from companies in different EC states;
(c)   Establishment of low cost legal procedures for consumers seeking compensation for minor damage caused by product inadequacy;
(d)   Provision of education on consumer matters to young people.

Evaluation

To evaluate the effectiveness of EC advertising expenditures you must either rely on feedback from local distributors (or other representatives) or hire the services of a marketing research agency. The work of European MR agencies is described in Chapter 2. Two special difficulties arise:

1.   Deciding evaluation criteria, given that national EC markets differ in many fundamental respects.
2.   The absence in several EC regions of research facilities for interviewing message recipients, assessing advertisement recall, defining the product and company images your advertisements are projecting, and so on.

These issues are so problematic that you will probably have to make intuitive rule-of-thumb evaluations, or rely heavily on specialist external advice.
   Ultimately, of course, the success of all advertising has to be measured against increases in sales, but you need to be quite sure that it is the additional advertising that is causing higher turnover and not some other factor.

Patents and branding for EC markets

Through giving a particular trade name or logo to your product and then seeking through advertising and other promotional activities to associate certain attractive characteristics with the now 'branded' good, you enable EC consumers to recognise your output and – having once purchased and been satisfied with it – to avoid needing to re-evaluate its worth before buying it again. Your EC customers can continue choosing your branded goods which they already know and trust.

Thus, having created a brand identity in a Continental market your subsequent advertising and other promotions may then be directed towards establishing 'brand loyalty' via the reinforcement of existing favourable images. People will immediately identify the branded product: you need not provide fresh information about it in each and every advertisement. All this requires your acquiring 'intellectual property' in brand names and identities.

Intellectual property
The term 'intellectual property' covers patents, trademarks, industrial designs and any other copyright material. Information on existing patents and trademarks in other EC countries is available from the Science Reference Library, which is located in the Patent Office building. Names and addresses of patent agents can be obtained from the Chartered Institute of Patent Agents.

Chartered Institute of Patent Agents
Staple Inn Buildings
High Holborn
London WC1V 7PZ
071-405 9450

Originally, each European country had its own law on intellectual property, so that it was necessary to register trademarks, patents, etc in every country where protection was required. Today, however, it is possible to obtain patent protection throughout Europe with a single application, and member states have further promised to standardise their domestic patent law in order to avoid contradictions regarding what will or will not infringe a patent.

You apply (via the UK Patent Office) to the EC Patent Office in Munich specifying which Community countries the patent is to cover. Then you receive a bundle of national patents relating to those countries. Renewals of these patents can be undertaken through the Patent Office here in the UK.

Patent Office
State House
66–71 High Holborn
London WC1R 4TP
071-831 2525

Also, a system for registering Community-wide trademarks will be established to operate in parallel with existing domestic trademark arrangements. For details of the new system contact:

DTI Industrial Property and Copyright Department
1–19 Victoria Street
London SW1H 0ET
Telephone: Patents 071-829 6944
Trademarks 071-829 6134
Copyright 071-829 6020

A body concerned entirely with trademarks and related issues is:

The Institute of Trade Mark Agents
4th Floor
Canterbury House
2–6 Sydenham Road
Croydon
Surrey CR0 9XE
081-686 2052

Registering (and protecting) brands and trademarks will continue to cost money so you need to balance their usefulness (as a means of differentiating your firm's output from that of competitors) against this expenditure. Factors influencing the decision include:

- the importance of the brand or trademark as a selling point for the product;

- how easily an alternative yet equally effective brand identifier could be devised;

- whether sales of the branded product are increasing or in decline.

If you discover that a European (or other) competitor has trespassed upon your intellectual property you may be able to use the good offices of the DTI to achieve a negotiated settlement – provided that legal proceedings have not been initiated by either side. Chambers of Commerce can also be useful for these purposes, eg by suggesting a route for arbitration.

Chapter 4

European Direct Marketing, Exhibitions and Sales Promotions

Direct marketing (DM)

Direct marketing covers direct mail, telephone selling, catalogues and 'off-the-page' selling via cut-outs in newspaper and magazine advertisements. All these are now possible on a Community-wide basis.

The DM industry itself distinguishes between 'suppliers' and 'consultants'. The latter are concerned with:

- planning and testing direct marketing programmes;

- suggesting new administrative arrangements to deal with the increased volume of enquiries and/or orders that a campaign will generate;

- integrating DM into the client's total marketing strategy;

- estimating the costs of DM exercises;

- drafting profiles of possible DM customers (lifestyle, reading habits, propensity to purchase using mail order, etc);

- training the client's staff in DM methods; and

- evaluating alternative approaches to direct marketing (maildrops versus off-the-page advertisements, for example).

'Suppliers', conversely, consist of telemarketing agencies, fulfilment houses, computer bureaux, list brokers and mailing agencies. Note that suppliers will also provide advice and general DM consultancy services whenever required.

Finding help

Many DM firms belong to trade associations, such as the Direct Mail Producers Association, the British Direct Marketing Association and the European Direct Marketing Association (EDMA), which issue lists of members to prospective clients. EDMA also operates a (chargeable) international list search and co-ordination service.

Direct Mail Producers Association
34 Grand Avenue
London N10 3BP
081-883 7229

British Direct Marketing Association
Grosvenor Gardens House
35 Grosvenor Gardens
London SW1W 0BS
071-630 0361

European Direct Marketing Association
34 rue du gouvernement provisoire
B–1000 Brussels
010 32 2 2176309

DM businesses also advertise extensively in the magazines *Direct Response* and *Direct Marketing International.*

Direct Response
4 Market Place
Hertford SG14 1EG
0992 501177

Direct Marketing International
Ferrary Publications
Boundary House
91–93 Charterhouse Street
London EC1M 6HR
071-250 0646

For detailed advice on how to select a DM company see Chapter 10 of my book *Choosing and Using Management Consultants,* published by Kogan Page.

Direct mail to Europe

Direct mail – the transmission of a personally addressed item of advertising through the postal system – offers a flexible, selective and potentially highly cost-effective means of reaching Continental consumers. The UK Post Office offers a variety of facilities for these purposes, and there is a constantly expanding range of commercially available European customer lists (see page 68). Your message can be addressed exclusively to a target market; advertising budgets may be concentrated on the most promising market segments; and it will be some time before Continental competitors realise that you are after their customers. Also, the size, content, timing and geographical coverage of maildrops can be varied at will: you can spend as much or as little as is necessary to achieve your objectives. There are no media space or air-time restrictions, and no copy or insertion deadlines to be met.

Direct Mail activity in Community nations is buoyant, and set to expand. Germany and Belgium head the league table of number of direct mailshots received per person per year; followed by France, Denmark and the Netherlands, with the UK some way behind. When off-the-page direct mail is taken into account Germany still heads the list, leading France and, in third place, Britain. Collectively, these three countries account for over two-thirds of all EC direct mail measured by value of order. Clearly, therefore, there is enormous potential for the development of direct mail in other EC nations, especially in the larger markets of Italy and Spain. All aspects of the process are subject to your immediate control, and you can experiment by varying the approach used in different EC markets. Direct mail is particularly valuable for entering foreign markets circumspectly, since local competitors will not realise you are canvassing their customers until some time after the event.

Telephone responses to maildrops
These are possible through British Telecom's 0800 service which enables you to quote an 0800 freefone telephone number so that your Continental customers can ring you free of charge in response to direct mail and other advertising campaigns to make enquiries or place orders direct. Another option is to have the caller pay only the cost of a local call in his or her own country.

The 0800 service enables you to rent one or more dedicated numbers in most EC countries. Use of a Continental 0800 number means you can interact personally and directly with EC customers, remembering, of course, the need to have a multilingual telephone receptionist to take foreign calls and deal with enquiries. (BT offers a separate service for this – see Chapter 3.) Freefone numbers may also be used by the firm's own staff, agents or distributors when calling head office from Continental locations.

Quoting a freefone number demonstrates to everyone your commitment to EC customer service and your total dedication to doing business in Continental markets. Sales should increase as a consequence of your enhanced accessibility and the fact that customers can respond immediately to maildrops and other advertising literature. International 0800 does not require additional equipment: calls come straight through on existing lines. Customers dial a number commencing with the local freefone dialling code (normally 0800) in the caller's country. Diversion facilities are available whereby International 0800 calls to your premises can be automatically transferred to some other UK (or Continental) location at set times each day.

Cost of the service

A small quarterly rental (currently less than £100) has to be paid. Thereafter, calls are charged per second or part second of connected time, regardless of the time of day. Currently, the charge varies between 50 pence and 70 pence per minute depending on the country from which the call originates. A 10 per cent discount applies to usage exceeding 2000 minutes per quarter. Details are available from:

British Telecom
International 0800
Freepost
London EC2B 2EA
0800 890800

0800 fax

Freefone 0800 numbers may be linked to fax machines. Hence customers and others can transmit complex specifications, technical drawings, etc to your UK headquarters free of charge. The great advantage of 0800 fax is its ability to bridge time zones: it does not matter if a message is transmitted at a time the UK office is closed. For urgent queries sent via fax it is possible to divert messages from machine to machine in different EC countries so that, for example, a distributor in a Continental EC country can deal with the enquiry.

European Telemarketing

Currently, EC telemarketing campaigns focus on business-to-business contacts, essentially because of the combined telephone/fax/telex/database facilities that an increasing number of companies possess and, in consequence, the greater reliability of business-to-business communications. The telephone can be used both to obtain orders and to conduct fast low cost EC market research.

However, you will almost certainly need to use the services of a commercial telemarketing agency to achieve a satisfactory outcome. Language skills are required, plus considerable skill and experience in identifying decision makers in target firms. Telemarketing agencies, moreover, can be engaged to receive the incoming calls resulting from a Community-wide 0800 number maildrop campaign. Switchboard operators taking such calls have to be competent to respond in any one of the EC languages and then pass the call to someone sufficiently *au fait* with the caller's language to be able to follow up the enquiry (eg by discussing the customer's requirements, offering a brochure, arranging a visit, etc). Note that the major telemarketing agencies now have transnational arrangements enabling the local country processing of incoming calls.

To find a telemarketing agency contact the Direct Marketing Association and/or the Institute of Sales Promotions (see page 78). Agencies are listed in Yellow Pages under 'Marketing and advertising consultants'. Also they advertise in the direct marketing magazines referred to on page 69.

Help with writing sales letters

Drafting EC sales literature is a specialist field for which specific copywriting skills are required. Promotional materials must:

- be convincing and attractively presented;

- relate to the needs of target audiences;

- contain clear and explicit procedures for responding to messages (filling in an order form, making a telephone call, visiting a show-room, etc).

The commonest method is to draft a basic version in very simple English, avoiding colloquialisms, puns or idiomatic expressions. Sentences should be short and not contain English words that have several different meanings. Then the draft has to be translated into appropriate EC languages, preferably by native copywriters in the countries concerned (or certainly by a UK translator fluent in the relevant language). Sources of information on translation services are given in Chapter 3. Direct Mail firms active in European markets are themselves increasingly adept at arranging translation.

Generally, a response address in the customer's own country is greatly preferable to one here in Britain, especially if cash with order is required. Advice and help with the production of direct mail materials are available from the Direct Mail Producers Association (see page 65) which publishes a list of its members (at present about 100 firms) and the services they provide.

European mailing lists

These can be obtained from commercial list brokers, many of which now carry European lists. Brokers' names and addresses are available from the British List Brokers Association.

British List Brokers Association Ltd
Springfield House
Princess Street
Bedminster
Bristol
BS5 4EF
0272 666900

Otherwise you can use trade directories (see Chapter 2), and/or examine the Yellow Pages of a particular EC country. The Royal Mail publishes a guide, *International Mailing Lists: How to Use Them, Where to Find Them,* which can be purchased from the Post Office. Another useful book is Euromonitor's *European Directory of Marketing Information Sources.*

Euromonitor Publications Ltd
87–88 Turnmill Street
London EC1M 5QU
071-251 8024

An excellent source of names and addresses of potential customers is lists (frequently available at very lost cost, or even free of charge) of attenders at recent trade fairs and exhibitions (see page 73) relevant to your product. Exhibition organisers are regularly asked for these by firms which are considering exhibiting at next year's event.

The magazine *Direct Marketing International* (see page 65) carries advertisements for European list broking firms plus occasional features on the current availability of international lists. Recent articles have contained news of:

- updates to lists of job titles and named individuals in major EC companies;
- freshly prepared lists of EC consumers who have purchased certain types of item via direct mail;
- lists of Europeans who regularly contribute to charities;
- the latest consumer lifestyle and demographic classifications (see Chapter 2);
- lists of EC firms according to number of employees and geographical region;
- lists of high value shareholders in large European companies;
- lists of EC consumers interested in health foods and environmentally friendly products.

Other magazines that sometimes carry list brokers' advertisements and information on current developments are *Direct Response* (see page 65), *Precision Marketing, Marketing,* and *Marketing Week.*

Precision Marketing
Marketing Week
Centaur Publications Ltd
50 Poland Street
London W1V 4AX
071-439 4222

Marketing
Haymarket Publications Ltd
30 Lancaster Gate
London W2 3LP
071-413 4078

Lists cost between £50 and £200 per 1000 addresses. Sometimes the terms of sale of a list will specify that it may be used once only. Such lists are 'seeded' by their suppliers, ie, the list will contain a few plausible-looking but bogus names and addresses which, if contacted more than once, will inform the supplier of the excessive use of the list.

Lists in Germany
Germany leads the way in list availability. At the time of writing, about 5000 business-to-business lists are offered for sale in that country, and about 500 consumer lists can also be purchased. Two-thirds of German lists consist of compiled lists, ie names and addresses taken from trade directories and similar published sources. The rest are 'responder lists' comprising details of customers who replied to previous promotions.

Note that the German Data Protection Act is more stringent than its UK or other EC equivalents. One effect of this is that, if you purchase a list from a German broker, you may be required to sign a declaration that the resulting maildrop will be conducted through a recognised German direct mail agency and not directly to end users from your own firm. You might even be asked to sign a statement that you have read and understood the German Data Protection Act, although this is not a legal necessity. As in other countries you will not be allowed to resell the list to third parties without the owner's permission.

Other EC countries
In Belgium the majority of purchasable lists are for individual named consumers rather than for named firms. The Belgian Post Office keeps lists of households that wish to receive information on products in various fields. Accordingly, the Post Office can deliver publicity materials to its list of all people in Belgium with a certain interest, without the items having to be individually addressed. For an introduction to the Belgian postal authorities contact:

Commercial Section
Belgian Embassy
36 Belgrave Square
London SW1W 9AB
071-235 5422

List broking is a rapidly expanding European industry, with France, the Netherlands and Italy experiencing exceptional growth in list availability during recent years. Currently, there are few lists covering potential customers in Spain, Portugal or Greece.

Details of brokers based in various Community countries can be obtained from national direct marketing associations, the names and addresses of which can be obtained from the European Direct Marketing Association.

Mail despatch services

You can use either the Royal Mail or a private carrier. Royal Mail services include a *Printflow* facility for sending printed papers to European destinations. Printflow is available for maildrops, brochures, booklets, catalogues, directories, price lists, etc, though not for magnetic media such as computer disks or video tapes. The latter are handled through a similar scheme, the *Contract Airmail Packet Service*. Printflow has two forms:

(a)   *Printflow Air,* which guarantees the fastest possible transit times (three to five working days door-to-door) using scheduled air services. You have the option of presenting the letters sorted or unsorted. Large discounts are available for mail that you sort yourself according to EC destination. The Royal Mail will provide bags and labels, and will take care of documentation. Mail going to each EC distribution centre (where it is fed into the local postal service) has to weigh at least 5 kgms. Further discounts are based on volume. Normally, items must be unsealed or 'Sealed Under Permit' (ie you pay [currently] £250 per year for a special licence to seal the envelopes, subject to making certain declarations about their contents).

(b)   *Printflow Surfacesaver,* which uses any convenient mode of transport to deliver mail which, again, may be sorted or unsorted at source. Transit time is five to seven days for near European destinations and seven to 14 days for longer journeys.

Envelopes used for Printflow mailings must carry special endorsements. Details are available from:

Royal Mail International
52 Grosvenor Gardens
London SW1W 0AA
071-681 9410

A further Printflow option is the use of Royal Mail 'M-Bags' whereby all items going to a certain EC destination are placed into bags sealed and labelled by the customer rather than by the Royal Mail. The customer also completes a customs document, although the Royal Mail will advise on how to do this.

Unsorted Printflow materials must be bundled separately from the rest of your mail, and have to weigh more than two kgs in aggregate.

Airstream

Airstream Europe is for really large mass mailings to Europe of presorted printed paper – paid for on a kilogram weight basis. The Post Office will collect the mail from your premises. Postage rates are based on *total* weight and the number of letters. This saves having to weigh and stamp individual items. Airstream flies at least twice a day to key European destinations.

Swiftair

This is a priority airmail service for individual letters, using the international postage network and hence avoiding the costs of a courier service. Swiftair mail receives special attention at each stage in its journey. Insurance is available on packages. Prepaid Swiftair packs may be purchased over the counter at Post Offices.

Reply paid services

A European business reply service is now in operation. You pay a small annual licence fee plus a set charge per reply returned (currently 25 pence per letter for more than 1000 items), although the first 1000 replies are covered by the annual licence fee (£250 in 1991). All replies are sent to you via airmail. Cards and/or envelopes are acceptable. The weight of reply envelopes including contents must not exceed 20 grams. A standard design has to be used for cards and envelopes carried by the service. For details contact:

Royal Mail International Sales
International Business Reply Service
Freepost
7th Floor
Impact House
2 Edridge Road
Croydon
Surrey CR9 9ER
081-681 9154

Note that newcomers to overseas direct mail marketing are normally entitled to an introductory offer (eg 3000 free items on a 10,000 item mailing).

Private services
Private direct mail distribution services have their own collection and air transport systems through which they:

(a) assemble sacks of mail for various destinations from client companies;
(b) fly the sacks to distribution centres in various EC countries;
(c) stamp the mail where it arrives and post it through the local system.

The problems involved
Although direct mail is potentially the easiest and most cost-effective means of selling to Europe it is important not to lose sight of the many practical difficulties involved. These include different postal rates and regulations, language problems, fulfilment of orders (locally or here in the UK), having to address prospects in certain countries by two or three family names, and the need to use a variety of typeface accents. Note, moreover, that bulk discounts for inland mailings differ from country to country so that the final cost per letter mailed can vary significantly between member states.

Exhibiting in Europe

Exhibitions are a key device for promoting goods in European markets. There are, nevertheless, several problems associated with exhibiting, including the following:

- Most consumers visit exhibitions to browse rather than to buy. How do you obtain the names and addresses of those callers on your stand who, subject to a follow-up letter or telephone call, are actually likely to purchase your products? And how can you identify important people who influence major buying decisions within their companies?

- Gimmicks may be highly effective in attracting visitors to your stand, but can attract the wrong people. An audience may be greatly impressed by the music, dancing, demonstration or whatever it is that you provide, yet not be remotely interested in your products.

- What criteria will be used to determine how big a display to mount at any given exhibition?

- Having a large and attractive stand at an exhibition could induce your competitors to do the same, thereby wiping out the benefits of exhibiting.

- How can the employees who staff your stand at an exhibition be prevented from treating the exercise as a holiday – paying more attention to the social aspects of their involvement with the exhibition than to finding customers? What specific targets can the staff be given and how can the attainment of targets be measured?

- How is exhibiting to be dovetailed into the company's general marketing plans? What marketing objectives does exhibiting seek to achieve?

- What is known in advance about the numbers and characteristics of the people who will visit the exhibition, their lengths of stay, needs and buying habits?

- How can you ensure that the proposed stand will be well located *vis-à-vis* the layout and illumination of the exhibition centre and the anticipated traffic flow?

Advantages of exhibiting
The advantages of exhibiting are that:

- you have face-to-face contact with potential major customers;

- you can size up the competition;

- visitors' names and addresses may be used for subsequent maildrops;

- agents and distributors of your type of product will be among the visitors;

- you can obtain an initial idea of local consumer reaction to your output;

- orders might be obtained on the spot;

- buyers from other EC countries (whom you can subsequently contact with a view to extending the scope of your European operations) might attend the exhibition.

Government help with exhibiting
Financial assistance for exporters wishing to attend foreign exhibitions is available via the Fairs and Promotions Branch (FPB) of the DTI.

DTI Fairs and Promotions Branch
Horseferry Road
London SW1P 2AG
071-276 2414

Each quarter the Branch publishes a list of the promotions it is prepared to support. Assistance is given to *groups* of British exporters attending an overseas fair, and covers 50 per cent of the following:

- The cost of hiring exhibition space.

- Design and construction of stands.

- Display materials.

- Access to a group interpreter.

- Publicity for exhibitors' products through the Central Office of Information.

Note that the cost of travel is *not* recoverable for European destinations. Also, it is only possible to claim support for the first three exhibitions in a certain country. Three further conditions attach to the scheme:

- You have to arrive at the foreign destination at least a day before the exhibition opens in order to set up your stand.

- The stand must be properly staffed at all times.

- Travel arrangements, insurance and hotel bookings are your responsibility.

Overseas stores promotions
The Fairs and Promotions Branch will also provide financial help to major foreign retail outlets wishing to mount in-store promotions of UK goods. The DTI advises British firms on how to participate effectively in such a promotion and informs buying offices in the local market of the occurrence of the event. News about forthcoming in-store promotions is distributed by the FPB.

Overseas seminars
If a Chamber of Commerce or trade association arranges a seminar aimed at bringing together influential people capable of stimulating the overseas sales of its members' products, the DTI will meet 45 per cent of the following costs:

- hire of an auditorium plus supporting services;

- translation and printing of papers;
- local publicity;
- the fee of one internationally known speaker;
- stand construction and associated costs of an exhibition attached to the seminar.

Exhibition planning
The specific matters you need to address include:

- whether to undertake pre-exhibition promotions (eg maildrops to people likely to visit the exhibition);
- visual presentation of the stand: colour scheme, headlines, staff uniforms, etc;
- the best ratio of staff to stand space;
- style and quantity of leaflets, brochures and other literature required;
- how to evaluate the effectiveness of the firm's exhibition efforts (eg how to measure the sales resulting from stand enquiries);
- budgetary control over exhibition activities: stand erection and removal (including electrics and water, where appropriate), cleaning, insurance, printing of leaflets, hotel reservations for staff, hire of furniture, etc;
- booking of interpreters;
- deciding an exact position for your stand.

Further duties relate to the hiring of local stand erectors; the design and submission of plans for stands; determining requirements for telephones, furniture, lighting, etc; and arranging a Carnet (see Chapter 5) for the temporary import of sample goods.

You must plan these matters well in advance of the exhibition. It is especially important to prepare high quality publicity material for inclusion in the exhibition catalogue (together with an advertisement if appropriate) and to have printed adequate supplies of promotional literature for distribution on the stand.

Information on forthcoming EC exhibitions is available from the DTI and from some of the large airlines and travel agents (which will book your flight and arrange for hotel accommodation near the exhibition).

Deciding which exhibitions to attend
Not all exhibitions are worth attending, and for certain types of product

there are so many exhibitions in European countries that it is physically impossible to attend all of them. Use the following criteria to decide which to support.

(a)   The degree of overlap between target consumers and likely visitors to the exhibition.
(b)   Whether the exhibition is well established (recently inaugurated exhibitions usually attract small attendances).
(c)   The extent of the availability of (1) useful information on the composition of past audiences, (2) lists of attenders and previous exhibitors, (3) amounts of new business generated, and so on.
(d)   How many orders you need to secure to cover the cost of exhibiting at the venue.
(e)   Whether the leads obtained from exhibiting can be easily followed up.

Sales promotions in the European Community

Sales promotions can be extremely effective as a marketing tool in European countries. They may be used to:

- stimulate impulse purchasing;
- encourage customer loyalty;
- attract consumers to an exhibition or showroom;
- penetrate new markets;
- increase the frequency of repeat buying;
- shift slow moving stock;
- smooth out seasonal demand, and generally draw attention to your firm and its products.

Promotions may be recommended and organised by European agents or distributors, or initiated by yourself. A wide range of promotional devices is available, including:

- money-off coupons
- competitions
- free draws
- coupons redeemable against the next purchase
- in-store promotions

- free samples
- premium offers (eg send in a certain number of packet tops plus a small amount of money and receive the offered item at very low cost).

The problem is that different laws apply to sales promotions in different EC states. For instance, at the time of writing a money-off voucher is legal in Spain but not in West Germany; a 'lower price for the next purchase' offer is legal in Belgium, illegal in Denmark and could be illegal in Italy; cross-product offers (buy one item and get a big price reduction on something else) are illegal in Luxembourg; and free draws are illegal in the Netherlands.

Coupons and door-to-door free samples cannot be used as easily in France as in most other EC states, while in Germany free gifts and premiums are forbidden if they constitute a genuine incentive to buy (on the grounds that they represent unfair competition).

To date, the European Commission has made two attempts to harmonise member countries' sales promotions laws and practices. The first occurred in 1974, the second in 1988. Neither succeeded, yet some degree of harmonisation is urgently required and it is to be expected that further and perhaps more serious attempts will soon be made.

The trade association for the sales promotion industry is the Institute of Sales Promotions, which will issue a list of its members interested in European consultancy work.

Institute of Sales Promotions
Arena House
66–68 Pentonville Road
London N1 9HS
071-837 5340

Typically, SP consultants will implement as well as suggest promotional strategies, so you can ask to see examples of previous work prior to making your choice. To brief an SP consultant you need to provide full details of the characteristics of your brands, package sizes, markets to be covered, product distribution system (including the whereabouts and calibre of retail outlets) and how much you are willing to spend. Then the consultant will devise a set of promotional techniques to achieve the specified aims (free samples to enter new markets, reduced price offers to encourage repeat purchase, money-off coupons to attract customers to the premises, etc). He or she will estimate redemption rates, suggest an appropriate number of customer proofs of purchase, look after the legal aspects of the promotion (competitions are especially complicated in this regard), and may arrange for the production of coupons and/or other promotional literature.

The 'New Products from Britain' (NPB) service

This is intended to generate foreign interest in British firms' products by encouraging overseas magazines and journals to publish feature articles on new British products as they are launched in local markets. A press release describing your product is written by a professional journalist and then translated and targeted at suitable foreign publications. All you have to do is provide the UK Central Office of Information (which organises the scheme) with brochures and other publicity materials, and to respond to telephone calls if further information is required. The product must be newsworthy in order to attract foreign attention. At the time of writing the cost is £60, which covers up to 15 selected target markets. Press releases are normally available to local British Diplomatic Posts within eight weeks of a decision to use the service. Information about NPB is available from the DTI.

Chapter 5
Getting Goods to the Continent

Goods can be sent to the Continent by road and ferry, rail, parcel post, airfreight or, for more distant European destinations, conventional shipping services. The extent of the firm's direct involvement in arranging transport can be varied according to your needs, resources and experience of international distribution. You could, for example, simply hire a freight forwarder (see below) to manage everything from the collection of goods from your premises right up to their final delivery abroad. At the other extreme you might opt to do everything yourself, especially if you have transport vehicles suitable for long European journeys and have a volume of European business sufficient to justify regular large deliveries. Another possibility is to arrange transport up to and including an EC airport, dock, rail terminal or other point of disembarkation and then contract a foreign third party to assume responsibility for the remainder of the journey.

Regardless of your precise arrangements someone, somewhere, must organise the following:

- physical carriage of the goods;

- insurance of the consignment (see Chapter 8);

- loading goods into containers and the movement of containers to relevant distribution centres;

- booking cargo space;

- warehousing;

- completing and despatching all the forms necessary to move goods between EC countries;

- final delivery.

Parcel post

The Royal Mail will deliver large parcels up to 20 kilos in weight door to door to Continental destinations. An 'all in' rate is charged which covers all transport and documentation. Insurance is available for an extra fee. If you are sending small consignments to numerous destinations, parcel post can be an attractive possibility. Contact the Post Office for details.

Freight forwarders

These are businesses which specialise in the international movement of goods. Forwarders provide advice on:

- which modes of transport are most suitable for carrying a client firm's output taking account of its size, weight, characteristics and the urgency of the delivery;
- packaging and labelling;
- how and where to store consignments on arrival in EC countries.

A forwarder will assume full responsibility for documentation and insurance; will book air freight or ferry space for consignments; arrange for the collection of goods from sea ports, railway stations or container depots in other countries; and organise final road delivery. Major forwarders have their own transport fleets. Otherwise they subcontract the actual carriage of goods to third parties in various countries. Forwarders take their profits from fees charged to client companies; from commissions taken from the airlines, shipping companies, etc with which they book space; and from bulk discounts given by carriers and commercial warehouses in consequence of forwarders' groupage (consolidation) services.

Groupage

A major reason for engaging a forwarder is its ability to provide groupage facilities, meaning that at its collection depots it can consolidate numerous small shipments into a single large consignment going to a particular destination, typically using a container. The larger forwarding companies possess their own container deposit and pick-up facilities throughout the Continent. They also subscribe to an international clearing house system that enables containers to be left (and reused) at final destinations rather than having to be returned empty.

Substantial discounts are available for the bulk transportation of consolidation consignments, part of which the forwarder will pass back to small business clients in the form of lower freight prices. Moreover, a forwarder can often avoid the losses resulting from lorries having to return from particular destinations empty, since forwarders continuously liaise with each other and swap counter-directional loads.

The problem with groupage is that a specific consignment may be stored at the forwarder's collection depot for several days awaiting a consolidation into which it conveniently fits. Express service is always available, but only at a considerably higher fee.

Finding a forwarder

You have to be careful when selecting a freight forwarder; indeed, one survey revealed that nearly half of all users of forwarding firms were dissatisfied with the service provided! This is perhaps unfair to freight forwarders because exporters do not always appreciate the complexity of the documentation that has in the past been needed to transport goods across national frontiers and the extent of the administrative red tape and sources of delay that are entirely beyond the forwarder's control. Few air journeys, for example, take more than two hours to EC destinations; yet at least two or three working days may be necessary to clear the consignment – perhaps even a couple of weeks if dangerous goods are involved.

To find a forwarder contact the Institute of Freight Forwarders, which is the industry's professional body and which seeks constantly to improve the standard of service provided by its members. The official name of the IFF is the British International Freight Association, although it chooses to continue to be known as the IFF.

British International Freight Association
Redfern House
Browells Lane
Feltham
Middlesex TW13 7EP
081-844 2266

Otherwise, look in Yellow Pages under the heading, 'Freight forwarding and warehousing' which contains several sub-divisions for forwarders specialising in particular fields.

Doing-it-yourself

Using a forwarder enables you to arrange delivery via a single contract with a UK firm, and the procedure is fast and simple. Yet following the completion of the Single Market the volume of paperwork needed for EC delivery should reduce drastically, and you ought at least to investigate the costs and feasibility of organising transportation yourself. After all, the main purpose behind the Single Market's creation is to enable UK (and other European) businesses to sell their output in Paris, Brussels or Milan as easily as in (say) Manchester, Glasgow or Leeds.

Transport cost analysis

The following sections explain basic procedures for sending goods to EC destinations using various types of transport. Examine the options carefully, and then conduct an analysis of the costs of each alternative relative to customer needs (speed and frequency of delivery, reliability of delivery dates, convenience of collection, etc). Compare freight rates, insurance costs, intermediate handling and storage charges (warehousing, for example), special packaging costs, documentation expenses, expected pilferage, spoilage rates, stockholding costs, and (most important) the interest on capital forgone through having money tied up as goods in transit for various journey times.

Rail and the Channel Tunnel

The Channel Tunnel will create continuity of transport between Britain and the Continent and provide direct access to combined EC road/rail transport systems. These mainly rely on standardised detachable interchangeable 'swap body' containers equally suitable for road haulage vehicles and the European 'road train' system.

Swap body containers are self-contained trailers on their own wheels that can be exchanged between cabs, as opposed to 'flat' trailers on to which containers have to be loaded. The entire swap body can be uncoupled from a cab, rolled on to a road train for long haul rail transport, and rolled off and attached to another cab at its final rail destination.

Direct 'piggyback' transport (ie the carriage of road vehicles by train) will also be possible for long journeys to the Continent, especially for trips to Germany, Italy, southern Spain and Greece. Piggybacking is already widely used by Italian, German and French exporters and as the Tunnel system develops it is sure to assume ever-increasing importance for businesses in the UK.

How the Tunnel link will operate

Half the Tunnel's capacity has been leased to the British and French Railways. The owner (Euro Tunnel Ltd) will use the remainder for its own shuttle services, which will run between the Tunnel's two portals (at Folkestone in England and at Coquelles to the west of Calais in France). Track gauge is the same as the European main railway lines so that services can operate from all principal UK industrial centres to Continental rail destinations. Note, however, that although the French TGV (*très grande vitesse*) will run right up to the French terminal at Coquelles it will not thereafter run on to London or other UK destinations.

Goods will be shifted either on container freight trains travelling from the UK to various Continental destinations, or in lorries carried on special shuttles between Folkestone and Coquelles that will operate around the clock and for which no prior booking will be required. Between two and four shuttle services per hour are envisaged. Drivers will travel in an air conditioned lounge with refreshment facilities. A journey of about one and a quarter hours from leaving the M20 to joining the French motorway at Calais is predicted.

Rail freight through the Tunnel is to be handled by Railfreight Distribution (RD):

Railfreight Distribution
Enterprise House
167–169 Westbourne Terrace
London W2 6JY
071-922 4385

Existing rail services

Currently RD offers multimodal (road-rail-road) door to door or terminal to terminal Freightliner services. Containerised traffic travels via Harwich-Zeebrugge; otherwise, train ferries (see below) operate four times a day from Dover to Dunkirk. RD containers have capacity for 33 to 69 cubic metre loads, with some containers being able to accommodate two Europallets (see page 102) side by side. Warehousing, break bulk and specialised handling services can be provided if required. RD is a member of the European Intercontainer Pool (see below), which particularly benefits RD customers who only need one-way delivery to the Continent.

RD Trainferry

Each of RD Trainferry's four daily return sailings carries up to 30 high capacity rail wagons on 600 metres of track. Wagons can take up to 63 tonnes of goods (double the maximum permittable payload of a UK road vehicle) and follow the Roll On/Roll Off principle. Total loading/unloading time is approximately one hour. A computerised cargo tracking system operates. This is linked up to HERMES, the Continental rail cargo tracking scheme. RD Trainferry will arrange Continental door-to-door distribution if required.

Following the Tunnel's completion, RD plans to run (initially) 54 trains to and from the Continent (27 each way), more if there is sufficient demand.

Intercontainer
RD and the other European railways have formed a joint subsidiary, Intercontainer, to carry and administer Continental container traffic. Containers may travel directly in train loads to (currently) 17 main centres for transfer to local rail networks and then on to road vehicles for door-to-

door delivery. Until now, most UK Intercontainer traffic has been with Italy and Germany, but it is set to expand sharply following the opening of the Channel Tunnel. Intercontainer plans 10–12 dedicated trains per day through the Tunnel carrying swap bodies and containers. They will leave UK railway stations on the evening of day one, travel during day two and be ready for local Continental pick-up and door-to-door delivery early in the morning of the third day. Details are available from RD or directly from:

Intercontainer
Margarethenstrasse 38
CH–4008 Basle
Switzerland
010 41 61 452525

The Channel Tunnel hub and spoke system
The Tunnel distribution system is to be organised on the 'hub and spoke' principle and will exhibit the following characteristics:

(a)   Timetabled 'through trains' will run between main distribution centres (the exact locations of which have yet to be determined), normally on a daily basis, but at least three times per week. Britain will have eight to ten of these centres, the Continent 12 to 15. Note how the guarantee of a train leaving for a particular destination at a pre-specified time – whether it is fully loaded or not – will avoid some of the groupage problems (see page 81) sometimes associated with other modes of cross-Channel freight transport.

(b)   Although the need for customs clearance should soon be abolished for intra-community trade, it is almost certain that some (simplified) documents will still be necessary, especially for goods originating outside the Community. The processing of these documents will be undertaken inland at the departure terminal. Each member country's customs authorities will provide facilities for this. For shuttle and other portal-to-portal services, goods that need to be processed by Customs and Excise will be cleared on the UK side at an inland depot at Ashford in Kent – ten miles from the Folkestone terminal. Similar inland clearing facilities will operate at Coquelles. All documentation, immigration and other controls will be dealt with at the departure terminal, so that vehicles can drive straight on to the motorway at the other end.

(c)   In addition to through trains, eight trains per day comprising 3 60-foot wagons destined for various centres will run in either direction through the Tunnel. Each of these trains will go to one of the 'hubs' of the system (eg Willesden for the south of England, Lille for northern France). The exact number and whereabouts of all the hubs have yet to be decided.

At the hub, wagons from these trains will then be transferred to other engines in order to make up complete wagon sets for transportation through a system 'spoke' to a particular distribution centre. If there are sufficient volumes of freight bound for certain destinations, 'full block' trains will be made up and run direct to those destinations on an *ad hoc* basis, without entering the hub and spoke system.

(d) A computerised tracking system will be introduced to enable customers to monitor the movement of their goods through the entire network and to ascertain the precise location of consignments at any given moment.

Advantages of the Tunnel system

Using the Tunnel will offer two major advantages over alternative means of transport: speed and a significant reduction in the need for intermediate handling during transit, as it will no longer be necessary to transfer goods from rail to ship and *vice versa* at UK and Continental ports. Other benefits the Tunnel should bring are as follows:

(a) A common distribution system with standard procedures for accessing all parts of the Community. The same documents will apply to the movement of goods to any member state.

(b) Only one mode of transport will be needed to reach selected markets.

(c) The ability to reach most EC destinations within 72 hours.

(d) It will take some traffic away from the ferry operators and airline services thus enabling ferry and airline companies to reduce their cargo despatch and processing times.

(e) The threat of aggressive competition from Euro-Tunnel is already causing ferry and airline firms to improve their services, hold their prices and generally pay greater attention to customers' needs.

(f) Services will be fast, convenient, reliable and unaffected by high seas, fog and other climatic conditions.

Transit times

Freight transit times will fall dramatically (eg London to Paris in 12 hours, Liverpool to Milan in 36 hours). Railfreight Distribution Channel Tunnel express services are scheduled to travel at speeds of up to 75 mph, cutting transit times to most European destinations by at least 24 hours. The following indicative journey times are quoted.

From London:		
	Lyons	18 hours
	Frankfurt	24 hours
	Turin	30 hours
	Valencia	48 hours

From Birmingham:	Strasburg	18 hours
	Roux	24 hours
	Bologna	42 hours
	Vienna	42 hours
From Manchester:	Brussels	18 hours
	Hanover	30 hours
	Munich	36 hours
	Barcelona	42 hours
From Glasgow:	Lille	18 hours
	Marseilles	36 hours
	Stuttgart	36 hours
	Salzburg	48 hours
From Cardiff:	Bordeaux	24 hours
	Basle	24 hours
	Milan	36 hours
	Madrid	48 hours

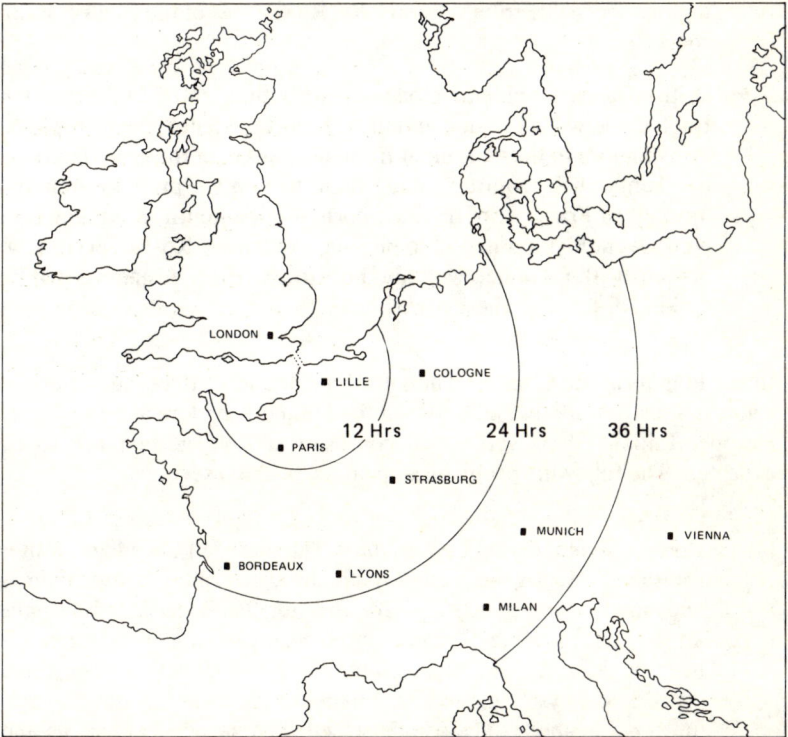

Figure 5.1 *Anticipated freight journey time zones based on a London departure*

Limitations of the proposed network

It is important to realise, however, that the Channel Tunnel will not solve every UK business's Continental distribution problems overnight. The following constraints and difficulties should be noted:

- Rail transport is more economical the longer the distance involved. Thus, for journeys shorter than 250–300 miles, road/ferry freight services will probably continue to be substantially cheaper than rail, especially as the latter begin cutting their prices in response to the challenge to their business that the Channel Tunnel presents. This is particularly true where door-to-door delivery is required.

- Certain areas will not be easy to reach via the Tunnel hub and spoke system and, in consequence, BR freight charges will not be competitive in comparison with alternative modes of transport to such regions. These areas will probably include most of the Netherlands and north west Germany (served as they are by the highly efficient sea port at Rotterdam), Normandy (see Chapter 9) Brittany and other regions accessible from the ferry Ro-Ro services of the English south coast.

- British Rail is not planning to have distribution centres in the south of England between London and the UK portal. Hence, the transportation of goods to the Continent from locations near the south coast via the Tunnel will require sending them to London prior to their rail journey to France. South coast ports – Portsmouth, Southampton, Newhaven, Plymouth, and so on – have extensive Ro-Ro services, so obviously the Tunnel will not be attractive to businesses within striking distance of these towns.

In the long term the Channel Tunnel will profoundly affect the pattern of trade and distribution in and between the United Kingdom and the rest of Europe. Initially, however, much confusion and congestion are to be expected. The following problems appear particularly severe:

(a)   *Political indecision and uncertainty.* The intended UK inland routes for trains servicing the Tunnel system have been altered several times and, at the time of writing, are still not finally settled. Nor have arrangements for the documentation and processing of consignments been finalised. Businesses need time to establish new transport and distribution systems, and the inability of firms to obtain hard information about the eventual structure of the network means that they cannot plan ahead to obtain maximum benefit from Tunnel facilities.

(b) *Inadequate rail capacity.* The UK railway system, it has been announced, is not to be modernised in order to cope with the extra freight traffic the Tunnel will generate. This contrasts sharply with the situation in France, Germany and a number of other Continental countries, which are investing heavily in international high-speed rail systems. Hence, British Rail will not connect directly with the new Euro-rail system at present being constructed.

(c) *Road congestion.* Certain UK terminals for incoming Tunnel traffic are in areas already experiencing severe road congestion. The effects of greatly increased lorry traffic around these areas as vehicles collect consignments from off-loading rail depots are, to say the least, disturbing. Morever, the bulk of passenger traffic is planned to pass through London Waterloo, which has poor quality rail links with surrounding areas and is not directly linked to the north of England, Wales or Scotland.

Ferry and road

This is currently the commonest method of transporting UK goods to the Continent. About 85 per cent of all road/ferry consignments are carried by third party commercial road hauliers, the rest by vehicles owned by exporting firms. Complete vehicles, or the trailers of articulated lorries, are transported on Roll-on Roll-off (Ro-Ro) ferries from UK ports. (An articulated lorry is one that comprises two separate parts: cab and trailer, connected by a bar or some other linking device.)

A great advantage of door-to-door European road haulage is the avoidance of the need for transhipment of goods (ie having to unload and reload consignments between different modes of transport), thus reducing handling costs and pilferage losses. Final delivery by road is convenient for customers and flexible (routes and destinations can be altered quickly and at will). Road/ferry transport, moreover, can be entirely self-contained: consignments may be moved in sealed loads direct from supplier to consignee. The problem, of course, is the possible absence of loads for return journeys. Road hauliers need to make the fullest use of vehicles especially the cabs ('tractors') of articulated lorries and will incorporate the costs of any time a vehicle is not earning money into quoted delivery charges.

Ro-Ro ferries

Use of cross-Channel Ro-Ro ferries has tripled during the last ten years, and further increases are inevitable following the completion of the Single Market. Ro-Ro services exist along the entire European coastline – from Spain to Scandinavia – and for many years have eliminated the need for intermediate checking of vehicles and/or handling of goods.[1] An entire vehicle may be driven straight on to the ferry and off again at the port of destination or (more commonly) the trailer of an articulated lorry is detached from its cab, tractored on to the ferry, then tractored off and coupled to another cab on the other side. The latter method is popular because it allows the transmission elements (cabs) of articulated vehicles to be continuously used for making deliveries rather than standing idle at docks and on ferries for hours at a time.

Ro-Ro is cheap because goods handling is reduced to the absolute minimum (no lifting gear is required, and marshalling is easy) and because (multi-million pound) ferries can turn around extremely quickly. However, the effective payload of the trailer of an articulated lorry transported in this manner is substantially lower than (say) a rail or conventional sea container in consequence of the extra weight of the wheels and frame of the vehicle and the additional space these occupy.

The large ferry companies themselves provide integrated door-to-door collection and delivery services throughout the Continent. P & O Ferry-masters, for example, has a fleet of 120 vehicles serving central Europe (Germany, Benelux and Italy, plus surrounding non-EC states). It operates two sailings per day through Ipswich and Rotterdam, and will arrange customs formalities plus all necessary documentation, including EDI (see page 107). Similar facilities apply for southern Europe and Greece. Direct sailings to several European ports also occur via associated companies. P & O has UK groupage points at Warrington, Nottingham and Manningtree, with counterpart depots in 36 key European destinations including an Eastern European hub at s'Heerenberg on the Dutch/German border.

P & O Ferrymasters Ltd
Whitehouse Industrial Estate
Goddard Road
Ipswich
Suffolk IP1 5NP
0473 42222

Rates for Ro-Ro services depend on the length of the vehicle and whether it is accompanied or unaccompanied, empty or loaded. Freight forwarders negotiate discounts with ferry operators based on a guaranteed volume of business over a long period. These discounts can then be passed back to customers.

[1.] An international transport agreement, known as the TIR (*Transports Internationaux Routiers*) convention, has for many years enabled road hauliers to seal their vehicles here in the UK, travel across national frontiers without interference, and have all documentation processed at the final delivery point. Until now special TIR documents were needed for this procedure. Today, however, the SAD (see page 104) is all that is required for EC road transport.

Advantages of ferry transport

Ferry companies will, of course, respond ferociously to the new competition resulting from the Channel Tunnel. The following advantages of ferries over rail carriage are claimed by the ferry operators:

(a) *Frequency of operations.* Already there are about 30 sailings *each day* from Dover to Calais, and only slightly fewer daily sailings between other main UK and Continental ports. Dartford, for example, now offers 24-hour operations, is fully equipped for swap body trade (see page 83), and can have two large vessels in dock and working side by side regardless of the state of the tide. Currently, most of its traffic involves Zeebrugge in Belgium and Esbjerg in Denmark, with an increasing volume of shipments to France. There is an adjacent 36-acre trailer park area with capacity for 1200 units. Dartford has a throughput capacity of 250,000 trailers per annum.

    Dartford International Ferry Terminal
    Stone Marshes
    Dartford
    Kent DA2 6QB
    0322 92111

(b) *The continuing expansion of the demand for ferry services* has enabled ferry operators to obtain economies of large-scale operation which have lowered cross-Channel transit costs to a level the railway will find hard to beat.

(c) *Reliability.* The ferry companies are well established; possess tried and tested loading and disembarkation procedures; and perhaps would claim to be better organised and generally more efficient than British Rail.

(d) *The ability to carry hazardous cargo* (a service the Channel Tunnel system cannot provide). Ro-Ro vessels have built-in driver accommodation and documentation facilities.

(e) *Coverage.* Ferry services operate from ports all over the UK. Major Ro-Ro facilities exist at Felixstowe, Hull, Poole and Plymouth. (For a complete list of Ro-Ro services in and out of Britain, see Appendix 1 of Nicholas Mohr's book, *Distribution for the Small Business,* published by Kogan Page.)

(f) *The time taken for a channel crossing through the Tunnel will only be 45 minutes less than using a ferry* (assuming Ro-Ro vehicles loaded on to Tunnel shuttles require the same clearance time as ferry vehicles). And the ferry environment – with restaurants, amenity rooms, recreational facilities, and so on – is arguably more attractive than a Tunnel journey. Vehicle drivers can genuinely rest while on a ferry and thus will require fewer relaxation periods on the other side.

The threat of competition from British Rail has engendered much new investment by parties with vested interests in the survival of ferry crossings.

Harbour Boards in particular are spending unprecedented amounts on new facilities: extra berths, direct roadways to embarkation points, additional warehousing and office space, etc. 'Superferries' with room for 100 lorries per crossing are being introduced, and the French Railway has built a train ferry capable of transporting 600 metres of rail freight on one deck and 700 metres of Ro-Ro freight on another!

Using your own lorry
If you intend using your own vehicle to deliver goods to European customers you need to contact the Department of Transport's International Road Freight Office, and obtain its (free) booklet entitled *Your Lorry Abroad.* Further detailed information about European road transport is available from the Freight Transport Association, which publishes a *Driver's Handbook,* plus guides to the specific operational requirements (weight restrictions, traffic rules, etc) of all European countries.

> Department of Transport
> International Road Freight Office
> Westgate House
> Westgate Road
> Newcastle upon Tyne NE1 1TW
> 091-261 0031

> Freight Transport Association
> Hermes House
> St John's Road
> Tunbridge Wells
> Kent TN4 9UZ
> 0892 26171

Legal and procedural road transport matters are scheduled for early harmonisation across the Community.[2] Eventually, permits to drive commercial vehicles through other EC member states will not be required.

Your ordinary UK motor insurance is sufficient for third party cover on all EC roads, although you could be compelled to produce evidence of third party cover if a country's traffic authorities so insist. Accordingly, you need to carry your UK Insurance Certificate with you on all European journeys – or the old 'Green Card' if you prefer. Green Cards are obligatory if your journey will take you beyond the EC.

---

[2] Until recently, international lorry trips in Europe were controlled by complicated and restrictive bilaterally negotiated permit systems between EC member states. The permit system is scheduled to end quickly. Prior to abolition, however, it is necessary to harmonise road tax, HGV driving licence requirements, drivers' working conditions and insurance arrangements across the EC.

Using a commercial road haulier

Many UK road hauliers provide complete door-to-door collection and delivery services to and from Continental destinations, including all the necessary documentation. You can find road hauliers in Yellow Pages, or by contacting the Road Haulage Association, which will actively help potential exporters to contact suitable hauliers.

> Road Haulage Association
> Roadway House
> 104 New Kings Road
> London SW6 4LN
> 071-736 1183

A road haulier's receipt for accepting a consignment is called a CMR note (*Convention de Marchandises par Route*). This records the contract of carriage, but does not provide evidence of ownership of the shipment. Additional documents are required for the road transportation of dangerous goods. Details are available from RHA, FTA or SITPRO (see page 105).

The CMR convention lays down standard international contractual conditions for road transport, covering liability for loss or damage to goods and the maximum value of insurance claims against the haulier. You need, however, to check carefully who precisely will be responsible for extra costs incurred through ferry strikes, border delays, etc.

Airfreight

Airfreight is fast and convenient. Insurance costs are slightly lower than for other means of transport (goods are at risk for shorter periods), and airfreight rates themselves are poised to fall in consequence of intended deregulation.[3] In the past, airfreight has been restricted to the transport of high-value low-bulk consignments. Increasingly, however, new and inexpensive aircraft are available capable of carrying larger and heavier loads. Indeed, it is now cheaper to send certain goods by air than any other method. Moreover, speedy delivery means less stockholding, faster settlement of invoices and hence better use of working capital. Certain intermediate warehousing costs may also be avoided since goods can go straight from the airport to customers' premises.

Airfreight is especially useful, therefore, for goods where demand is seasonal or highly variable, as it becomes possible to meet new orders

---

[3] Most European airlines belong to the International Air Transport Association (IATA) which sets common airfreight rates that in theory apply to all IATA members. In practice, however, price competition between airlines does exist (via special discounts and so on) and there is a considerable spread of airfreight prices.

immediately without having to store goods in local warehouses. (The cost of warehousing may average as much as one-third the value of the stored items.)

Heathrow accounts for more cargo than any other UK airport, and the volume of airfreight passing through Heathrow is increasing by about 5 per cent each year. More than 100 airlines operate at Heathrow, and there are at least 400 freight forwarding agents in the area.

Airfreight procedures

Sending cargo by air is relatively straightforward compared to other modes of transport. You can deliver goods direct to the cargo terminal of the airline with which you have booked space, or you can engage a freight forwarder (see page 81) or 'cargo agent'. The latter help consignors to arrange shipments and documentation, and will organise goods collection services if required. Airlines will provide lists of their approved agents. The major airlines themselves also offer customer collection facilities. For certain airports you can deliver to airport container depots in city centres rather than to the actual airport.

The British Airports Authority publishes a useful *Information Directory* that lists contact points and addresses of (a) cargo agents based around the three BAA airports (Heathrow, Gatwick and Stanstead) and (b) members of the Road Haulage Association's Airfreight Carriers Group who provide collection and delivery services in the London airports area. This Directory is available from:

British Airports Authority (Air Cargo)
Building 554
World Cargo Centre
London Heathrow Airport Ltd
Middlesex TW6 1JH
081-745 7134

Procedures are simple: you need (a) to book cargo space, (b) to get your goods to the airport, and (c) to arrange for their collection or delivery to the customer from the receiving airport.

Booking space

You can offer your cargo directly to an airline (British Airways or Lufthansa, for instance) or to a freight forwarder – who will almost certainly provide a consolidation (groupage) service.

(a)   *Direct booking.* To book directly you contact the airline and state when the goods will (definitely) arrive at the airport. The airline sends you a booking form (which might be called an 'instructions for despatch of goods' [IDG]) on which you specify who will be responsible for the payment of loading, freight and other fees and who will collect the goods on their arrival. Otherwise a straightforward letter containing this information will normally be acceptable *in lieu.*

(b)   *Using a freight forwarder.* The advantage here is the (substantial) cost saving available to a forwarder who can consolidate the shipments of several clients into full container loads for transport on wide bodied aircraft. Space on the latter is sold at large bulk discounts which forwarders may in part pass back to customers via lower freight prices. If a forwarding company finds that it has purchased too much air cargo space, it simply sells off the surplus to other forwarders.

At present about two-thirds of all air cargo is carried in the holds of passenger aircraft, which are increasingly suitable for this purpose as aeroplanes are made wider to accommodate more passenger seats – resulting in extra space beneath the passengers.

Getting goods to the airport

Airports and forwarders have their own depots to which you deliver your consignments. Alternatively, you can have a forwarder pick them up from your premises (for which service an additional fee is payable). At the depot the goods will be loaded into a Unit Load Device which is then weighed and presented for shipment. Unit Load Devices may be conventional rectangular containers or, more commonly, 'igloos' designed to fit exactly the peculiar dimensions of the fusilages of different makes of freighting aircraft. ULDs are supplied free to shippers who possess the capacity to handle them. They provide greater protection and security, minimise labour and handling requirements, and enable users to claim large discounts on airfreight rates. Moreover, the larger airlines (British Airways, for instance) operate trucking services specially designed to ease the transfer of igloo containers to and from aircraft, both here in the UK and abroad, hence providing a complete door-to-door igloo transport service to certain foreign destinations.

Airlines will also collect and deliver goods to an airport. Self delivery (or hiring a local road haulier to shift the consignment) is not necessarily cheaper than using a freight forwarder or airline company because the latter might be able to collect loads from several different customers in the same area on a certain day, and you do not have to pay for the return empty journey from the airport.

Freight rates

Airfreight rates are quoted by weight and volume, with the customer paying according to whichever is the higher value. In other words, for a given amount of money you get either so much space or a certain number of kilos. If, therefore, you are freighting a bulky yet light consignment you pay by volume and not by weight, and *vice versa*.

Discounts apply to cargo size, type of product, the route taken, and the sizes and shapes of containers (bulk loading of wide fuselage aircraft is much easier and cheaper than when peculiarly shaped igloo ULDs are required). The airlines will not normally insure cargos. This you have to do separately yourself. Also, they will not usually accept cash on delivery business.

The European Commission has announced its displeasure at air transport price fixing arrangements, and has threatened deregulation. If this occurs, freight rates should fall dramatically, especially for large long-term contracts.

Price fixing does not apply to consignments big enough to justify chartering an entire aircraft. Rates for this vary widely depending on (a) the type of aircraft chartered, (b) the urgency of the trip, and (c) the time of year the aircraft is required. However, a chartered aircraft is not necessarily cheaper than scheduled freight services, since the charterer may have to pay for the entire round trip if the chartered plane needs to return empty.

The air waybill

This is a consignment note issued by the airline. It is not a document of title. However, provided the goods are addressed to the person (customer, agent, distributor) named on the air waybill and that person settles any outstanding freight or airport charges, the goods will be handed over on landing if the consignee has the order number and offers proof of identification. The air waybill is given to you by the airline company for completion by yourself (or your forwarder), and a copy of it accompanies the consignment. Three copies are required. One acts as an instruction to carry the goods; the second is a receipt for their safe transfer on to an aircraft; the third is for the consignee and must be signed by the latter as evidence of collection.

ACP 90

This is the computerised air cargo processing system used by the London airports. The computers of 40 airlines, five bonded warehouses, about 400 freight forwarders, and HM Customs, are linked to provide a cargo tracking procedure through every stage of a consignment's journey to its final destination, with customs documentation handled automatically via EDI (see page 107). Customers, freight forwarders and agents can book space through the system and follow the progress of a consignment 'on-line'.

Arranging collection

When the goods arrive the airline will notify the consignee (by telephone, fax or letter) or await collection depending on your initial instructions. Airports keep their own warehouses into which unclaimed goods are placed. A storage fee is then demanded if and when the goods are eventually collected.

Airports are located on the far outskirts of industrial conurbations, so intermediate goods handling plus a secondary journey are required for air consignments. If you are not using a freight forwarder the final delivery options are as follows:

1.   Quote the customer on the basis of delivery to a named EC airport (see Chapter 8) specifying that the customer is responsible for collecting the consignment from the airport.
2.   Instruct your local agent or distributor to pick up the goods.
3.   Contact a UK freight forwarder and have its representative in that EC country deal with collection and final delivery.
4.   Have the airline or airport arrange for local delivery, provided this service is available. (Numerous cargo agents operate from airports.) Within Europe, competition from road and rail hauliers has caused airlines to improve their door-to-airport and airport-to-door services enormously in recent years, and the major airlines (notably Air France and Lufthansa) have large fleets of collection/delivery vehicles.
5.   Contact a local EC road haulier directly and advise it to collect and deliver the consignment.

Your choice should depend on cost, customer preference, convenience, speed of delivery and reliability of service.

Packaging for air transport
Airfreight packaging is typically less robust than for most other means of transport. All packages must carry the air waybill number, destination, total number of items in the consignment, weights of the individual pieces, and the full name and address of the consignee.

Dangerous goods
Common sense should indicate whether a particular type of good is 'dangerous'. However, apparently innocent products can contain dangerous substances. Examples are electrical apparatus incorporating alkaline batteries, barometers containing mercury, and anything with compressed gases, bleaches and/or magnetised materials. If in doubt the Dangerous Goods Section of the Civil Aviation Authority will advise whether special packaging is needed and, indeed, whether air transport is possible.

Civil Aviation Authority
Dangerous Goods Section

Aviation House
129 Kingsway
London WC2B 6NN
071-405 6922

Need for accurate documents
Aim to present your goods for transportation with all documents fully and
accurately completed, properly packed and precisely labelled. Then the
consignment may be immediately allocated to the booked flight or, at worst,
the next available. Inadequate documentation means that the goods have to
be stored while errors are corrected. Moreover, the manifests of other
aircraft will then need to be carefully examined in order to find alternative
cargo space, adding further to the hold-up.

Courier services
Air cargo, on average, spends four times as long on the ground at airports as
it does in the air. For certain consignments speed is vital, especially where
customers operate Just-In-Time production systems or where the benefits of
faster delivery greatly outweigh the additional cost. Express (courier)
services already account for nearly 10 per cent of EC airfreight and are
expected to increase their market share significantly in the years ahead.

These services use light aircraft to shift consignments to local airports
close to the end customer. This has proved highly cost effective for small
high value cargoes, and gives suppliers using such services a competitive
edge over rivals. Express services, moreover, have led the field in the
introduction of computerised systems for tracing and quickly locating
consignments. These are essential for meeting tight delivery schedules –
with perhaps only minutes to spare between connections. The express
services either employ their own aircraft for short-haul flights or block-book
(at a premium) priority space on scheduled airlines. For door-to-door
delivery they use company vehicles and, when these cannot meet demand,
subcontract external road transport services.

Speedbird
This is British Airway's door-to-door express delivery service. It covers
collection of the consignment, documentation, customs clearance and
(guaranteed) final delivery. Courier service is available for an extra charge.
For details contact your local BA cargo office (see your local telephone
directory) or ring Freefone 0800 181777.

Seafreight

Longer journeys to certain European destinations – Hamburg, Marseilles, or the coastal regions of southern Spain, Greece or Italy, for example – may conveniently be undertaken via conventional sea transport.

Seafreight includes scheduled services (referred to as 'liner' services) which sail according to a strict timetable (so that you know exactly when the ship will depart) and other vessels, sometimes referred to as 'tramp' ships, that depart only when they have a full cargo.

Liner services charge uniform rates applicable to all shipping companies. Tramp rates vary between vessels. As for airfreight, seafreight charges are quoted on a unit weight/volume basis so you pay a certain rate for either so many kilograms weight or a corresponding number of cubic metres.[4] Supplementary charges may also be specified, eg for additional fuel or extra unloading costs owing to port congestion, so be sure you know the total amount you may be called upon to pay.

To book space for a consignment you write to or telephone a shipping company (look in Yellow Pages under 'Shipping companies and agents') which then sends you a booking form and standard shipping note (SSN). The latter advises the shipping company regarding what is to happen to the goods on arrival at the foreign port, eg who will pick them up, who will pay unloading charges, whether the consignment is to be placed in a warehouse within the docks, etc. An SSN also acts as a request to the destination port authorities to receive and handle the shipment. Accordingly, the port authorities must sign a copy of the SSN and return this to the exporter as proof of delivery.

LCL services

LCL stands for 'less than full container load'. LCL groupage services are offered both by the major shipping companies and by freight forwarders.

Bills of lading

The contract between you and the shipping company is set out in a document known as a bill of lading. This also functions as (a) a receipt for the goods specifying whether they were loaded in a satisfactory or damaged condition, and (b) a document of title, meaning that the consignee named on the bill of lading has the legal right to claim the consignment. A clean bill of lading refers to goods received on board in apparently good condition and with no shortages. A short form bill of lading is one that does not show the shipping company's terms and conditions of carriage on the back. At least three copies are required: for you, for the shipping company and for transmission to the customer. The customer can transfer the right to collect the goods by

---

4. Most rate cards equate one cubic metre to one metric tonne. You measure your load in these terms and pay according to which is the highest. Suppose, for example, the basic unit charge is £10 and your consignment is ten cubic metres and weighs three tonnes, you pay £100 for the shipment.

endorsing the bill accordingly. Hence, a bill of lading is a 'quasi-negotiable' document of title.

Data freight receipts (DFRs)

For small loads and/or short journeys you could be issued with a data freight receipt (sometimes called a sea waybill) rather than a bill of lading *per se*. DFRs are the sea transport equivalent of air waybills in that they act merely as receipts for goods and as evidence of contracts of carriage and do not relate to the ownership of goods.

Seafreight procedures

Inevitably, conventional sea transport is slower than Ro-Ro ferry services since (substantially) more handling and documentation are required. For large consignments (and it is here that sea freight is most economical) you deliver the goods ready packed in a container or palletised (see page 102) for rapid loading. The goods have to be discharged at a dockside warehouse where they are stacked and recorded. When the ship arrives they are unstacked, transferred to the quayside, hoisted on board, stowed and again recorded. The procedure is reversed at the port of destination.

Shipping companies specify the latest dates by which goods must be received at the docks to guarantee shipment on a particular sailing. Delivering as near as possible to these deadlines secures the shortest overall transit time, and consequently gives your business the maximum period for production and processing. Unfortunately, however, other companies will be acting similarly, and your load may be passed over in the rush to meet the deadline – long queues of vehicles awaiting the opportunity to discharge their loads are still depressingly common at UK docks and harbours. Lamentably, early despatch to the docks can also create problems. Storage charges may be incurred and your goods could lose precedence to consignments that arrive later.

Contracts for sea transport adhere to an international convention, which is now legally binding on UK shipping companies. Under this the shipowner must *inter alia:*

- properly load, handle, stow and discharge the goods (for which service a handling fee is payable);
- ensure that holds, refrigeration chambers and other parts of the ship are fit and safe to receive consignments.

Packaging

Normally your chosen carrier (British Rail, a road haulier, shipping company, airliner, freight forwarder) will advise on how to package your goods for foreign delivery. If you are doing your own transport contact the Paper Industries Research Association (PIRA). This body will provide up to date information on packaging suppliers, national standards and regulations, costs and properties of various packaging materials, etc. It publishes *Abstracts* on packaging processes and equipment and on specific hazards and distribution techniques. PIRA is the only approved UK body for testing and certificating packages for the transport of dangerous goods. Its fees are low and related to the size of the client company.

Paper Industries Research Association (PIRA)
Randalls Road
Leatherhead
Surrey KT22 7RU
0372 376161

Further information on packaging is available from the Institute of Packaging, and the Institute of Physical Distribution Management. The latter publishes surveys of current packaging costs and practices.

Institute of Packaging
Sysonby Lodge
Nottingham Road
Melton Mowbray
Leicestershire LE13 0NU
0664 500055

Institute of Physical Distribution Management
Management House
Cottingham Road
Corby
Northamptonshire NN17 1TT
0536 204222

Package selection
Normally you will want the minimum packaging to ensure that goods reach customers in a reasonable condition; aesthetic considerations are not usually the main concern. To select a package you need to balance the expense of sturdy packaging against the extra costs of breakages and/or pilfering if cheaper packaging materials are used. Much depends on the length of the distribution chain; the more intermediate handling the packages will receive the more robust the packaging needed. The mode of transport is also relevant. Seafreight, for example, usually requires heavier packaging than freight shifted by other methods.

It is not a good idea to state the contents of packages on outside covers as this encourages stealing. Rather, each package should simply bear a unique consignment number, the address of the consignee, plus an indication of how many packages are contained in the shipment (eg 2/4 indicates the second package of four). For high value consignments it may be appropriate to use a false name for the recipient. Otherwise a potential thief might know that the addressee regularly imports expensive items and might be inclined to steal anything addressed to that customer. There are internationally accepted symbols to indicate hazardous goods and/or special handling requirements. Your carrier or PIRA will advise.

Palletisation
A pallet is a flat tray upon which articles can be placed and secured, eg by bolting or lashing. Carriers may request that even small items be palleted to allow mechanical handling (by fork lift truck, for example). Freight forwarders and some road hauliers operate pallet pools to ensure the re-use of pallets after they reach their destinations. Otherwise you may have to write off the cost of pallets as an inevitable expense of distribution.

Palleting greatly assists the speed, safety and general efficiency of loading and unloading procedures at docks and airports. Consequently, less dockside/airport warehousing facilities are necessary and aircraft/sea vessel turnaround is faster. Unfortunately, there is a difference between the size of the standard (Euro) pallet, which is 1000mm × 800mm, and the standard UK pallet which is 1000mm × 1200mm. It is likely that in future the Euro pallet will be adopted throughout the Community, including the UK. The trade association concerned with palleting is:

The Timber Packaging and Pallet Confederation
Heath Street
Tamworth
Staffordshire B79 7JH
0827 52337

Acquiring and using containers
Firms that regularly transport bulky deliveries to Europe should consider buying or leasing their own containers. The initial cost is substantial, and the acquired containers need to be insured. Yet the overall cost of transportation to European destinations will thereafter fall significantly as economies in storing, handling and not having to hire containers from outside carriers are experienced. The obvious problem is what to do with an empty container after the load has reached its destination. Possibly you could share the container with a local exporting company in the importing country, enabling that business to use the container for its shipments to Britain, or (at a cost) join one of the container pools operated by freight forwarders and other major carriers.

Although the transportation of containers is easy, their loading for shipment sometimes creates problems for the smaller business. If your consignment justifies the use of an entire container it is usually cheaper to load at your own premises than to send your output to a container depot for loading there. Either you have to (a) fill the container (normally using pallets) at ground level and subsequently fork lift or jack it up to the back of a lorry, or (b) wait for the lorry to arrive and then load the container on site (which ties up an expensive vehicle that ought to be working elsewhere), or (c) load the container while it is on the trailer of an articulated vehicle, consequently hooking the trailer to a cab when loading is complete.

Documentation

A research study commissioned by the European Commission estimated that documentation typically accounts for between 4 and 7 per cent of a business's export costs – rising to a staggering 15 per cent if the documents contain errors. This is not really surprising when you consider the many public and private bodies requiring information about shipments of goods between European countries. Interested parties include:

- government departments that collect data on imports and exports;
- VAT authorities;
- handlers of the goods who need to identify particular consignments;
- banks instructed to release money needed to pay for goods only after evidence of their shipment has been transmitted;
- carriers of goods (road hauliers, airline companies, ferry services, etc);
- dock, railway terminal or airport authorities;
- managers of container depots or marshalling yards;
- foreign agents and distributors;
- employees of warehouses where goods are to be stored;
- final recipients of consignments.

The greater the number of intermediaries (hauliers, ferry companies, distributors, etc) handling the goods the greater the importance of accurate documentation. Differences in goods descriptions, discrepancies in order and consignment numbers, uncompleted boxes on customs forms, absence of instructions for disposal of shipments on completion of their journeys, and so on, may cause long delays and serious financial losses. Goods arriving at sea ports or rail or air terminals without proper identification will be placed in local warehouses which charge storage fees to the parties eventually collecting them. And late delivery to consumers creates bad customer relations and eventual loss of orders.

The essential documents for a European delivery are a consignment note (an air waybill or a shipping or CIM/CMR note, for example), an insurance certificate (see Chapter 8), an invoice, the Single Administrative Document (see below), and possibly a number of documents relating to the method of payment (see Chapter 8).

The invoice

An export invoice should include all the commercial information used for a domestic transaction plus the following:

1. Full details of the method of carriage and where and when the goods will arrive.
2. Details of the markings and contents of packages.
3. Weight and measurements of each delivery.
4. Precise terms of sale.

Terms of sale

Normally you should quote a Delivered Duty Paid (DDP) price, expressed in local currency. This means that you will deliver the goods to the customer's premises having paid import tax (see Chapter 8) and all transportation and insurance charges. DDP pricing enables you to compete equally with local firms. European customers are not usually interested in having to collect goods from docks, airports or railway stations, especially as they do not have to do this when buying from local businesses.

Of course, certain customers prefer to undertake some (perhaps all) transportation themselves in order to secure lower prices, particularly if they have their own delivery vehicles and/or special expertise where transport is concerned.

The Single Administrative Document (SAD)

There is now a single document for clearing goods through the customs and excise departments of Community members, provided that the goods originated in the Community (or have already paid duty on their initial entry). Import duty on goods originating outside the Community is paid just once (although VAT and internal excise duty is still payable as normal). Thereafter the goods are free to move wherever necessary.

The form itself – which you obtain from HM Customs and Excise, the Post Office or a commercial stationer – conforms to agreed international standards and comes in two versions: an eight part SAD for manual completion or a four-part document for transmission via computer. For detailed step-by-step instructions on how to fill in the SAD, see Largent Brown's book, *Customs 88*, published by Kogan Page.

At the time of writing the future of the SAD is open to question. It was never intended to be anything other than a transitional stage towards complete freedom of movement of goods within the Community, and is likely to be abolished soon.

The Community Carnet

A Carnet is a document which enables you to move goods temporarily between different countries without having to pay any tax or customs duties. Carnets are used extensively for shifting exhibition materials, samples to be shown to customers, demonstration equipment and other working materials. Previously, businesses wishing to show goods to potential customers in several Community countries required a separate Carnet for each nation. Now, however, a single document can be used throughout the Community.

EC Carnets are available free of charge from HM Customs and Excise or from Chambers of Commerce. The need for them will, of course, disappear as soon as the Single Market is fully operational and all goods can move freely around the Continent.

Customs declarations

No customs duty is payable on imports originating within the European Community. However, import tax equivalent to the domestic rate of VAT in the importing EC country is normally required and you have to declare all exports (via the SAD) to HM Customs and Excise for the recording of balance of payments data. Details on VAT requirements and the procedures involved are available from any Customs office (see your local telephone directory for the address and telephone number). Otherwise contact:

HM Customs and Excise
King's Beam House
Mark Lane
London EC3R 7HE
071-626 1515

Advice on documentation

Most UK banks offer extensive advice on export documentation. Chambers of Commerce are also extremely helpful in this respect. There is a government department – the Board for the Simplification of International Trade Procedures (SITPRO) – specifically established to simplify international trading documents and procedures and to provide useful (free) advice on export documentation to UK businesses. SITPRO also produces and sells standard forms guaranteed acceptable to the authorities of foreign states, plus the software needed for computerised systems. If you belong to a Chamber of Commerce you may be able to purchase these standard

SITPRO documents (eg shipping and dangerous goods notes, airfreight letters of instruction, bank letter of credit forms [see Chapter 8], and so on) at a reduced price.

DTI Country Desks can also be approached for information about documents. Freight forwarders and international road hauliers are, of course, expert in this field.

SITPRO systems

SITPRO publishes a series of do-it-yourself manuals for export documentation, each containing sample forms, checklists, information on shipping marks, etc. It also produces a booklet explaining how to cut the costs of export administration, plus extensive material on letters of credit (see Chapter 8) and other methods of financing international trade.

The purpose of SITPRO standard forms is to enable the exporter to complete just one or two core documents which can then be photocopied and used for multiple documentation purposes. You type all the necessary information on to the basic form (the SITPRO master) and then apply the various plastic overlays supplied in the SITPRO package to photocopy relevant information on to particular documents. The invoice overlay, for example, will block out all material not required for a commercial invoice, while positioning the information that is actually needed into appropriate places, leaving you with a headed and neatly constructed invoice.

All SITPRO documents are designed to satisfy international specifications (the International Chamber of Commerce, European customs agreements, the United Nations plus the various regional trading blocs) and can be generated using either an ordinary photocopier or a laser printer controlled by a desk top computer. The basic package contains everything you need for documenting consignments to Europe and North America. A further pack is available for European parcel post deliveries.

Simplification of International Trade Procedures Board (SITPRO)
Almack House
26–28 King Street
London SW1Y 6QW
071-930 0532

Commercial systems

Privately constructed systems are also available. Suppliers advertise in export magazines and in the publications of trade associations and Chambers of Commerce. See also Cornhill Publication's *Export Manager's and Freight Forwarder's Handbook* which is a useful source of information regarding these matters.

Cornhill Publications Ltd
4–7 Nottingham Court
Short's Gardens
London WC2H 9AY
071-240 155

Using a computer for documentation

The better organised your documentation the faster the delivery. If you intend selling to many customers in several different EC countries it may eventually be worthwhile investing in a computerised facsimile documentation system. This will ensure that invoices and air waybill numbers coincide, that identical goods descriptions apply to all documents, that booking sheets relate to the proper loads, etc.

SITPRO's computer software will automatically assemble all the information necessary for documenting a consignment to a known customer or of a particular product type. Databases hold customer records, freight rates, discount information, and so on. SITPRO occasionally runs training courses to instruct users on its currently available packages.

Electronic data interchange (EDI)

This is the fully integrated electronic mail exchange of documents between exporters, customers, public authorities, banks, carriers, agents and distributors. Nowadays dock and airport authorities, Customs and Excise, freight forwarders and many European customers have fax machines (and if they do not they probably have telex) so it is increasingly common to link computerised documentation systems to a fax or telex facility and transmit documents in this way. Indeed, British Telecom (a major supplier of EDI systems) estimates that by the mid 1990s up to three quarters of all UK export business will be handled using EDI.

An international standard for EDI documentation and technical terminology (which can be extremely confusing) is currently being negotiated via the United Nations. It is called EDIFACT (Electronic Data Interchange for Administration, Commerce and Trade), and will produce standard messages using common technical terms for most types of business transaction (invoicing, issue of purchase orders, transport documentation, etc). EDIFACT messages are broken into short coded 'data elements', linked together using an EDIFACT 'syntax' that is transmitted from one computer to another through a standard computer communication system known as OSI (Open Systems Interconnection).

Integrated computerised systems offer faster payment cycles, a general reduction in clerical costs and far fewer serious errors in export documents. A major advantage of EDI is its avoidance of the need to rekey information into different computers at various stages in the chain of distribution. Hence there is no chance of errors (which cause transport delays and hold-ups in payment) creeping into documents through frequent rekeying. The main problem, of course, is the incompatibility of computer hardware and systems making it difficult for computers in different countries to inter-connect.

Chapter 6

Logistics, Agents and Continental Distribution

Logistics concerns the analysis of the costs, efficiencies and feasibilities of the various modes of transport and temporary storage needed to shift goods to their destinations – safely and with minimum pilferage and other materials loss – at the right time. Products have to be available for purchase where and when they are required.

The management of logistics is a critical administrative task, since mistakes in this area can be extremely expensive. Once you select a particular means for distributing your output you enter long term agreements with third parties that cannot be cancelled at will, and substantial compensation will be payable if you renege on contracts.

Distribution channels

These are the routes that goods follow from suppliers' premises to end consumers. Decisions regarding distribution channels are critically important; they affect pricing and product quality policies, the volume of clerical work undertaken and the extent of potential bad debt. The major alternatives are as follows:

1. *Direct sale distribution* via direct mail (see Chapter 4), or through your own staff or other representatives making personal contact with potential consumers. Here you assume total responsibility for all stages of distribution and hence (advantageously) retain complete control over the process. Thus you can ensure that the product is attractively priced, properly advertised and adequately presented to customers. This is especially important in highly competitive markets and/or for technically complicated output.
2. *Sale to retailers*. This requires a mechanism to guarantee continuous supply to local retail outlets, eg local warehousing (see page 120), and/or the ability to transport goods quickly and at short notice (by airfreight, for instance). Local representatives canvass department stores, hypermarkets, supermarket chains, etc. Additionally, you need to contact the UK buying offices of major foreign purchasing groups. They may be located through procedures described in Chapter 2.

3.   *Sale to intermediaries.* A UK or foreign intermediary may be prepared to buy your output in bulk and thereafter assume complete responsibility for warehousing and sale. Such businesses are sometimes referred to as export houses. This is a generic title applied to a variety of foreign trade intermediaries. Export merchants will buy your goods in the UK and resell them in European markets. They act as principals in export transactions and perform a wholesaling function as far as the exporter is concerned. Some specialise in particular countries, others in certain types of goods. Merchants carry all the risks of failure and you are relieved of all responsibilities for transport, insurance documentation, etc.

Confirming houses represent, as principals, foreign buyers who are not sufficiently well known in the UK for British firms to supply them on credit terms. The confirming house guarantees ('confirms') payment for the goods and hence assumes the risk of the buyer's default, charging the buyer a commission for this service. Many export houses belong to the British Exporters Association (BEA), which each month issues to its members a list of exporting businesses seeking assistance. A small fee (about £35) has to be paid in order to appear on the list. Additionally, BEA publishes a directory giving details of its members' interests, facilities and services.

British Export Houses Association
69 Cannon Street
London EC4N 5AB
071-248 4444

British Exporters Association
16 Dartmouth Street
London SW1H 9BL
071-222 5419

Information on the activities of confirming houses – particularly when they are instructed by foreign buyers to look for certain types of goods – can be obtained via the Export Intelligence Services of the DTI (see Chapter 2).

Use of an intermediary reduces your profit margin (big discounts are typically required), and you lose control over product pricing and presentation. Equally, however, intermediaries possess expert knowledge of local markets, and your sales administration and transport costs are kept to a minimum. You avoid the need for foreign warehousing, make a smaller number of deliveries, issue fewer invoices and incur less bad debt.

Selecting a system

Choice of distribution system depends obviously on the nature of your product (direct mail is not suitable for bulky and/or high value items), and on the following factors:

1. *Duration of the total order cycle.* For each of the available options you need to compute the average period likely to elapse between the product being required at an EC destination and the actual delivery of the goods. Estimation of these lead times requires your breaking the order cycle down into sub-divisions for order processing, documentation, warehouse packing, loading/unloading and intermediate handling, and final delivery.

2. *Effects of non-availability in local EC markets.* Occasional stockouts in foreign warehouses or retail outlets may be acceptable provided stock replenishments are quickly available. Warehousing is extremely expensive so you have to balance cost against the possible bad image that the odd stockout may create for your firm.

3. *Frequency and size of customer orders.* You need to examine carefully the pattern of local demand for your type of product, and analyse the extent and periodicity of sales fluctuations, market growth trends, geographical dispersion of purchasers, etc.

4. *Distribution costs.* Evaluate these with respect to transport costs, warehousing expenses, clerical workload, the interest loss attributable to having capital tied up in the volume of stock necessitated by each distribution option, order processing, and packaging and breakage expenditure.

5. *Degree of control over the system.* Certain types of distributor assume control over product pricing, advertising and presentation. How reliable are such distributors in these matters? Might they price your goods at inappropriate levels? Technically complex goods and/or those requiring specialist after-sales service are perhaps less suitable than others for distribution through numerous intermediaries.

6. *Spread of the market.* The method selected should provide adequate geographical coverage of the market.

7. The *share of the target market* that each alternative commands, and the *effectiveness of the various options* for penetrating the market.

8. The *extent and character of the after-sales service* (if any) that you will be expected to provide.

9. *Promotional costs* (including advertising, merchandising and related expenditures).

10. Whether the *distribution channel considered enhances or detracts from the image* of your product.

Direct representation is essential if merchandising is required. The techniques of merchandising used on the Continent are basically the same as in the UK, involving suppliers' representatives seeking to advise retailers on such matters as:

*   the best shelf positions for products;
*   use of dump displays;

- how to present the product effectively;
- special offers, deployment of point-of-sale literature, etc.

Agents and distributors

Most UK businesses in fact use agents or distributors to sell their outputs in European markets. It is essential to understand the difference between an agent and a distributor.

Distributors

A distributor is an independent business that you authorise to sell your goods – normally to other businesses and/or retail outlets – within a certain territory. Distributors differ from agents in that they actually purchase your products prior to resale. Hence they own the goods and assume full responsibility for their condition, for contracts of sale and for bad debts. The advantages of using a distributor (rather than an agent) include:

- fewer credit risks (you sell to just one distributor in each area);
- not having to supervise the distributor's operations;
- foreign customers possibly regarding the goods as originating locally;
- absence of the need for local stockholding (the distributor buys and warehouses the goods);
- ability to negotiate deals with end consumers on the spot without the need to refer back for direction on selling policy.

The disadvantages are loss of ultimate control over product presentation, and the fact that many distributors of goods sold to them by smaller businesses will handle competing lines. Nevertheless, as independent businesses distributors are legally bound by the distribution agreements they enter; there is (usually) no question of a court implying additional rights. Thus, a distribution contract can specify selling procedures and product prices, territorial restrictions, the types of outlet to which the goods may be sold, and so on. National variations on this matter are discussed in chapters covering individual EC states.

Distributors typically demand exclusivity. This is fair enough, but try to obtain a contribution towards local advertising and sales promotion expenditures as a quid pro quo. Note how exclusivity clauses in a distribution agreement can create legal difficulties, because exclusive trading arrangements are not generally permitted under EC law. And even if no exclusivity arrangement is specified a distributor will almost certainly insist on receiving more favourable terms than other purchasers, again causing legal problems. Legal aspects are discussed on page 138.

Agents

Agents undertake tasks on the client's behalf, usually by putting the client in touch with third parties. However,the agent then drops out of consequent contractual relationships, so that agreements are between the agent's client and third parties, without the agent being further involved. An agent will find foreign customers for your products; but if the goods are defective, damaged or delivered late it is you and not the agent who is responsible. Agents operate on a commission basis and may be either *brokers,* who simply bring together buyers and sellers without ever taking physical possession of the goods, or *factors*, who do hold stocks of the goods (eg in showrooms and/or warehouses) until customers are found and who some-times sell under their own names and decide on final selling prices. A *del credere* agent is one who, in return for a higher commission, indemnifies the supplying firm against customers' bad debts.

Factors (or distribution agents as they are sometimes called) are normally preferred when the product is:

- frequently required at short notice;
- sold in small quantities but has to be transported in bulk;
- one that sells better in showroom surroundings; and
- normally sold after inspection and/or requires a spare parts service.

Clearly, the distinction between an agency and a distribution agreement can become blurred, especially if the agent is acting as a factor. It is essential that the precise legal position is clarified at the outset of the arrangement to prevent subsequent disputes and interpretation difficulties.

Size of the agent's firm

Agency size can vary from the one-person business (eg the French VRP – see Chapter 9) to a large company with sub-distributors, warehouses, its own delivery vehicles, product testing and assembly facilities, etc. The advan-tages of a big agency are its abilities to:

- store and process large quantities of goods;
- arrange for after-sales service and immediately deal with customer complaints and queries;
- conduct or commission local market research on behalf of client firms.

Selecting an agent

The essential criteria to apply when choosing an agent are as follows:

- The agent's proved knowledge of local business conditions and practices.

- The agent's ability to conduct local marketing research.

- Whether the agent has contacts with local businesses capable of supplying specialist services to the exporting company (repair and after-sales service, for example).

- How easily the agent can be contacted.

- Whether the agent will represent competing firms and, if so, the incentives needed to encourage the agent to promote the exporter's products enthusiastically.

- How much information and feedback on matters such as consumer responses to the product, the quality of local delivery arrangements, whether local translations of operating instructions are satisfactory, etc, the agent can provide.

- How easily the calibre of the agent's work can be evaluated.

- The agent's track record, how long the firm has existed and its general business reputation.

- How extensively the agent covers the market; how many branch offices it has, their location, and whether the agent can genuinely cover an entire EC country.

- Whether the agent possesses sufficient resources for the task: staff, showrooms, technical competence, storage facilities, etc.

- The ease with which the firm can control and motivate the agent. What control and motivational devices (eg submission of market reports, inspection arrangements, commission and other incentive systems) can be built into the deal. Normally, the agent will be asked to prepare quarterly sales forecasts and to explain significant deviations of actual sales from these predictions. The agent should keep a record of enquiries received, calls made, customer complaints, etc, and submit details on a monthly basis.

- Will the agent require a large amount of technical training about the product and sales training for promoting it effectively?

No serious agent will accept a client's assignments without first assessing the work of the client company and its long-term commitment to selling in the local market. Accordingly, you should expect to supply detailed information not only about your products but also about your recent performance here in the UK, your business's strengths and the particular selling points of your output.

Because the agent is far away from your premises he or she will inevitably need to make some decisions on your behalf without clearing them with you in advance. Accordingly, your agent has to be fully conversant with your company's policies regarding price, credit, delivery terms, cash and bulk purchasing discounts, availability of after-sales service, etc.

Agency contracts
It is easy to fall out with an agent, so agency agreements must be carefully drafted and if you have no experience of these matters you should consult a solicitor or other specialist before proceeding. Make sure the contract contains full details of:

- the parties to the agreement;

- goods covered (especially whether the agent is to be allowed to repackage or otherwise alter items);

- product sales prices;

- the period of the deal and the territory involved;

- how disputes between the exporter and the agent shall be resolved, which country's laws shall apply and whether and in what circumstances the dispute might go to arbitration;

- commission rates and payments for additional services;

- responsibility for:
  – collecting debts
  – transport of goods to customers
  – breakages and other spoilage
  – local advertising and promotion
  – after sales service;

- whether a probationary period is to apply;

- whether secrecy is expected in relation to confidential information and the protection of intellectual property;

- requirements to disclose all relevant facts and to pass all sensitive documents back to your company on termination of the agreement;

- your right to inspect the agent's accounts and other records relating to your business;

- the precise extent of the agent's discretion to offer discounts, credit or special terms;

- responsibility for credit checks on potential customers;

- whether the agent is to participate in drafting promotional literature (if so, the agent will want a payment for his or her contribution);

- how the agent's work will be evaluated (target setting arrangements, for instance) and the consequences of poor performance;

- whether you will pay commission on orders received from the agent's territory that did not pass directly through the agent but which might be indirectly attributable to the agent's work (repeat orders, for example). Note how regular EC customers will often seek to circumvent your local agent in order to obtain a lower price by dealing with you directly.

The agreement should spell out the meaning of key words and phrases (what is meant by 'exclusivity', for example), and detail when and in what circumstances the contract may be terminated.

Paragraphs specifying the rates of commission payable are particularly important. These should state the percentages available on various types of order, and the nature of the prices on which commissions will be calculated (eg DDP, CIF, Ex Works, etc – see Chapter 8). Specify also exactly when commission is payable: on receipt of an order, on delivery of the goods, or on final settlement of the resulting invoice. Is commission still payable if an order is cancelled at a late stage or if the customer's firm goes bankrupt? How frequently will accrued commissions be handed over – monthly, quarterly, semi-annually or when?

After-sales service
This can be arranged by your agent or undertaken by third parties whom you contract direct. The arguments for having your agent provide after-sales service are that:

- agents are near to end consumers and can communicate with them in language they understand (fear of inadequate after-sales service from a British company could be a major incentive for local customers to choose domestically manufactured products);

- the agent has an incentive to ensure that goods are delivered in first class condition;

- the agent becomes 'locked into' dealing with your business.

However, the investment necessary to provide sound after-sales service can be extensive and agents who furnish these services must be trained; will require more extensive communications with your business than otherwise would be the case; and need guaranteed continuity of supply of spare parts. And the agency contract stipulating who precisely shall be responsible (and financially liable) for the service will necessarily be complicated.

Using agents to conduct local market research
This is cheap and convenient, but has several disadvantages.

1.   Agents and distributors will not normally have received any training in market research.

2.   Your demands for information may cause them to respond flippantly, without conducting proper investigations, and hence to supply you with misleading information.
3.   Agents and distributors obviously want your product to succeed in the local market, so their evaluations may lack objectivity.

Nevertheless, agents have direct and immediate access to final consumers and can observe at first hand their buying habits and demands. Agents are ideally placed to analyse competitors' strengths and weaknesses. Another advantage is that customers will probably be more willing to respond to questions put to them by an agent (with whom they may regularly do business) than by outside research bodies. Indeed, customers may be pleased that your local representative is taking an interest in their special requirements.

Agency law
There are, unfortunately, a number of significant differences between the agency law of various EC countries. Examples of disparities are given in chapters dealing with individual countries. Nevertheless, certain general principles of agency law apply regardless of the country concerned. The most important of these are as follows.

- Conflicts of interest between agents and clients are unlawful. Thus, for example, an agent cannot take delivery of your goods at an agreed price and resell them for a higher amount without your knowledge and permission.

- An agent cannot act for third parties without disclosing that this has occurred. It is unlawful, therefore, for an agent to accept a commission from one of your customers (to secure priority delivery, for instance) unless you are informed of that fact.

- Your agent is obliged to maintain strict confidentiality regarding your affairs. Equally, the agent must pass on to you any relevant information. Thus, for example, an agent engaged to sell something on your behalf must tell you about every offer received. If you accept an offer price lower than the highest submitted and the agent concealed the fact that a higher price could be obtained, you are legally entitled to recover the difference from the agent.

- You are liable for damages to third parties for wrongs committed by an agent 'in the course of his or her authority', eg if the agent fraudulently misrepresents your firm.

The essential difference between UK and Continental agency law is that, in general, the latter regards agents more as if they were employees of client organisations rather than as separate and independent businesses. In consequence, Continental agents are able to secure substantial compensation if you terminate (or simply fail to renew) an agreement. And in most EC countries an agency contract can be deemed to exist even if it is not in writing.

Arguably it is only fair that agents receive such compensation. An agent might work extremely hard and spend a lot of money in order to build up a client's business in a certain area, only to find that the client dispenses with his or her services as soon as the client has acquired sufficient experience to be able to operate independently in that particular market.

Britain is the 'odd man out' where Community agency legislation is concerned, and the harmonisation of EC law in this area will inevitably cause UK rather than Continental rules to alter. The UK has until January 1994 to change its domestic law relating to compensation for agents.

In general, EC agents are legally entitled to the following:

- Adequate notice of intention to terminate the agreement (provided the agent has not committed misconduct). The period required increases in proportion to the period the agent has been with the principal.

- Recompense for lost commission on sales to existing customers, especially if the agent was undeniably responsible for attracting these customers in the first place. Compensation is payable for a 'reasonable period', the length of which, ultimately, is determined by a commercial court.

- Proper support from principals, including full information about potential customers, product developments, quality changes, intended advertising campaigns, etc.

Particular differences in the agency laws of various Community members are mentioned in the chapters that deal with individual countries. Further information on the agency laws of EC states is available from (a) the relevant country desks of the DTI, (b) a guide published by the International Chamber of Commerce, and (c) specialist textbooks. If you belong to a trade association, it should be able to help in this respect. For serious problems you will need to contact a lawyer with detailed knowledge of Continental agency and commercial practice. A list of lawyers specialising in these matters is available from the UK Law Society.

The Law Society
113 Chancery Lane
London WC2A 1PL
071-242 1222

Finding an agent

You can use the services of a private agency-finding consultant or the facilities of the DTI's Export Representative Service. Under the latter scheme, information about an exporting company and its products is transmitted to the commercial department of the appropriate British Embassy or Consulate which then reports back (normally within eight weeks) with a list of suitable agents (or distributors if required). Embassies and Consulates already possess extensive data on local agencies, some of which they contact on receipt of information about your firm. You may have to supply the Embassy/Consulate with packages of your trade literature (brochures, price lists, credit terms, etc) plus sample products where appropriate. The more accurate the information provided the faster the response from relevant prospects. Potential partners for joint ventures, contract manufacturing (see page 129) and licensing agreements can also be located. The fee (currently) is £300 for enquiries that take less than 24 hours' work and £600 if more than 24 hours' work is required. Reports do not evaluate the credit worthiness of the agents, although credit checks can be obtained separately through the DTI's Overseas Status Report Service (see below). However, the report will detail listed agencies' interests, capacities, territories covered, warehousing facilities, after-sales service offered and other agencies held. A simple list of names and addresses of local agents, without any comment on them, is available under the DTI's Market Information Enquiry Service (see Chapter 2).

Overseas Status Report Service
This provides UK companies with information concerning the financial status and resources of foreign firms. The commercial department of the appropriate local British Diplomatic Post will report on a foreign business's trading activities, facilities, technical know-how, credit rating, and so on. Reports take about four weeks to complete and cost (currently) between £60 (for up to four hours' work) and £180 (for more than eight hours' work). Where the investigated firm is an agency, the report will list (where known) the other agencies it holds, its facilities, its capabilities, experience, etc.

Further options
Other avenues for contacting potential agents include:

- the UK banks (which will also undertake status checks on likely prospects);

- the UK branches of foreign banks in target EC markets;

- organisations jointly representing UK and foreign Chambers of Commerce (eg the Franco-British Chamber of Commerce) or the branch offices of foreign Chambers of Commerce here in the UK;

- exhibitions and trade fairs in various EC markets;

- trade directories and journals which carry advertisements placed by potential agents;

- sister companies (see Chapter 7) in other EC countries.

Location of warehouses

Continental storage points for your output should be carefully selected at the outset of your European exporting effort and not emerge haphazardly. Immediate candidates are the (often subsidised) warehousing facilities owned by airports and by docks and harbour authorities. The Port of Paris authority, for instance, lets out storage space at highly competitive rates (see Chapter 9). Some freight forwarders and large European road hauliers also provide warehousing facilities.

Otherwise you have to consider renting (perhaps eventually buying) one or more storage depots at strategically determined distribution points. In choosing a site for a depot you must take into account the following factors:

(a)   The centre of gravity of the market. To establish this, imagine the market area as a flat surface on which weights have been placed at each customer location. (Weights are proportional to each customer's anticipated annual purchases of your goods.) Now pretend you can physically lift the flat surface. On which spot would it balance evenly on the end of a pointed stick? This place is the centre of gravity of the market area.

(b)   Ease of transport to major outlets, taking into consideration local traffic congestion, road and rail links, etc.

(c)   Availability of government and/or local authority grants for establishing warehousing operations in alternative EC locations.

(d)   Nearness to railway terminals or European motorways that facilitate bulk transportation to the depot.

The decision to have one or many depots is subject to a number of influences. If you establish several storage points you can get your goods to customers quickly, but only at higher cost. There is more administration, and much intermediate handling may be required. Accordingly, you need to consider:

- depot acquisition costs;

- staffing requirements;

- the cost of having additional amounts of working capital tied up in stock as a result of establishing several different warehouses;

- possibilities of increased losses through breakage and pilferage;

- whether important priority customers are located in particular areas.

Advice and information on these matters is available from:

- large UK estate agencies, which are increasingly active in the European commercial property field;

- regional development authorities of various EC states (see Chapters 9–15);

- the UK Institute of Directors (see Chapter 2);

- the quarterly bulletin *Corporate Location Europe,* which contains extensive information on EC enterprise zones and location incentives, surveys of local rentals, differences in countries' property law, etc.

Corporate Location Europe
Century House Publications Ltd
22 Towcester Road
Old Stratford
Milton Keynes
Buckinghamshire MK19 6AO
0908 560555

Chapter 7

Establishing a Permanent Presence in the European Community

Communication difficulties with *ad hoc* representatives, lack of commitment on the part of commission agents, costly margins taken by independent distributors, and escalating administrative costs as EC markets develop may cause you to consider seriously the option of setting up subsidiary businesses in Community countries – each with its own employees, premises, warehouses, delivery vehicles, and so on. A permanent local presence enables you to trade as if you were a local firm. This might be necessary or desirable:

- if local assembly or part-manufacture is required;

- to maximise the benefits available from regional EC investment grants (see Chapters 9–15);

- if local agents/distributors are unreliable and/or difficult to find;

- to exercise close control over local market research, the granting of credit and promotional activities;

- where a regional identity is needed to create a credible image for the exporting firm.

Local EC subsidiaries can recruit local staff who are expert in the nuances of particular Community markets – but who nevertheless are subject to your direct and immediate control. Alternatively you could send UK staff to work in European subsidiaries, although this is expensive. Numerous costs are involved, including:

- removal costs and the need to find fresh accommodation for transferred employees;

- boarding school fees for employees' children while their parents are abroad;

- compensation for possible loss of a spouse's earnings;

- higher salaries necessary to induce people to live in an unfamiliar foreign country;

- language training and other settling-in costs.

Conversely, nationals of the foreign country in which you are doing business are already fluent in the local language, will (or should) have wide-ranging contacts with local businesses and institutions, and already possess accommodation in the area. The problem is how to control and appraise local nationals.

Branches

EC branches (ie subsidiaries which are not quasi-autonomous incorporated bodies) may not be the most cost-effective means of establishing a permanent presence in another Community country, compared to alternative organisational forms. Branches are easy to set up and close down, but complicated tax situations arise because the tax authorities of many EC countries are empowered to tax branch offices on profits that the authorities deem to accrue to the parent business's *entire* worldwide operations (including those in the UK and other quite separate countries) in consequence of the branch's activities in the country concerned. For example, if the tax authorities of a particular EC nation believe that 15 per cent of your UK firm's aggregate profits are due to operating in that country, they may impute a figure for these total UK profits and tax you on 15 per cent of that amount!

Legally, a branch is nothing more than a direct extension of your existing business into another country. Most foreign branches of UK firms are concerned with transport and storage of goods, marketing and the provision of spares and after-sales service. Local assembly and/or manufacture is normally undertaken by other means (see page 129). You may or may not have to register the existence of a branch with governmental or local authorities, depending on local laws. Later chapters which describe the markets of individual countries deal with this point. All the operations of the branch will be subject to the business law (including the law of contract and employment regulations) of the host country.

Buying an existing business

A principal tenet of the Single Market is that no restrictions shall exist on the ability of any EC national to buy a business anywhere in the Community. And it is indeed the case that EC nationals can now freely purchase existing businesses in any member state. The advantages of buying a local business outright – rather than incorporating an entirely new company – include:

- avoidance of start-up delays and expenses;

- immediate possession of a functioning administrative structure;
- possibly the acquisition of an existing distribution system with staff, transport vehicles, etc.

On the other hand, the acquired business will have to be integrated into your current organisation system, and implementing changes in the purchased firm's management methods may prove difficult.

Setting up a company in Europe

The establishment of a self-contained legally constituted subsidiary company in a local market is frequently the best way to create a permanent presence. You can set up a company from scratch under the laws of a particular EC country, buy one that already exists or enter into a collaborative venture with other EC companies.

Double taxation

To the extent that you sell to a country rather than operate within it, the promotional and other expenses (hire of agents, local EC advertising, field visits, etc) attached to the selling process are fully deductible from your firm's UK profits, and you pay no tax in the country concerned. Once you establish a permanent presence via a branch or subsidiary in a European country, however, you become subject to local taxation, so you pay tax twice – once on your UK profits arising from EC operations, and again on the local profits that accrue (or are deemed to accrue – see page 123) in the EC country itself.

The procedure is for you to declare to the UK authorities the tax paid to foreign governments by your European subsidiaries so that it can be deducted from your local UK tax bill. Hence you are taxed only once. The problem is that the UK tax relief is applied at the UK rate, which is considerably lower than elsewhere. Thus, for example, if you have a subsidiary in Germany that pays German corporation tax at (currently) 50 per cent, you only get (assuming you are a small business for UK tax purposes) UK relief at the rate of 25 per cent.

Forming companies under the laws of various EC countries

The fundamentals of company formation are essentially similar in most EC states, although administrative details (and hence the costs of company incorporation) differ. Audit requirements also vary from country to country. Generally, European states have audit rules which are less stringent than in the UK, though audit requirements and procedures are currently being harmonised across the entire Community. Other national differences in company legislation occur in relation to:

- shareholders' voting rights (especially *vis-à-vis* the protection of minority shareholders);
- restrictions on share transfer in private companies;
- contents of Memoranda and Articles of Association;
- registration costs;
- dissolution procedures.

All EC countries have company structures broadly similar to UK private and public companies. Details are given in the chapters dealing with each country. Further information on company formation matters is contained in *Setting Up a Company in the European Community*, by Brebner and Co, published by Kogan Page. Table 7.1 on page 126 summarises some of the major differences.

European companies

A new type of limited liability organisation is being created for the European Community. Subject to agreement, there are to be European companies governed not by the laws of any one member country but by a set of fresh rules and procedures applicable throughout the EC. The European Commission proposes that these companies will have compulsory worker participation, although the precise details have (at the time of writing) still to be worked out.

A critical proposal is for European companies to be able to offset profits and losses between activities in various member countries, hence avoiding complications arising from double taxation (see page 124).

Harmonisation of EC company law
Company legislation regarding accounting systems, disclosure requirements, incorporation arrangements (eg minimum capital requirements, and so on) is scheduled for harmonisation across the entire Community over the next few years. Of immediate interest to small UK businesses is the new procedure whereby private limited companies can be formed easily and with just a single member.

Harmonisation of national company legislation is being effected through EC Directives which, once agreed, have to be incorporated into each country's law. To date, Directives have concerned such matters as the requirement to file accounts, shareholders' rights following takeover bids, the format of company accounts and auditing requirements. Other Directives are still being negotiated and involve, *inter alia*, provisions for compulsory employee participation in management decision making and rules concerning the accounts of branches of companies established in other member countries.

Table 7.1 *European Community company formation: some major differences*

	Do minimum capital requirements apply?	Is official notification required for foreign companies?	Rate of Corporation Tax	Is employee participation compulsory?	Are non-voting shares allowed?
Belgium	Yes	No	43% for small firms	Yes	No
Denmark	Yes	Yes but only for large companies	50%	Yes	Yes
France	Yes	Yes	45%	Yes	No
Germany	Yes	Yes	50%	Yes	Yes
Greece	Yes	No	49%	No	No
Ireland	Public companies only	No	50%	No	Yes
Italy	Yes	No	52.6%*	Yes	No
Luxembourg	Yes	No	36%	Yes	No
The Netherlands	Yes	No	42%	Yes	Yes
Portugal	Yes	Yes	Sliding scale from 30% upwards	No	No
Spain	No	No	35%	Yes	Yes

* Includes compulsory local income tax of 16 per cent.

Sister companies

Completion of the Single Market is causing large numbers of UK businesses to seek sister companies within the EC. Sister companies are foreign firms offering similar products which are of similar size and structure to the one seeking a partner. They not only act as a foreign agent but also advise on local conditions, translate documents, and generally provide support and comfort when things go wrong. The UK firm offers reciprocal facilities to the foreign business. There are regular meetings and exchanges of information, and possibly exchange of staff for short periods.

Ideally the sister company should be engaged in complementary rather than competitive lines of work and face the same sorts of problem as your own business. Above all, however, it needs to consist of people with whom you can communicate easily and establish a good rapport. Language abilities are, of course, critically important in these respects. The EC has consistently encouraged sister company arrangements and offers a clearing house (the Business Co-operation Centre – see page 129) for this purpose.

European Economic Interest Groups (EEIGs)

These are combinations of European businesses (companies, partnerships or sole traders) which extend over at least two EC states. Their purpose is to pool common research and development or marketing activities, or to manage particular projects. However, the EEIG must not seek to make profits 'in its own right'. To the extent that an EEIG does earn profits, each member business will be taxed on them in its own country according to its share in total profits.

An EEIG has a separate legal identity (established via a procedure laid down in an EC regulation of 1985), but individual members have unlimited liability for the debts of the entire group. EEIGs need not have any capital and are not required to file annual reports or accounts.

Advantages and problems with EEIGs
Benefits accruing to EEIGs include:

(a)   economies of scale available from combining the operations of several businesses;
(b)   the retention of independent status by each member organisation;
(c)   the provision of a means whereby small firms may collectively bid for large contracts;
(d)   the ability of a small business to enter new lines of work and unfamiliar territory;

(e)   the pooling of risks;

(f)   groups can be set up by different forms of organisation (companies, sole traders, partnerships, etc) and different sizes of business;

(g)   the ease with which an EEIG can be formed and disbanded. A group can be wound up by a unanimous decision of its members, or will automatically end on expiry of a stated contract period or when the purpose for which the group was set up has been accomplished.

The contract that establishes an EEIG must specify its name (which has to include the words 'European Economic Interest Group' or their initials), address, the objects for which the group is formed, details of participants, and the duration of the contract (unless this is indefinite). The contract is then registered in the member state where the EEIG has its head office. Member businesses must decide how the group is to be financed and its revenues distributed. If there is no explicit agreement on this point it is assumed that all participants will contribute equal shares and receive equal revenues.

Problems with EEIGs are that they:

● cannot raise money from the general public;

● must not control the activities of any member firm;

● are taxed in line with national laws just like any other business;

● cannot trade and attempt to make profit on their own accounts.

Joint ownership ventures

These are useful for firms seeking a permanent presence in an EC country but lacking the financial, material or managerial resources needed to operate independently. You take an equity stake in the joint venture (or form a partnership with local interested parties) and help to manage the business. Returns are higher than for indirect market entry and you exert close control over the venture's operations. There are, however, a number of difficulties attached to joint ventures. Some examples are listed below.

● Working methods in member companies may not be compatible.

● The establishment of a joint venture could transmit a signal to competitors that they too should enter that particular market.

● There could be arguments about how underperformance by any one of the participants is to be dealt with. For instance, should equal compensation be payable to each of the parties if the project is abandoned?

- Members may disagree about the long-term goals of the operation, eg whether earnings should be reinvested in the venture or returned to participants.

Further problems could include:

- disagreements regarding which participants shall provide the bulk of finance for expansion;

- partners who turn out to be less technically knowledgeable than was first supposed;

- 'who-does-what' disputes among participants;

- inability to change working arrangements quickly and at short notice;

- policy disagreements concerning (say) pricing strategies, the markets to be served, etc;

- participants not wishing to divulge confidential business information to other members.

Local manufacture

If transport costs are high relative to the selling price of the product, or if skilled labour is abundant in the local market, you may wish to consider making or assembling your output in EC countries rather than in the UK. Alternatively, you could enter into contracts with local manufacturers to produce goods which you then sell in the local market. The latter method is sometimes referred to as contract manufacturing.

Local assembly or manufacture attaches a 'home grown' image to the goods, and delivery and customer service mechanisms should improve. The major difference between establishing your own manufacturing facilities and contract manufacture is the ease with which operations can be terminated. Local manufacturing requires substantial capital investment that cannot be sacrificed easily, whereas cancellation of a contract manufacture agreement is (subject to the details of the contract) cheap and straightforward. Note, however, that the foreign contract manufacturing firm acquires expertise in making your product, which it may subsequently use by competing against you, and quality levels may be lower.

The Business Co-operation Centre (BCC)

This is a sort of 'marriage bureau' established to encourage co-operation between EC businesses, particularly for the transfer of technology, the setting up of joint distribution and after-sales service systems, and for the pooling of financial resources.

Business Co-operation Centre
89 Rue Froissard
B–1040 Brussels
Belgium
010 32 2 2304091/2303949

To achieve these objectives, BCC has implemented a computerised information network, BC-Net.

The Business Co-operation Network (BC-Net)
The purpose of BC-Net is to help small and medium sized-enterprises easily find contacts for collaboration. It acts as a clearing house for requests for co-operation from firms in various Community countries. The Network's database also includes names and addresses of management consultants and business advisers active in the European field.

To use BC-Net you have to approach an adviser who is a member of the system. (Many UK Chambers of Commerce and trade associations now undertake this function.) The adviser enters the nature of the co-operation sought plus your business's particulars on to a standard pro-forma 'company profile' which is then instantly and automatically compared with the existing stock of offers within the system. In the case of a positive outcome to the search, both the applicant company and the firms offering co-operation are informed immediately. Otherwise, all business advisers within the geographical area covered by the request are sent a 'flash profile' advising of the opportunity in case an adviser has a company on its books that may be interested in the application. Note that BC-Net extends beyond the frontiers of the European Community.

Other co-operation initiatives
In addition to BC-Net the BCC occasionally operates *ad hoc* co-operation schemes. These have included the following:

(a)   The 'Europartnership' scheme, to encourage commercial, financial or technical co-operation in underdeveloped or declining regions. Projects suitable for company co-operation were listed in a catalogue distributed throughout the Community.

(b)   The establishment of databanks of sub-contractors in various industries and the publication in nine European languages of vocabularies of sub-contracting terminology in those industries.

(c)   The Venture Consort project to promote the availability of venture capital across national frontiers within the Community.

Information on these matters is available from:

European Commission Task Force for Small
 and Medium Sized Enterprises
200 Rue de la Loi
B–1049 Brussels
Belgium
010 32 2 2303949

Limited information on these matters is also available from UK based EC information offices (see Chapter 2).

Licensing

This enables you to enter EC markets at minimal risk. You offer a foreign firm the right to produce and distribute your branded product (normally protected by a patent or registered trademark) for a royalty or lump sum fee. No capital investment or exporting know-how is required, but you necessarily sacrifice profits through allowing others to make and sell your goods.

Licensees benefit in that they avoid product research and development costs while acquiring experience of manufacturing the item. Normally the licensee will demand exclusive rights in the country concerned (possibly in several countries) and may request the right to sub-contract to other local businesses. Licensing is appropriate where:

(a)   you have firm legal control over your intellectual property (see Chapter 3) through patents and registered trademarks;
(b)   transport costs or the cost of establishing local manufacturing facilities would be prohibitive;
(c)   'home-grown' product images will improve sales;
(d)   rapid installation of a manufacturing capability in a particular market is necessary in order to beat the competition;
(e)   the licensee will have to purchase input components or materials from your business;
(f)   you are already exporting directly to more markets than you can conveniently handle.

Licence agreements need to specify, *inter alia*, details of:

 • ownership of technical developments and inventions resulting from the licensee's involvement with the product;

- the geographical area covered by the agreement;

- minimum production levels, and your remedy if the licensee firm fails to meet its obligations;

- rate and frequency of payments;

- quality control requirements;

- the licensee's ability to become involved with competing products;

- permissible selling prices;

- provisions for terminating and/or renewing the contract.

Types of licence

There are various types of licensing agreement. With an 'assignment', for instance, you hand over *all* your intellectual property rights in relation to a particular patent, trademark, design, or whatever, to a licensee. The latter may then use these rights as it wishes. If you issue a 'sole' licence, however, you retain rights but agree not to extend licences to anyone other than a single licensee during the period of the agreement. 'Exclusive' licences require licensors not to use their patents, trademarks, etc., for their own businesses while licensing contracts are in force, leaving these rights entirely to licensees for pre-specified periods. Non-exclusive licences allow licensors to distribute licences to several licensees simultaneously.

Know-how licensing

Know-how is confidential non-patented technical knowledge, and it can be licensed. Arguably, know-how (and patent) licensing is a barrier to free competition and could be used to sustain a monopoly. Equally, however, licensing is a major vehicle for the fast and efficient transfer of new technologies across national frontiers and, in recognition of this (plus the reasonable rights of those who research, initiate and develop new methods), the Commission has created a block exemption (see page 137) for know-how and patent licences. In consequence it is permissible for know-how licence agreements to restrain licensees from exploiting the licensor's know-how in territories not covered by the contract. The details of the exemption are quite extensive. For further information see the book by DM Jacobs and J Stewart-Clark, *Competition Law in the European Community*, published by Kogan Page. Clearly, it is essential that any patent or know-how agreement is drafted in such a manner that it falls within the block exemption. Specialist advice from a qualified patent agent would be necessary to ensure that this is the case.

Chartered Institute of Patent Agents
Staple Inn Buildings
High Holborn
London WC1V 7PZ
071-405 9450

Problems with licensing include the following:

(a) The risk of a licensee company setting up in competition once it has learned all your production methods and trade secrets and the licence period has expired.

(b) Deciding how to control the licensee in relation to quality standards, declaration of production levels, and methods of marketing the product.

(c) Ambiguities and interpretation difficulties *vis-à-vis* minimum and/or maximum output levels, territory covered, basis of royalty payments (including the frequency of payment and the currency to be used), and the circumstances under which the agreement may be terminated.

(d) The possible need to spend large amounts of time and money to protect your product's reputation if the licensee is less competent than you expected.

Franchising

Franchising is sometimes more appropriate than licensing *per se*. With a franchise, the foreign firm adopts your complete business format in the local market – your name, trademarks, business methods, layout of premises, etc. Additionally, you provide (in return for a royalty and lump sum fee) a variety of supplementary management services: training, technical advice, stock control systems, perhaps even financial loans. Hence you retain complete control over how your product is marketed, but the franchisee carries all the risks of failure and your capital commitment is typically low. Franchising is relatively new to the Continent. In most EC countries it is the consequence of the example set by the European operations of United States franchising companies. Accordingly, the legal arrangements that apply to franchise business invariably conform to the American model. Hence, the following rules normally apply:

(a) Franchisees rarely possess rights against a parent organisation in the event of either the entire system or just an individual outlet collapsing.

(b) Franchisees are self-employed, not employees of the parent firm. Thus, franchisees will be highly motivated to succeed in their own businesses. There are no strikes, go-slows, work-to-rules or other industrial relations problems.

(c)   Franchisees are usually tied to supplies from the parent organisation, at supply prices determined by the latter (which buys raw materials in bulk at big discounts).

The nucleus of your distribution system remains small, and immediate overheads are minimal. However, you need to be fully capable of advising foreign franchise outlets about product presentation, layout of premises, stock control and related matters. Detailed agreements are necessary in respect of:

- exclusivity of franchisee rights in a particular area;
- extent of franchisor control over outlets;
- duration of contracts and what happens when they expire (eg whether higher royalties may then be determined);
- the franchisee's ability to engage in other business activities;
- restrictions on the franchisee's right eventually to compete with your business.

The franchising block exemption

Since franchising is potentially a restraint on free competition, it could violate EC competition law. However, there exists is block exemption (see page 137) to cover distribution franchise agreements. At the time of writing there is no exemption in relation to industrial or manufacturing franchises.

Under the block exemption it is permissible for distribution franchise agreements to restrict franchisees' abilities to:

- sell or use competing products during or up to one year after the termination of the contract;
- seek custom outside the designated territory;
- decline to sell the entire range of the franchisor's products;
- scale down the extent of the operations of their outlets;
- engage in independent advertising;
- disclose to outsiders the know-how gained during the period of the agreement.

Franchisees, moreover, can be compelled to inform the parent company of any new and additional know-how they acquire through their experience of operating the franchise.

Piggy-backing

Large firms which already operate in certain foreign markets are sometimes willing to act as agents for businesses that wish to export to those markets. This enables them to use fully their sales representatives, premises, office equipment, etc in the countries concerned. An example is the Tradeway system operated by ICI, which currently handles the work of 300 UK companies (mostly small businesses) that sell to ICI's 150 overseas markets. The system operates as a conventional agency, using ICI's extensive network of office and sales organisations in foreign countries, although the company will only offer its services for the marketing of chemical products which complement its own product range.

Piggy-backing has the following advantages:

(a)   'Riders' can export conveniently without having to establish their own distribution systems. They can observe carefully how the 'carrier' handles the goods and hence learn from the carrier's experience – perhaps to the point of eventually being able to take over their own export transactions.

(b)   Carriers broaden their product range without having to manufacture extra products.

(c)   Economies of scale in bulk distribution become available.

(d)   The carrier's overall business image may be enhanced through being seen to carry additional products.

EC laws on competition

The European Commission has in the past exhibited somewhat ambivalent attitudes towards the restriction of free business competition. On the one hand, the Treaty of Rome expressly forbids restrictive trade practices and/or monopolies likely to interfere with trade within or between countries. Simultaneously, however, the Commission recognises the need for Europe to possess large economic units able to achieve economies of scale and compete effectively in world markets. Thus, in recent years new regulations have been introduced which allow cross-frontier amalgamations enabling large firms to organise themselves on a Europe-wide basis. Taxes which discriminate against cross-frontier mergers (compared to mergers within a single country) have been abolished, and many legal barriers to international amalgamations of EC businesses have been removed. In general, the Commission now seems to favour larger European firms.

Community law in these respects is embodied in Articles 85 and 86 of the Treaty of Rome. Article 85 prohibits trade practices which prevent, restrict or distort competition. Agreements by firms to carve up the European market among themselves are void and thus unenforceable in the courts of member nations. Article 86 prohibits firms which already occupy a dominant position in an EC market from abusing that position. A dominant position is defined as a position of economic strength which enables an enterprise to prevent effective competition by being able to operate independently of its competitors and customers. There have been cases in the European Court where abuse has occurred through firms increasing their market shares by taking over competitors, or through gaining control over the supply of raw materials and then cutting off supplies to competing firms.

Additionally, the Treaty of Rome defines the following business practices as abuses of a dominant position:

- imposition of unfair prices for purchase of raw materials or sale of final goods;
- restrictions on production;
- restrictions on distribution;
- holding back technological development;
- charging different prices to different consumers.

This is a formidable list. And Articles 85 and 86 are directly enforceable via the laws of member countries and/or the European Commission. The latter is empowered to investigate any complaint registered under either of these Articles and, if proved, will ask the firm involved to alter its behaviour. If it refuses, the Commission will issue a formal warning – accompanied by reasons for its decision – and if this fails to achieve the desired change the Commission will approach the European Court for a ruling. If the ruling goes against the company, the Commission can impose substantial fines (although it cannot dismember the business).

Nevertheless, the Commission has been extremely anxious to encourage co-operation among smaller firms in order to enable them to compete with bigger units. Accordingly, the Commission does not regard the following agreements as violating Articles 85 and 86:

- exchanges of opinion or experience;
- joint market research;
- joint collection of trade and market statistics;
- co-operation on the preparation of accounts, or on matters relating to tax;
- provision of trade credit;
- joint debt collecting.

Also, the Commission has issued block exemptions covering small firms that enter into exclusive dealership, licensing, materials supply and certain other business arrangements.

Minor agreements and block exemptions

A wide range of practices common among small firms could be caught by EC competition law, notably:

- exclusive dealership arrangements;
- joint ventures with other businesses;
- licensing of intellectual property rights;
- franchising.

Community law extends, moreover, to any 'concerted practice' that prevents, restricts or distorts competition. A concerted practice is where businesses do not enter a formal agreement but where their collective actions imply collusion.

In recognition of the fact that co-operation between small firms will not distort competition appreciably, the Commission has issued a Notice on Minor Agreements exempting from Articles 85 and 86 all situations where:

(a)   the goods or services covered by an agreement represent less than 5 per cent of the total market for these goods or services; and (additionally)

(b)   the aggregate turnover of the parties to the agreement is less than a certain threshold (currently 200 million ECUs).

An agreement that breaks EC competition rules is regarded in law as null and void and thus unenforceable.

Even if these criteria are not satisfied the Commission may exempt agreements that:

(a)   contribute to improving the methods of producing or distributing goods or to the promotion of technical or economic progress; and

(b)   give consumers a fair share of resulting benefits; and

(c)   will not significantly reduce competition across the entire Single European Market.

Applications for exemption must be submitted to the Commission unless the following are involved, in which case an automatic block exemption applies and no formal application is needed (provided, of course, that points (a) to (c) above are met):

(a)   exclusive distribution or purchasing agreements;
(b)   patent and (unpatented) know-how licensing;
(c)   research and development agreements;
(d)   motor vehicle agreements;
(e)   franchising.

The situation of large firms

Individual exemptions for large firms engaging in restrictive agreements (eg to fix price or carve up a market) are available provided:

(a)   the restrictive agreement is registered with the Commission; and
(b)   the Commission sees no grounds for action given the facts in its possession.

A negative clearance will then be issued.

Comfort letters and oppositions

The time period typically taken by the Commission to consider negative clearances is so long (usually two to three years) that, in order to avoid chaos within applicant businesses, the Commission is prepared to issue informal 'comfort letters' which express the view that (initially at least) the Commission can see no reason to intervene. In consequence, the firm cannot be fined during the period the matter is awaiting formal resolution.

Another device for relieving the Commission's administrative burdens is the opposition procedure whereby, if an agreement that falls just partly outside a block exemption is *not* challenged by the Commission within six months of its notification, the agreement automatically becomes valid.

Agents and distributors

Since an agent is merely an extension of the employing firm, agency agreements are outside the scope of Articles 85 and 86. Exclusive dealerships whereby an independent trader actually takes possession of your goods are, however, covered by Article 85. The distribution block exemption enables nearly all these exclusivity contracts to continue provided they apply to small businesses and, of course, are not detrimental to the aims and development of the Community. Under the exemption, agreements between pairs of undertakings, whereby one agrees to supply exclusively to the other pre-specified goods for resale in a certain area and which require the distributor to obtain goods only from the other party, are legal. However, the following restrictions apply:

(a)   There have to be alternative sources of supply of that type of product in the area covered.
(b)   Customers in the distributor's territory must be free to obtain the goods from at least one other source apart from the exclusive distributor. This source could be a distributor in an adjacent territory, or direct supply from your own premises.
(c)   Manufacturers of the same type of product cannot appoint each other as exclusive distributors in order to carve up the total European market, eg if a British manufacturing firm has its French counterpart as its exclusive distributor in France, and *vice versa*, so that consumers only have one source of supply in either country.
(d)   At least one of the parties must have a turnover less than (currently) 100 million ECUs per annum.

Hence, you could legitimately refuse to appoint more than one distributor in a certain area, and could insist that your distributor in one territory not actively seek to sell in others. However, distributors cannot be prevented from responding 'passively' to unsolicited orders from customers outside the allotted territory.

Note that businesses are entitled to complain if larger EC firms unfairly prevent them from competing in a particular market, eg by imposing unfair materials input prices or other unfair trading conditions, threatening retailers with withdrawal of supplies if they take your products, or applying exceptionally onerous obligations on contracts. You are not required to prove that an infringement has occurred; it is up to the Commission to investigate the issue and reach a conclusion. Nevertheless, you are expected to provide extensive background information on the details of the complaint, including a precise statement of why and how the infringement prevents fair competition. You complain in the first instance to:

DTI Competition Policy Division
Room 647
1–19 Victoria Street
London SW1H 0ET
071-215 7877

The Commission itself has wide powers of investigation. Its employees can enter business premises without permission, may remove and/or photocopy documents, and are empowered to demand on-the-spot oral explanations from anyone in the accused company.

Enforcement
If you believe another company (or any other body) is acting unlawfully or that your business is being unfairly victimised by Community actions there are a number of means of remedying the situation, as follows:

(a)   You can ask the European Court of Justice to annul the EC Directive, Regulation or Decision that created the problem in the first instance. This is possible only if you have a direct and immediate interest in the situation. Such actions are extremely important in cases of alleged restrictive practices, since the European Commission prohibits perceived restrictive practices via Decisions that are served on the parties to the agreements. Often the latter will ask the ECJ to annul the original Decision. This request must be registered within two months of the Decision's publication.

(b)   You can sue the Community for damages, provided you are able to prove that it acted unlawfully and that, in direct consequence, this unlawful behaviour caused you financial harm.

(c)   You can ask the UK courts to seek a preliminary ruling from the ECJ on a question concerning Community law. This enables UK firms to challenge indirectly the validity of EC Regulations, Directives and Decisions without having to bring an action in the ECJ.

(d)   You can approach a UK court for an injunction to prevent a breach of Community law. If you suffered damages as a result of the breach you can sue – through the British courts – for compensation.

Ultimately, all complaints are heard by the European Court of Justice. The workload of this Court is extremely heavy and it can take two or three years before a case is heard. Thus there is now a Court of First Instance attached to the ECJ empowered to deal with minor cases.

National barriers
EC rules on competition prohibit the creation of unfair barriers against entry to national markets by foreign EC firms. If you consider that unfair barriers have, in fact, been erected against your doing business on equal terms with local firms in any EC market (eg through the imposition of unnecessarily stringent technical standards, testing requirements, special labelling rules, etc) you can seek UK government assistance in removing the unfair practice by complaining to:

DTI Single Market Compliance Unit
Room 405
1–19 Victoria Street
London SW1H 0ET
071-215 4648

The UK Office of Fair Trading can offer guidance on the procedures involved in making a complaint about alleged breaches of EC competition law.

Office of Fair Trading
Competition Policy Division
Field House
15–25 Bream's Buildings
London EC4A 1PR
071-269 8824

Chapter 8

Pricing, Insurance and Getting Paid

Whenever possible, have your EC customers pay for your goods in the same way and on essentially the same terms and conditions available from their local suppliers. Why otherwise should they bother buying from you rather than from nearby businesses? Thus, you need to quote local currency prices, give whatever credit is customary and (where appropriate) accept payment by cheque.

Export pricing

This needs to incorporate details of the price of the goods, parties to the sale, delivery terms (CIF, DDP, etc – see page 145), the latest despatch date, the mode of transport to be used and the method of payment. The contract of sale needs to specify:

- which country's law is to apply to the contract;
- the documents required by the buyer prior to payment;
- the currency to be used to settle the transaction;
- for sales involving letters of credit (see page 154), the names and addresses of the buyer's and seller's banks handling the transaction, and who is to be responsible for bank charges.

Normally you should specify local currency Delivered Duty Paid (DDP) prices (see page 145), so that goods are handed over at the customer's premises with no charges outstanding. This enables the customer immediately to compare the price of your output with prices offered by domestic competitors. And from the customer's point of view there is no currency exchange risk attached to the transaction.

In assuming the currency exchange risk you may need to incur the cost of a forward exchange transaction (see page 150), which you must incorporate into your initial pricing computations. Successful DDP pricing requires the accurate estimation of all export transport, handling and insurance costs, and you should not prepare quotes or invoices until these have been properly analysed.

Payment by cheque

Customers' cheques will usually be drawn on customers' own local banks, thus creating delays in payment as cheques are returned to source for clearance. Delays can be minimised, however, using the bankers' SWIFT (Society for Worldwide Interbank Financial Telecommunications) system, which is a computerised means of speeding up international payments. SWIFT is based in Belgium and jointly owned by the large European and North American banks. Transactions carried by banks linked into the SWIFT network are much faster than others. Other possibilities are for the customer's bank to authorise a UK bank, by airmail or (more satisfactorily) fax or telex, to pay you the money.

Other means of payment

Payment by cheque (or direct debit, telegraphic transfer of funds, or other method that relies entirely on the buyer's eventual willingness to settle the debt after the goods have been forwarded) is known as open account settlement of international transactions. It is risky, but inevitable in many situations. However, if you have serious reservations about a customer's financial standing you need to look for a safer alternative, eg post-dated bankers' drafts, documentary collections or acceptance credits (see page 153), perhaps even cash on delivery if you can persuade customers to pay in this manner.

Currency accounts

You may open a bank account in any EC country, and can open foreign currency accounts (including accounts denominated in ECUs – see page 151) with any major UK bank. Foreign bank accounts are useful for a number of reasons:

(a) European interest rates are often considerably lower than rates in the UK. Accordingly, you might borrow at low cost from a Continental bank, convert the funds into sterling (to acquire working capital), and repay the amount borrowed using local currency cheques received from European customers.

(b) Residual balances in Continental accounts can be used to meet incidental trading expenses, hence saving currency conversion costs when obtaining money for field trips, payments to local advertising media, etc.

(c) Possession of a portfolio of currencies is a hedge against UK currency depreciation.

Another means for hedging against sterling depreciation is to ask for ECU payment (see page 152).

Credit control

Collecting debts in other countries can be enormously difficult because different and unfamiliar foreign procedures and legal systems are involved. Accordingly, most exporters choose to insure against non-payment for their shipments and, as it is not possible to obtain 100 per cent indemnity on credit insurance policies, to conduct credit checks. Credit status reports are available from:

- the ECGD (see page 147) which has an extensive database on the credit standing of customers throughout the EC;

- your own bank, which can contact its branch or correspondent bank nearest the intended customer's address;

- private credit agencies (Dun and Bradstreet is the best known; for their local telephone number look in Yellow Pages).

Reservation of title (RT)

An increasingly common (though somewhat complicated) hedge against non-payment is the incorporation of reservation of title clauses into international contracts. When you sell to a foreign customer on credit you accept that the purchaser can sell the goods to a third party prior to your being paid. If your credit customer then reneges on the debt, you must try to collect the money from that person or firm; you cannot normally approach the third party and reclaim the goods, which in law now belong to the third party. The exception is where you build into your terms of sale a reservation of title clause whereby you retain legal ownership of the goods until you have been paid. This is not a straightforward matter; the circumstances in which international courts will accept the legitimacy of such contracts are complex and you must consult a solicitor before attempting such a sale. However, the possibility is perhaps worth investigating if your output is high-value and of such a nature that its reclamation from customers in a resaleable condition is practicable.

Types of RT clause

An RT clause (sometimes referred to as a *Romalpa* clause, after the name of the court case in which the legitimacy of RT arrangements was first established) makes the transmission of ownership of property conditional on receipt of payment. There are two types of RT clause: simple and extended. The former occurs in the circumstances already outlined, ie where the seller retains ownership until cash payment is received or a cheque is cleared. More difficult are extended RT clauses, which come in two varieties:

1. The buyer is regarded as an agent of the supplier and, if the goods are sold to a third party, the money received is viewed as being 'held in trust' on the supplier's behalf. Thus, should the first buyer become insolvent before paying the supplier, the latter has a claim on that firm's assets even to the point of being able to reclaim the goods in question from the third (or subsequent) parties to whom they were resold.

2. The clause may state that if the goods supplied are used as inputs (eg as raw materials) to other goods the original supplier retains a financial interest in the final goods that result, unless the final goods possess a different 'commercial identity' from the original goods' input. For example, a supplier of leather to a handbag manufacturer was held not to have title to handbags sold to the public by the manufacturer, despite the existence of an extended RT clause.

Choosing an export price
In deciding a price for selling in EC markets you need to consider all the normal costs of production, promotion and transport, plus the special pricing requirements of the particular markets concerned. The latter could include:

- brand images of the product (an item regarded as up-market in one country may be considered down-market in others);

- the strength of local competition and the ability and inclinations of competitors to change their prices quickly and by substantial amounts;

- whether the product is entirely new to a market (in which case a higher price might be charged);

- local conventions regarding discounts for bulk purchases and prompt payment;

- mark-ups and profit margins demanded by local retailers.

Define carefully your long-term objective in the market. Do you want a large market share (implying the need for a low price in conjunction with extensive advertising and sales promotions), or are you offering a high quality top-end-of-the-market version of a locally available low priced product? In the latter case the 'Britishness' of your output might allow the establishment of a prestige appeal for the product and enable you to charge a higher price.

If you succeed in Europe the consequent increase in your business's total output could lead to economies of scale (fuller use of equipment and labour, integration of processes, ability to buy in bulk at high discount, etc) which result in lower unit costs and hence possibilities of reducing prices at home as well as abroad. Note that the determination of an appropriate export price is a critical aspect of the market research you need to undertake before entering the European market.

Incoterms

The International Chamber of Commerce (see page 156) has drafted a set of definitions of export delivery terms for use in international trade. They are widely quoted, and have a legal status in some countries. Definitions are updated periodically and details of recent revisions are available from the ICC.

Wherever possible, specify a Delivered Duty Paid (DPP) price in the buyer's national currency. This means that you assume *all* the risks and expenses involved in delivering the goods to the customer's premises. (DDP used to be known as Franco Domicile pricing.) Other Incoterms are listed below. For the purposes of explanation it is convenient to begin with Ex Works where the buyer shoulders the maximum obligation to collect and then transport consignments.

(a) *Ex Works (EXW)*. The goods are made available for the customer to collect from your premises here in the UK. Buyers take full responsibility for all transport and other risks and charges from the moment their consignments are collected. Note that EXW and similar terms of delivery are increasingly unacceptable for European business and should not be used unless specifically requested by the customer.

(b) *Free on Board (FOB)*. A freight forwarder (see Chapter 5), shipping company or other carrier arranges for the consignment to be loaded on board a ship at a UK port named in the sales contract. The buyer assumes responsibility for the goods the moment they pass over the ship's rail.

(c) *FOB Airport (FOA)*. Goods are delivered to an agreed UK airport. The customer pays airfreight charges plus all other expenses from that point.

(d) *Free on Rail (FOR)/Free on Truck (FOT)*. These are the FOB equivalents for rail and road transport.

(e) *Free Carrier (FRC)*. This is the same as FOB but applies where the mode of transport cannot be clearly defined, eg when goods are loaded on to a trailer or into a container for collection by another firm.

(f)   *Free Alongside Ship (FAS)*. The consignment is placed alongside a ship on the quay of a UK port and a port employee signs a declaration that this has been done. From that moment onwards the customer is liable for losses resulting from theft, natural deterioration, fire or other damage. The customer has to pay for loading the goods on to the ship.

(g)   *Ex Ship (EXS)*. Goods are made available to the customer on board a ship at a named foreign port of destination. Normally, the customer is responsible for unloading the goods. If not the term used is *Ex Quay (EXQ)*.

(h)   *Cost and Freight (C&F or CFR)*. You pay all the transport charges (excluding insurance, which is the customer's obligation) required to deliver goods by sea to a named destination. The customer assumes the risk of loss or damage to the goods from the moment they pass over the ship's rail at the UK port of embarkation. For CIF equivalents using modes of transport other than ships the term OCP might be used (or DCP if the goods travel in a container).

(i)   *Delivered at Frontier (DAF)*. The customer takes responsibility for the consignment the moment it passes through a named frontier.

(j)   *Cost, Insurance and Freight (CIF)*. This is the same as C&F but includes the requirement that you and not the customer insure the goods to their final destination. For methods of transport other than sea the term CIP might be used.

It is important to understand that the Incoterms are nothing more than guidelines and that any combination of delivery conditions can be written into a contract of sale. However, the domestic laws of Germany and France assume that Incoterm definitions represent normal trade custom.

Insurance

You can insure the goods themselves and the payment for them. Cargo insurance (often referred to as marine insurance, regardless of the means of transport used) is available from your usual insurance broker. Payments insurance may be obtained from a private insurance company (via your local broker) or from the Export Credits Guarantee Department (ECGD).

Cargo insurance
Cargo insurance typically costs about 1 per cent of the value of consignments, which are normally insured for CIF shipment plus 10 per cent (to cover incidental expenses attached to the loss).

When purchasing cargo insurance be sure you understand (or have your broker carefully explain) what exactly you are getting. In particular you need to know:

- when precisely your responsibility for the safe transit of the goods ceases;

- what you are covered for and exclusions from the policy;

- the extent of 'franchises and excesses'. A *franchise* in this context is any percentage loss beneath which the underwriter will not pay compensation, eg if the loss is less than (say) 5 per cent of the value of the goods, the exporting firm must bear this itself. An *excess* is an amount deducted from the compensation payable, eg if the exporter is liable for the first £250 of the total loss.

- the periods within which claims must be registered. These are quite short, eg 30 days for goods arriving by air.

Open cover is available for exporters who continuously despatch goods to foreign destinations. Here, a single policy applies to all consignments, which are declared to the insurance company on a monthly or quarterly basis.

Payments insurance and the ECGD
The Export Credits Guarantee Department (ECGD, a government-owned body due to be privatised) exists to provide UK exporters with low cost insurance against foreign customer default. Additionally, it provides much general information and advice on export credit and financing matters. About a third of all UK exports to Europe are insured by the ECGD.

Policies may be comprehensive or specific. Comprehensive policies offer guarantees against all short-term credit risks. Specific policies cover particular risks on long-term credit for projects involving major capital goods. Comprehensive cover applies to transactions involving up to six months' credit and will indemnify losses incurred through:

(a)   insolvency of the foreign customer;
(b)   failure of the customer to pay within six months for accepted goods;
(c)   the customer's failure to accept goods already despatched, for reasons which are not the fault of the supplier, and where the ECGD believes that legal action will not result in settlement;
(d)   extra handling or transport charges owing to the necessary diversion of a consignment from its planned route, if these cannot be recovered from the buyer.

Policies operate continuously and last for one year at a time. Normally, cover begins the day goods are shipped, though for an extra premium a transaction can be covered from the day the contract is signed (up to a limit of 12 months between signing and shipment).

The ECGD has never offered full indemnity to exporters, who must bear at least 15 per cent of losses caused by political factors, or 10 per cent of losses owing to commercial risk. Full indemnity might encourage firms to exercise insufficient care in choosing potential customers.

Comprehensive cover is cheaper than specific cover because by insuring all your business with a wide range of customers you are spreading risk. You pay either an annual premium computed according to your total expected export sales plus a further monthly premium or – if you are a small exporter whose foreign business is less than a certain annual amount – you can pay a single annual premium adjusted at a year's end to account for divergences between actual and anticipated EC sales. You are expected not to inform foreign customers that you have taken out ECGD cover, on the grounds that if the buyers know you are insured they might be less inclined to pay for the goods. ECGD cover costs between $1/2$ and 1 per cent of the value of export sales depending on the spread of risk and the volume of your export work.

The ECGD offers a variety of special policies, which alter periodically as circumstances change. Details are available from the ECGD head office. Note that since ECGD cover guarantees eventual payment your bank may be willing to lend you money to finance the deal, using the ECGD policy as security against your defaulting on repayment.

For an extremely large transaction involving a major project, the ECGD may even help your customer to finance the deal. Under its Buyer Credit Scheme your customer pays you 15 to 20 per cent of the value of the sale on signature of the contract, the remainder being paid to you by a UK bank from a loan made by this bank to the customer. The UK bank's loan is guaranteed 100 per cent by the ECGD. You have to pay a premium to the ECGD to cover its guarantee to the bank, the cost of which you incorporate into your quoted price. The facility is only available on finance of at least £1 million extending over at least two years. The ECGD publishes a useful and informative brochure on the subject, *Buyer Credit: Flexible Finance for Project Exports*, which you can obtain from the ECGD's London office (see below).

Obtaining cover

The first step in obtaining ECGD cover is to contact one of the ten regional ECGD Insurance Service Offices scattered around the UK. For their addresses contact the ECGD at either of its head offices:

London: ECGD
                Export House
                50 Ludgate Hill
                London EC4M 7AY
                071-382 7000

Cardiff: ECGD
                      Crown Buildings
                      Cathay's Park
                      Cardiff CF1 3NH
                      0222 824000

The ECGD claims that 80 per cent of all applications for cover are cleared within 24 hours of receipt of the enquiry.

Settlement of claims
The timing of claim settlement varies according to the cause of loss, as follows:

(a)   Immediately on proof of the buyer's insolvency.
(b)   Six months after the buyer has defaulted on accepted goods.
(c)   One month after the resale of the goods if the original customer refuses to accept them and they have to be resold to third parties at a loss.
(d)   Four months after the date of other causes of loss.

ECGD Lines of Credit
These are similar to 'buyer credits' (see page 148) except that they cover many transactions and not just one. Most important, Lines of Credit apply to individual contract values as low as £20,000, although several contracts with unrelated buyers will normally be involved.

Private credit insurance
State credit insurers no longer have a monopoly in EC countries and private insurers – UK and Continental – are increasingly active in the export field. Private insurers compete through seeking to provide superior services to state institutions. Key areas for improved service include:

●   faster turnaround of applications for cover;

●   speedier settlement of claims;

●   provision of tailor-made policies;

●   provision of 'catastrophe' policies, ie policies which for a much reduced premium cover only excessive levels of loss;

●   provision of credit ratings on potential customers.

Private companies have a significant advantage over the ECGD in that they can offer both domestic and export cover under the terms of a single policy, thus saving much administrative inconvenience for the exporting firm. Also, substantial discounts may be available on large combined policies. This is especially valuable for businesses with small volumes of export sales.

At the time of writing the biggest private UK export credit provider is Trade Indemnity PLC, from which further details of multi-market combined policies can be obtained.

Trade Indemnity PLC
12–34 Great Eastern Street
London EC2B 2FJ
071-739 4311

Your normal insurance broker should also be able to advise on private cover.

Insurance cover against currency exchange risk is not available from either the ECGD or from private sources. If, therefore, you are to be paid in a foreign currency against which sterling has appreciated, you stand to lose when you eventually convert the foreign balance into pounds. There are two ways to avoid this risk: use of the forward exchange market and payment in European Currency Units (ECUs).

Forward exchange

The invoices you send to customers will require them to pay you certain amounts of foreign currencies at future dates, eg one month or three months from now. To be sure of how much sterling your invoices will yield you can sell to your bank, in advance, the foreign currency your customers have been invoiced to pay. The bank will quote you a fixed forward exchange rate for these transactions. This predetermined forward rate will apply to the conversions regardless of the actual spot exchange rate in force one month or three months (say) from today.

The bank will demand a reward for its services and therefore will quote an exchange rate for forward currency transactions which differs from the current spot exchange rate by an amount sufficient to cover the bank's exposure to risk and make a profit.

If you expect the spot exchange rate to move in your favour, so that you stand to raise more sterling when you eventually come to convert than you would get if you converted today, you may decide not to bother with forward cover.

Option contracts
An exporter scheduled to receive payments from an EC customer over a long period can enter an option contract with a UK bank, whereby the

exporter is given the right to sell to the bank foreign currency up to an agreed limit at a predetermined rate at any time within the next 12 months. If the spot exchange rate moves in one direction the exporter will exercise the option; if it moves in the other the option will not be taken up – forfeiting thereby the fee paid to the bank to purchase the option.

The European Currency Unit (ECU)

This is the official monetary unit of the European Community. Its value is defined in terms of a 'basket' of the currencies of all 12 EC countries, weighted according to each nation's economic importance (measured in relation to its gross national product and the extent of its intra-Community trade).

Weightings are reviewed periodically (normally once every five years), or whenever the exchange rate of a member country changes by a large amount. Through the 1980s the Deutschmark, for example, carried a weight of about 30 per cent, the French franc about 20 per cent, and the UK pound about 15 per cent. These percentage weightings are converted into corresponding values of the national currencies that make up the ECU.[1] The 1990 composition of the ECU was as follows:

0.6242	Deutschmarks	0.008552	Irish punts
0.2198	Dutch gilders	151.8	Italian lire
3.301	Belgian francs	1.44	Greek drachma
0.1976	Danish krone	6.885	Spanish pesetas
1.332	French francs	1.393	Portuguese escudos
0.13	Luxembourg francs	0.08784	British pounds

To compute the value of the ECU as (say) UK pounds it is necessary to convert each component part into sterling at current exchange rates and then add the 12 resulting amounts. In 1990 the ECU was worth about 73 pence.

Since it is based on a variety of currencies and because most of the countries involved belong to the Exchange Rate Mechanism of the European Monetary System (which means they control movements of their exchange rates with other EMS members to within a very small band) the value of the ECU against any particular EC currency does not alter much over time. This inherent stability makes the ECU an attractive currency to hold.

---

[1] To illustrate how this may be done, suppose the ECU were composed of just three currencies: A, B and C. Suppose that country B is twice the size of the others, so that the weightings are 50 per cent for B and 25 per cent each for A and C. Let the currency exchange rates between the countries be 1A = 3B = 6C. Clearly the ECU comprises 0.25 units of A currency, 1.5 units of B currency (ie 50 per cent of 3) and 1.5 units of C currency (25 per cent of 6).

Uses of the ECU

ECUs have for some years been used to value EC countries' central bank reserves and to denominate debts and credit transfers between EC financial institutions. Increasingly, ECU valuations are applied to private commercial transactions and to the pricing and invoicing of goods.

Quoting a price in ECUs removes many of the trading risks connected with currency fluctuation, since a fairly predictable amount of money will eventually be collected from foreign customers, even if the exchange rate between the exporting and importing countries changes substantially. This can obviate the need to take forward cover (see page 150) on credit sales invoiced in foreign currencies. Consider, for example, the fact that the ECU has never fluctuated against the Deutschmark by more than 5 per cent during any one year, whereas (prior to Britain joining the ERM in 1990) annual sterling/Deutschmark fluctuations of 15 per cent were not uncommon. Furthermore, ECUs may be used (a) to denominate the bank loans and deposits of private businesses; (b) for forward exchange transactions (see page 150); (c) to value travellers' cheques, credit cards and similar personal financial instruments; and (d) to value mortgages.

Many European businesses now have ECU current accounts on which they draw ECU cheques. ECU debenture issues are possible and there are French unit trusts that invest exclusively in ECU denominated bonds. Some Continental companies now publish their annual balance sheets in ECUs. It is important to note, however, that ECUs are used more extensively in some EC countries than others. Italy, for example, recognises the ECU as a proper currency in its own right with a status equal to that of (say) US dollars or Japanese yen. Germany, in contrast, has in the past prohibited private German residents from holding ECU denominated assets and, in consequence, ECU valuations are (currently) used far less widely in Germany than in other European countries.

You can borrow in ECU units, with the money you receive being paid in whatever national currency you wish. Equally, your interest and capital repayments will be calculated as ECUs, which are then converted into a particular currency at the appropriate rate of exchange.

Bills of exchange

Payments other than by open account typically involve the preparation by the seller of a bill of exchange. The latter is a document, drafted by the seller of goods, instructing the buyer to pay the seller an amount of money either on receipt of the bill or (more commonly) on a specified date in the future (eg in three months' time). A bill that requires payment immediately or within three days of acceptance (see below) is called a sight bill or draft; one that is to be settled in the future is referred to as a term, usance or tenor bill.

Documentary collections

All the banks have their own standard format for bills of exchange and offer extensive help and advice on how to use them. The commonest application of bills is for documentary collections. Here, you make out the bill and give it to your own bank, together with various documents (eg the insurance certificate, invoice, transit documents [see Chapter 5]) required by the customer prior to taking delivery. Your bank now sends the bill to the importer's bank, which presents it and the relevant documents to the customer. If the bill is a sight bill, the customer settles it at once. If it is a term bill the customer accepts it by signing the bill (to acknowledge existence of the debt) and the bill is then returned to your bank, which now becomes responsible for collecting the money. All the documents which provide title to the goods are handled by your bank, which will only release them to the customer at the time of payment.

Technically, all bills of exchange remain drafts until they are formally accepted, though nowadays the word bill is generally used for all circumstances.

Further options

Other possibilities for an accepted term bill of exchange are as follows:

(a)   Sell it to your bank at a discount (bills of exchange are negotiable instruments) hence raising immediate cash to finance the production and delivery of the goods. Your bank then collects the money when the bill matures. Thus the bank assumes the risk of non-payment. This is sometimes called an acceptance credit transaction.

(b)   Keep the bill until it falls due for payment and collect the money yourself.

(c)   Borrow money from your bank using the accepted bill as security.

In the latter case your bank might want a guarantee that the bill will definitely be settled, eg by requiring the importer's bank to promise to honour the bill if the importer defaults. The term avalised bill of exchange is applied to a bill that carries such an undertaking. If the bill is not avalised and the buyer defaults your bank will still expect your company to repay the loan.

Protesting unpaid bills

If a customer defaults on a bill of exchange and it is your responsibility to collect the money, the first step towards recovery through local courts is to have the bill protested. This means getting a notary public (ie a local person legally qualified to attest and certify documents) to ask the customer for payment or reasons for non-payment. The latter are put into a formal deed of protest which your solicitor then places before a local court as evidence of dishonour.

The International Chamber of Commerce publishes a set of guidelines – *Uniform Rules for Collection* – for the use of bills of exchange, which can be legally binding if a contract so stipulates.

Documentary letters of credit

A letter of credit is an undertaking issued by the customer's bank to pay a stated sum of money to the exporter, provided certain pre-specified conditions are met. These conditions normally relate to the receipt by the importer's bank of a number of properly completed documents (including documents of title) relating to the transaction. The most important documents are as follows:

- Transport documents, eg bills of lading, air waybills, road or mail consignment notes, parcel post receipts, etc which give evidence that the goods are in transit.

- A commercial invoice (see Chapter 5) giving a full description of the goods and terms of payment.

- An insurance certificate. For letter of credit and documentary collection purposes you need a full insurance certificate; a broker's cover note will not normally do. However, if you use open cover (see page 147) you can draw up a certificate yourself on a standard form printed and already endorsed by the insurance company.

- Where appropriate, dangerous goods notices, packing lists, pre-inspection certificates, bank indemnities, etc.

- Bills of exchange.

The procedure for letter of credit settlement is as follows.

(a)   Your customer approaches his or her bank and asks it to open a letter of credit in your favour. The letter of credit will specify when payment is to be made (eg on presentation of documents, or at a later date) and which documents must be submitted prior to the paying bank releasing the money. On issuing the letter of credit the bank assumes liability for the debt.

(b)   You – or more commonly the local UK bank (known as the advising bank) that is handling the transaction – are informed that the credit has been opened and of the exact conditions to be met prior to releasing the money. You must read these conditions carefully, noting the expiry date, and any special terms relating to:

- place of payment (if the money is to be paid into a non-UK bank there could be a few days' delay before it is transmitted to Britain);
- liability for costs incurred over and above the value of the credit, eg for freight hold-ups or inspection fees;
- how claused transport documents (eg if a carrier writes on a consignment note that goods were received in a damaged condition) will affect the validity of the letter of credit;
- the means of transport to be used;
- the latest date for despatch of the consignment.

(c) The goods are sent off and the documents forwarded to the bank that is to pay the money. A bill of exchange may or may not be included in the documents depending on the precise terms of the credit.

(d) On receipt of the documents the paying bank checks them and, if they are in order, releases payment. Alternatively, if payment is to be through a bill of exchange, the bank accepts and returns this on behalf of the customer. In the latter case it is the bank and not the customer that honours the bill of exchange when it matures.

(e) The customer's bank passes the documents to the customer, provided the latter has paid in to the bank the amount due or has negotiated an overdraft.

The importer's bank may ask you for an indemnity against the buyer deciding not to pay for the goods, eg if they are short measure or of unacceptably low quality. If you give an indemnity you will be paid promptly, but must then reimburse the importer's bank – with interest – if anything goes wrong. Do *not* issue indemnities under normal circumstances, and never without carefully discussing the matter with your own bank.

A confirmed letter of credit is one the settlement of which has been guaranteed by a UK bank. You are paid direct by the UK confirming bank, which then collects the money from the foreign bank issuing the credit. The confirming bank has no claim on you if the credit is not honoured.

Currently, nearly all letters of credit are irrevocable, meaning that they cannot be arbitrarily cancelled by the customer. Nowadays, European banks outside the UK are well known and usually reliable, so unconfirmed irrevocable letters of credit are the norm for EC letter of credit transactions.

The International Chamber of Commerce has published a set of model rules for the use of letters of credit. These are binding on all parties if the credit bears an endorsement stating that it is 'Subject to ICC Uniform Customs and Practice for Documentary Credits'.

International Chamber of Commerce
103 New Oxford Street
London WC1A 1QB
071-240 5558

Problems with letters of credit
Do not expect European customers to respond kindly to demands for letters
of credit. Why should they? Such complications are not necessary when
buying from local suppliers, and customers' own banks will probably require
that appropriate amounts of funds are placed on deposit before issuing
letters of credit. Hence, working capital is forgone, and the foreign firm's
borrowing ability may consequently be affected! Letters of credit must
themselves be paid for, and the administrative work involved (especially for
arranging confirmation by a UK bank) can be expensive. There are
arrangement fees, bank and interest charges, all of which are conventionally
borne by the buyer.

Banks have a vested interest in not parting with money until the last
possible moment, so they will not remit payment unless the documents are
exactly correct. Thus, goods descriptions on invoices and advice notes must
tie up; dates must coincide; payment terms (DDP, CIF, etc) have to be
clearly stated, words and figures must tally, and so on. The following errors
are especially common:

- unsigned documents (though under international agreements photo-
  copies of signed documents are perfectly acceptable);

- mis-spelt company names and addresses;

- inadequate descriptions of the goods included in particular
  consignments;

- wrong addresses for goods destinations;

- contradictions in documents, eg mentioning a bill of lading (see
  Chapter 5) in one document and an air waybill in another.

A survey carried out by SITPRO (see Chapter 5) estimated that about half
of all letters of credit were not settled by paying banks on first presentation
because of errors in documentation.

Factoring

Many of the risks of customer non-payment can be avoided by selling your
export invoices to a credit factor in exchange for a cash payment (typically 75
to 80 per cent of the face value of invoices in the first instance, the remainder

when customers settle their outstanding balances). The factoring company then assumes full responsibility for collecting the money. You have a single transaction with the factor and are thus saved numerous clerical expenses.

Factors are expert in the laws and techniques of international debt collection. Usually they operate through international networks of credit factors, providing reciprocal services for fellow members. These networks enable factors in various countries to communicate with end customers in the latter's own languages and to apply collection procedures appropriate to the country concerned. Thus, local telephone calls can be made to remind customers to settle overdue accounts, local legal presentation can be arranged quickly in order to pursue recalcitrant debtors, and so on.

Most of the large UK banks now provide factoring services, and numerous UK credit management companies are interested in EC work (look in Yellow Pages under 'Factoring' for their names and addresses). The Association of British Factors will provide lists of its members currently active in the European Community.

Association of British Factors
25–28 Bloomsbury Way
London WC1A 2PX
071-831 4268

Cost of factoring services
How much you get for your invoices is subject to negotiation, but will depend ultimately on the monetary values involved, the degree of risk and the extent of the paperwork needed to collect payment. The cost of a factor's services typically divides into four components:

1. A service charge of perhaps 1 or 2 per cent of the value of sales to cover the cost of administering your invoices.
2. A financing charge (equivalent to loan interest) on the money turned over to you by the factor. This will normally be 3 to 5 per cent above bank base rate and is payable on the period between your receipt of cash from the factor and the dates that creditors settle their bills. If you invoice DDP in local foreign currency you can usually elect to have the residual 20 to 25 per cent of your total payment in the relevant local currency. This reduces the financing charge because interest rates in most EC countries are far lower than in the UK, and the effects of these lower rates are passed back to the client.
3. A premium of about 1 per cent to cover the cost of bad debts borne by the factor.
4. Extra charges for legal fees incurred by the factor while collecting money owed against your invoices.

If the customer ultimately defaults, the factor may or may not be able to reclaim part of the loss from you, depending on the precise terms of your contract. However, 100 per cent bad debt protection is available from most factors on payment of an additional premium.

Increasingly, factors offer ancillary services to their clients, eg information on customers; industry norms for prices and terms and conditions of sale; news about which regions and industries are experiencing recession (evidenced by exceptionally late payment by firms in these industries and regions), and so on. The large factoring companies provide this information via on-line computer viewdata facilities available on a monthly, weekly or even daily basis.

Forfaiting

Forfaiting is a means of financing the export of expensive capital goods which customers are not obliged to finish paying for until a long time in the future – as in the international construction industry, for example. Suppliers must invest large sums *now*, although buyers will pay by instalments as the project proceeds; with the final instalment falling due anything up to two years *after* the project's completion.

To raise money to pay for the initial investment the exporting contractor may draft not one but a series of bills of exchange – each with a different time to maturity – for acceptance by the purchaser. The first bill – representing the customer's first instalment – may be payable three months after beginning the project; the second bill (for the second instalment) may be due six months after that; the third a few months later, and so on. Following their acceptance, these bills may then be discounted *en bloc* by the exporter, today, at the exporter's bank in exchange for a cash payment.

In the past, forfaiting has been used exclusively for high value projects. Today it is used extensively for smaller amounts, although a minimum fee over and above the cost of funds for the deal will be required to ensure that administrative expenses are fully covered.

Forfaiting is especially popular for financing export deals of between two and five years' duration. It is 'finance without recourse' in that the bank purchasing the bills assumes full responsibility for collecting the money, and has no comeback against the exporter. However, the exporter's bank will probably insist that the bills of exchange be avalised.

The advantages of forfaiting are as follows:

(a)   Since bills of exchange are sold to the bank at today's known rate of discount the exporter pays what is in effect a fixed rate of interest on the money raised.

(b)   The cost of this finance can be quite low compared to other sources (eg a conventional bank loan secured against an ECGD credit insurance policy).

(c)   Finance is available for any period between six months and ten years.

(d)   The amount available to the exporter is known with certainty and there are no risks of currency exchange rate depreciation (critically important if you invoice in local currency).

(e)   Exporters avoid the (typically) 10 to 15 per cent non-indemnifiable risk normally required on credit insurance policies (see page 147), plus the lengthy delays typical of insurance settlements.

(f)   Forward planning and budgeting are made easier, since all costs and revenues are predetermined.

(g)   Although the exporter is effectively borrowing money to finance the project, the sale of a bill of exchange is not regarded in law as borrowing *per se*, and so does not appear as such on the exporter's balance sheet.

Nearly all the major banks offer forfaiting services, and you can shop around for the best terms. The field is increasingly competitive, with many Continental banks now bidding for UK exporters' forfaiting business.

When comparing various forfaiting facilities you need to consider the following:

(a)   The interest rate charged (ie the discount at which the bank will purchase the bills). Banks will quote different rates according to their assessments of the risk attached to your business.

(b)   Commitment fees. If you are uncertain about how and when the customer will eventually want to pay, you can ask a forfaiter to agree to purchase relevant bills of exchange as they arise, without determining a precise date for settlement. In this case a commitment fee will be payable from the date of your request until the moment you present the bills for purchase by the forfaiter.

(c)   Surcharges for delays in payment caused by administrative problems (errors in documents, postal delays, etc). Some banks add up to five days' extra interest for these.

VAT and customs planning

Currently, exports to the European Community are free of UK Value Added Tax, but are subject to import tax levied at the domestic rate of VAT applicable in the importing EC country. This tax is levied on the CIF value (see page 146) of the imported goods. There are no customs duties on goods moving between EC member states, although excise duties are payable on certain items (alcohol, for instance). Customs posts will continue to exist at national frontiers for the collection of statistical information on intra-Community trade and for health and police controls.

VAT rates differ between EC states and all negotiations aimed at harmonising VAT rates have broken down. However, the Commission has suggested the following scheme for use until the issue is finally settled.

(a)   Exports to other EC countries will no longer be zero rated for VAT purposes. Rather, VAT will be charged by exporters at the rate applicable in the exporting country. Foreign EC purchasers will then claim this back when making their annual VAT returns.

(b)   A clearing house system should be established through which end-of-year (say) aggregate imbalances between countries can be settled. Amounts owed by, or owing to, member nations would be computed from exporters' and importers' VAT returns, which would need to record intra-Community transactions separately.

Excessive taxation
Community law insists that imports into one EC state from another shall not be taxed more heavily than similar domestically produced items. If you believe your goods are being taxed excessively on crossing a border, you are entitled to challenge the taxes through the courts or (more conveniently) to write a letter of complaint to the appropriate department of the European Commission:

Commission of the European Communities
Department of Internal Market and Industrial Affairs
200 Rue de la Loi
B–1049 Brussels
Belgium
010 32 2 2351111

Examples of excessive charges are customs levies for administrative services, charges for quality inspections or special compulsory storage fees. Also prohibited under EC law are any kind of import restriction on conventionally traded goods (excluding firearms, narcotics, dangerous goods, etc), national campaigns to buy the output of a particular country ('buy British' campaigns, for instance) and any requirement that domestically produced items be used instead of EC imports.

Customs planning
The purpose of customs planning is to minimise the firm's exposure to VAT and excise and other taxes. This is achieved by:

- delaying payment of such taxes until the last permissible moment;

- applying that description of your goods (and hence HS number – see Chapter 2) which classifies your output in the category that bears the lowest rate of VAT and other tax;

- possibly selling your output as sub-assemblies rather than as finished goods.

Customs planning is particularly important (and complicated) for firms whose products include imported raw materials and/or components since the range of potential reliefs, scope for redefining the characters of goods, possibilities of altering the route by which items enter the EC (which can greatly affect their liability for duty), methods of valuing imported goods for tax purposes, and so on, increase greatly. It may be that you can figure out the tax minimising situation in respect of your product independently. Otherwise, specialist help is required. Many of the large national accounting firms have customs planning departments. These firms belong to the Management Consultancies Association, from which their names, addresses and further particulars may be obtained.

Management Consultancies Association
11 West Halkin Street
London SW1X 8JL
071-235 3897

Foreign payments jargon explained

Arbitration clauses. Clauses in documents which specify a particular third party to which disputes arising from a transaction shall be referred. The most frequently used arbitration bodies are the London Court of International Arbitration (LCIA) and the International Court of Arbitration (ICA), which is based in Paris.

Average. An insurance term meaning loss. Particular average is a partial loss caused accidentally. General average is a partial loss deliberately incurred, eg if an aircraft is in danger of crashing and the captain decides to jettison cargo to lighten the load. With general average, the loss is intended to benefit everyone; hence all parties are expected to contribute proportionately towards the cost, even if certain consignments have not been touched. Compensation for general average is available through standard cargo insurance policies.

Most policies are 'With Particular Average', meaning that partial losses accidentally caused are fully covered. Otherwise the policy is 'Free from Particular Average', so that claims for accidental partial losses will not be met.

Back to back credits (counter credits). These involve two separate letters of credit. The first is in favour of the exporting company, which now instructs its own bank to issue a second letter of credit in favour of one of the exporter's own suppliers (eg to provide raw materials necessary to produce the goods).

Beneficiary. The exporter specified in a letter of credit.

Clean bill of exchange. A bill of exchange sent to a foreign customer's bank without any transit or insurance documents. The latter are forwarded direct to the customer, thus enabling him or her to take possession of the goods prior to payment. Payment via a bill of exchange without the need to hand over shipping documents is called a clean collection.

Collecting bank. The foreign branch of a UK bank (or a foreign bank which acts on behalf of a UK bank) to which a UK exporter's bill of exchange and supporting documents are passed. The collecting bank presents the bill to the foreign customer for acceptance.

Consensus interest rates. Internationally agreed interest rates for government backed medium- to long-term export credit. Consensus rates were introduced to avoid interest rate wars between countries as national governments increasingly subsidised export finance. Currently, consensus rates are not available for sales to the EC or to other 'richer' countries. Also, the gap between consensus and commercial rates has narrowed considerably in recent years.

Deferred payment credit. A letter of credit specially designed to give importers extra time to pay. The deferment period may terminate on a predetermined date regardless of when the goods are despatched, or be due for settlement a certain number of days after delivery.

Demurrage charges. Storage charges incurred at docks and airports.

Dirty (claused) bill of lading. A bill of lading endorsed to state that goods were received on board a ship damaged or in short measure.

Finance without recourse. Money obtained from a bank to finance an export transaction in such a way that if the customer eventually defaults the bank cannot go back to the exporter and demand compensation. The bank assumes the entire risk of customer non-payment. Examples of finance without recourse occur in factoring, forfaiting and the discounting of bills of exchange.

Negotiating bank (accepting bank; paying bank). Other titles for an advising bank, ie a bank in the exporter's country that acts as an intermediary between the importer's (issuing) bank and the exporter. The advising bank collects documents from the exporter and receives funds from the importer's bank which are then passed over to the exporter.

Performance bonds (default bonds). An undertaking by a third party (usually a bank or insurance company) that it will pay the exporter an agreed sum of money in the event of the customer's default.

Red clause credit. A letter of credit which authorises the importer's bank to pay the exporter before presentation of documents.

Remitting bank. The (exporter's) bank which sends a bill of exchange (plus appropriate documents) to a collecting bank.

Revolving credit. A letter of credit used to cover a number of consignments when the exporter wishes to avoid opening a series of individual credits. Revolving credits apply to a number of different consignments within an agreed limit. Hence the credit amount is automatically renewed without formal amendment.

Stale bill of lading. A bill of lading that arrives at the customer's premises after the goods have arrived at the port of destination. In the absence of a bill of lading the customer can only obtain possession of the goods by giving the shipping company a bank letter of indemnity which protects the shipping company against subsequent claims.

Standby credit. A letter of credit with an extended period for payment. Under the arrangement the importer's bank stands ready to honour the credit if the exporter can prove that the importing firm has failed to meet its obligations. The purpose of a standby letter of credit is to allow the participating businesses to trade on an open account basis, so that the credit is never actually used except in the event of default by the buyer.

Standby credits are non-performance documents used only when the importer does not perform a contracted duty. The standard documentary letters of credit referred to in the text, conversely, are performance documents, ie payment occurs given the presentation to a bank of satisfactory documents proving export of the goods. In other words, a standby credit comes into play if something does not happen rather than when something does.

Through (transhipment) bill of lading. A bill of lading used when sea transport forms only part of a journey and it is more convenient to prepare a single contract document than separate documents for each carrier.

Transferable credits. Letters of credit used by intermediaries in the export trade which enable the intermediary to transfer part of the money released under the credit direct to the intermediary's supplier(s).

Chapter 9
The French Connection

France is just 20 miles from the British mainland and offers UK companies a potential market of at least 55 million consumers. Yet the French buy twice as much from Italy and three times as much from Germany as they do from British firms. Of course, direct overland access from Italy and Germany straight into the French market partially explains these differences, as does the physical separation of Britain from France. It has to be said, however, that Italian and German businesses are on average considerably more assertive and ambitious when dealing with France than their counterparts in the UK. British firms have much to do if they are to compete effectively in France in the aftermath of the Single Market.

Characteristics of the market

Paris has by far the largest population (about eight and a half million) of any French city, although there is today an annual net migration out of the city – notably towards the south (especially Toulouse and Montpellier) where many of France's newer microtechnology industries are situated. No single French conurbation outside Paris has a population exceeding one and a half million.

Increasingly, France is a high technology country with many demands for imported manufactured goods. And despite recent setbacks the country still represents a large and prosperous consumer market. Hypermarkets account for nearly 20 per cent of all retail sales. Chains of hypermarkets can place huge orders with suppliers, and so can the collective buying organisations (called *Supercentrales*) of the major supermarket chains.

France has a large public sector and there are many opportunities for selling to schools, hospitals, the armed services, social services, state owned industries, and so on. The French Government Procurement Agency publishes a booklet outlining its purchasing policies. You get this from:

L'Union des Groupements d'Achats Publics
Tour Paris-Lyon
209 Rue de Bercy
75585 Paris Cedex 12
010 33 1 43 46 11 70

Certain business practices are illegal in France. The main prohibitions are loss leading, unjustified price discrimination, refusal to supply goods and resale price maintenance (ie refusing to sell products to retailers who will not undertake to charge pre-specified minimum prices).

Advantages of selling to France

Arguably, France is one of the easier EC markets to enter, for a number of reasons.

- The French market is highly stable.

- There is already a substantial number of UK companies operating in France and you can approach these firms for advice and assistance (through a Chamber of Commerce, the commercial departments of British Diplomatic Posts in France, your own UK bank, etc) when commencing French operations.

- A strong demand for good quality British products continues to exist among French consumers. (France is the UK's third largest export market.)

- Extensive published statistics about France and French buying habits are available, so it is relatively easy to conduct preliminary market research.

- You can travel to all parts of France quickly and conveniently if problems requiring immediate attention arise unexpectedly.

- As French is widely taught in British schools and colleges it is not difficult to find translators of standard commercial documents, advertisements, etc from English into French.

- France has an excellent and wide-ranging rail network that can be used for onward distribution of products throughout Europe.

- French attitudes towards business are not dissimilar to those found in the UK.

What the French want from British goods

To market your goods in France successfully you must:

- project sound and concrete images of high quality products;

- wherever possible, enable French customers to obtain your goods direct from a local supply point (eg a retail outlet) rather than having to order them from an address in Britain;
- allow customers to pay in French currency, and on the same terms and conditions (including credit terms) available from local suppliers;
- provide effective customer care facilities and strong technical back-up services.

French versus British promotional images

Normally, it is best either to conceal the UK origin of your products – by marketing them under a French name and using quintessentially French promotional images – or to identify them as undeniably British, playing on traditional French perceptions of what the British are like, and using plenty of highly stereotyped English (or Scottish) characterisations.

On balance, it is perhaps rather more difficult for British goods to be sold simply under a 'Made in Britain' label in view of past difficulties concerning supply problems (real or imaginary) with UK firms: late deliveries, inadequate after-sales service, communication breakdowns, and so on.

Use of the French language

The French are encouraged to deal exclusively in their own language in consequence of a law of 1975 which required that all advertisements, guarantees, instructions for use of products and related information, etc be written in French. Indeed, many French managers expect foreign suppliers to do business as if they were French! Thus, wherever possible write invoices, advice notes, estimates and other commercial literature in French. Officially, all invoices submitted to French customers should be in French, although the rule is (obviously) unenforceable.

Always quote French currency prices for delivery direct to the customer's premises or nearby, eg a local railway station or container depot. A French business will be just as disinclined to pick up your goods from a UK port (say) as you would be to fetch a French company's goods from the dockside in Boulogne or Calais.

Translating sales materials into French

Translation services are discussed in Chapter 3, but the sensitivity of the translation issue in relation to the French market requires further comment. It is essential that the translator knows something about French business methods and social and other conventions affecting the effectiveness of advertising messages in France. Note, in particular, how the basic meaning of a promotional message may itself require alteration since, in France, an advertiser who is unable to substantiate a claim made about a product can be compelled, when challenged, to undertake 'corrective advertising' to point out the inadequacy – at the advertiser's own expense!

The following difficulties are especially troublesome when translating advertising copy from English into French.:

(a) Numerous English advertisements use alliteration (words beginning with the same letters) or assonance (words with parts that rhyme – Beanz Means Heinz, for example) that are impossible to translate into French.

(b) Puns and other forms of word play do not normally translate between the two languages.

(c) The definite article (ie the word 'the' in English) is necessary far more frequently in French than English, leading to longer slogans when writing in French, and to body copy being less punchy than is normal in Britain.

Researching the French market

To market your products in France successfully you need accurate and detailed market information. Fortunately, France is a much researched country and you can quickly locate data on:

- income per head by region and occupation;

- percentages of regional populations possessing various products, broken down with respect to age, occupation, type of residence, wage level, etc;

- controls on local investment and regional investment incentives;

- transport systems and, in particular, any changes in temperature and humidity conditions that make special packaging or product modifications necessary;

- age structure of the population, family size and other demographic characteristics.

France has its own marketing association, which you can contact directly to enquire about the facilities it offers.

Association Nationale du Marketing-Recherche
30 Rue d'Astorg
75008 Paris
010 33 1 42 26 51 13

The Franco-British Chamber of Commerce will, if you wish, arrange commissioned research into a particular French market on your behalf, but the cost of this is high (market research is much more expensive in France than in Britain), despite the availability of DTI grants (see Chapter 2).

Franco-British Chamber of Commerce and Industry
26 Avenue Victor Hugo
75016 Paris
010 33 1 45 01 55 00

The French Chamber of Commerce in Britain may also be able to arrange research facilities.

French Chamber of Commerce in Britain
197 Knightsbridge
London SW7 1RB
071-225 5250

Further information on possibilities for commissioned research may be obtained from the Market Research Society (see Chapter 2). UK members of the Market Research Society – operating usually through Continental sister companies and/or subsidiaries – will (for a price) collect data on local French purchasing habits, retail opportunities, effectiveness of various advertising campaigns, etc in particular markets. Also, they will test various French markets to ascertain their suitability for your product, advise on appropriate brand images, conduct market surveys, and so on.

Advertising in France

The French advertising industry has a similar structure to that in Britain, with full-service agencies that offer a complete range of services (media, liaison, account strategy, creativity, copywriting, research, production, etc) and specialist à la carte agencies which provide a single function. As in Britain, agencies that deal with the media take the bulk of their profits from media commissions rather than from client firms. However not all French advertising agencies are independent of media owners; some 'agencies', in fact, act mainly as space sellers for just a few publications – upon which they depend entirely for their incomes.

In addition to advertising agencies, there is in France a well-developed marketing services industry comprising public relations consultancies, mail order houses, list brokers, etc. You can obtain details of French advertising agencies, and of UK agencies that operate in France, from the French Association of Advertising Agencies.

> Association des Agences Conseils en Publicité
> 40 Boulevard Malesherbes
> 75008 Paris
> 010 33 1 47 42 13 42

Direct marketing to France

The geographical proximity of France (and hence the ease of fulfilment of premium offers, and so on) makes it a prime target for direct marketing and sales promotion activities. In the past France has lagged behind Britain in this field, essentially because of the relatively low cost of conventional advertising (about 30 per cent less than in the UK). However, recent increases in media rates, plus heightened awareness of the potential and benefits of DM methods, have led to a significant growth in the number of French DM and sales promotion agencies and consultancies. French law on sales promotions is broadly comparable to that of the UK, notably in relation to competitions. Prizes in a competition may be determined by chance provided no proof of purchase is needed. Otherwise, as in Britain, some substantial element of skill or judgement is required. Upper limits are imposed on the value of premium offers, which must not exceed 7 per cent of the price of low value items.

Distributing goods in France

French distribution systems parallel those of the UK, ie retail outlets (including franchises), wholesalers, direct sale via agents or mail order, and chain or multiple store groups. If you wish you can approach directly the trade associations and centralised buying groups representing the major French distributors; indeed, many of these have offices and/or buying agents here in the UK. Their names, addresses and fields of specialisation are available from:

- The British Diplomatic Post in your target sales area (you can get details of this from the French Desk of the DTI);
- The DTI's Export Market Information Library;
- UK Chambers of Commerce and the Franco-British Chamber of Commerce.

Transporting goods to France

A large proportion of the French population lives in Paris or in conurbations near the French coast. Chapter 5 describes how the Channel Tunnel hub and spoke system may not be cost effective for distributing goods in these areas. Thus, many deliveries to France will continue by air, road and ferry, and by conventional seafreight services, depending on the area to be served.

Ferries operate to Calais, Boulogne, Dunkirk, Caen, Cherbourg, Le Havre, St Malo and Roscoff. Paris is also a major shipping port in its own right. The Port of Paris Authority owns numerous warehouses along the riverside, which it lets out to local freight handling firms. And it is possible for UK firms wishing to export to France to use direct sea transport between most British small ports and Paris and then to store goods in facilities provided by the Port of Paris Authority for this purpose. Further information concerning these facilities is available from freight forwarders (see Chapter 5) or direct from the Port of Paris Authority. The port of Dieppe provides similar facilities.

Port of Paris Authority
2 quai de Grenelle
75732 Paris
010 33 1 45 78 61 92

Dieppe Port Authority
Chambre de Commerce et d'Industrie
4 Boulevard General de Gaulle
BP 62
76202 Dieppe
010 33 35 84 24 96

Normandy
To transport goods to Normandy you can use the Ro-Ro ferry facilities at Dieppe and Le Havre. These towns lie at the corner of the Single Market's 'golden triangle', comprising industrial West Germany, the Netherlands, Belgium and the Paris basin, an area that collectively offers a market of 60 million potential consumers within a few hours' driving distance. There are two main roads and several trains to Paris per day. Some of these trains are scheduled to connect with ferries from the UK. Dieppe has an airport that can be used for business purposes.

Lyons
Lyons – France's second city – is another major centre. It lies at the intersection of a motorway network that serves the south of France,

Germany, Italy, Spain and Switzerland. And it has an airport with direct routes to most major destinations in Europe and North Africa.

Agents

Few UK business owners are fluent in French; have the time to visit the country frequently; or know enough about French business institutions and methods to be able to operate in the market independently. Thus, most UK firms wishing to sell in France will need to consider appointing a local French agent to handle their French dealings – other than straightforward mail order transactions. General agency matters are discussed in Chapter 6. This section discusses only the special arrangements that apply to French agents. The rules of French agency are rather more complicated than for most other EC countries.

Commercial agents

These are agents who work on commission on behalf of their principals (ie the foreign businesses that employ them) and are bound to the latter by contract. The status of a commercial agent is clearly defined in the French Commercial Code (which forms the basis of French business law), and is substantially different from that which applies in Britain. The major features of the French commercial agent's situation are as follows.

(a)   In France, all agency contracts must be registered with the *Tribune de Commerce* (ie the French Commercial Court).

(b)   Agency agreements are fully enforceable even if they are not in writing.

(c)   Commercial agents are entitled to substantial compensation if their contracts are terminated before they are due to expire (although short probationary periods are permitted). There is (currently) a crucial difference between French and English law regarding this matter. In England it is possible to build into an agency contract a clause stating that the agency agreement may be terminated at the request of either party without any future financial liability being incurred by the side that initiates the request. This is not true in France, where agents cannot be arbitrarily dismissed without compensation regardless of the wording of the contract. Accordingly, a French agent might sue you for damages (computed as an estimate of the value of the goodwill the agent has brought to your business) and you might have to pay a couple of years' anticipated profits to the agent as compensation.

(d)   An agency contract may include an exclusivity agreement, subject to the provisions of EC competition law (see Chapter 6).

(e)   The agent may undertake agency work for other firms without your permission, but not for a direct competitor of your business.

Distributors

A distributor (sometimes referred to in France as a *concessionaire*) is an independent business which formally agrees to purchase your products in exchange for exclusive rights to sell in a predetermined area. Since the distributor buys and sells on its own account it is not an agent as such (see Chapter 6), and thus does not enjoy the protection of French agency law. Nevertheless, French distributors do sometimes act in an agency capacity on behalf of their clients as well as in their role as *concessionaires*. The following should be noted:

(a)   In France, distribution contracts are normally for a specific period and, under French law, they can only be renewed by *explicit* agreement between the parties – not tacitly.

(b)   A distributor is *not* entitled to compensation if you decide not to renew the contract, although it will be able to claim damages if you repudiate the deal prior to the agreed expiry date and without good cause. In the latter case, damages claimed could include amounts for 1. financial losses, 2. 'discredit' (a French notion referred to as *préjudice morale et commercial*, which is difficult to translate into English), and 3. damage to the distributor's business goodwill.

   You can cancel a distribution agreement without legal difficulty if the distributor fails to perform any of the conditions stated in the contract or takes any action detrimental to your firm. It is advisable, however, to include an explicit clause to this effect in the body of the contract.

(c)   French distributors normally expect to determine the selling prices of the goods they purchase, and they frequently handle several complementary products at the same time. Take care to ensure, therefore, that your distributor does not give precedence to other firms' products.

Commissionaires

These are French businesses which act – on commission – for (usually) several principals but under their own business name. Their role is to market goods sent to them by other firms for sale to customers who cannot be conveniently contacted by principals. However, *commissionaires* do *not* purchase your goods – they merely sell them on your behalf.

Under French law a *commissionaire* is at liberty to represent your direct competitors without disclosing that this is being done. The following aspects of the *commissionaire's* legal position are important:

(a) A *commissionaire* is regarded by French law as a 'merchant', ie a business that trades on its own account.

(b) Firms undertaking this line of work must register with the French Commercial Register and be issued with an identification number.

(c) Unlike a commercial agent, the *commissionaire* is a party to contracts entered into on behalf of clients (see Chapter 6 for a discussion of the significance of this point). Accordingly, the *commissionaire* incurs personal liability when contracting with third parties and is responsible for settling any debts to these third parties following the principal's insolvency.

The purchaser of the goods enters a contract with the *commissionaire* rather than the principal. This is not the case, however, if the contract carries the principal's name or is stated as being on the principal's behalf. Here the intermediary is regarded as a commercial agent and not a *commissionaire*.

(d) Any person or business can act as a *commissionaire*. Thus a commercial agent (see page 171), broker or VRP (see below) can be regarded as engaging in this work in certain circumstances. It is important, therefore, to establish from the outset the capacity in which your French representative/agent is acting in relation to your company.

(e) The agreement setting up the relationship with the *commissionaire* can be implicit and need not be in writing. You cannot terminate the agreement at will without paying substantial compensation. Equally, the *commissionaire* cannot cancel the arrangement without good reason.

(f) If the *commissionaire* is not able to sell your goods you can be required to take them back. In the absence of any agreement to the contrary the cost of returning them must be borne by you.

(g) A *commissionaire* must carry out your instructions exactly, and is obliged to act with skill and care when so doing.

Salaried representatives

French civil law defines a special status for salespeople who represent client firms – as agents – but who receive predetermined salaries (perhaps with a commission incentive in addition) even though their work is essentially similar to that of a commercial agent. These individuals are called VRPs (standing for *Voyageur, Représentant, Placier*) and come in two varieties:

1. The VRP *multicarte*, who works for a number of different employers.
2. The VRP *monocarte*, who works for a single employer.

To qualify as a VRP, the salesperson must not trade on his or her own account and must be bound by a service agreement. Thereafter, a VRP receives a professional identity card, and becomes legally entitled to (a) paid holidays and (b) notice of dismissal plus compensation for consequent damage to his or her reputation. VRPs and their employers must each pay government social security contributions. Employers' contributions are collected initially from the VRP, who then recovers the amounts paid back from his or her employer.

VRPs lose their right to compensation on termination of their contracts if they:

- are negligent, disloyal, incompetent or indulge in repeated misconduct (the burden of proving these allegations rests with the employer);

- do not canvass with sufficient vigour, eg failing to call on customers despite being instructed to do so;

- act for another employer in direct competition with the first employer without obtaining the latter's consent;

- fail to submit accurate reports on their activities.

Brokers

A French broker brings together other parties who wish to enter a contract, and in this capacity will tell each party of the other party's terms and acts as an intermediary in negotiations. However, a French broker is not regarded as an agent under French law. Brokers receive commissions from both parties to the contract. The commission is paid in equal shares by the parties, unless there is an agreement to the contrary.

Advice on French agency arrangements

You can obtain lists of lawyers expert in the French law of agency from (a) the UK Law Society (see below), (b) the Franco-British Chamber of Commerce, and (c) the British Embassy in Paris. Names and addresses of VRPs are available from the *Chambre Syndicate Nationale des Représentants d'Industrie et du Commerce* in Paris.

Chambre Syndicale Nationale des Représentants d'Industrie
  et du Commerce
30 Boulevard Bonne Nouvelle
75010 Paris
010 33 1 48 24 97 59

The Law Society
113 Chancery Lane
London WC2A 1PL
071-242 1222

Establishing a permanent presence

France is a bureaucratic country and, although the liberalisation of rules on intra-Community investment embodied in various Single Market agreements should ease existing constraints on foreign investment, you will still have to check carefully the extent of possible restrictions on your line of business in a particular region. Note in particular that:

(a)   the French government imposes many controls on businesses connected with road transport, financial services, insurance and the provision of public utilities;

(b)   in order to take over an existing French business you may be required to submit to the Ministry of the Economy an assessment of the impact of your investment on the local community;

(c)   local planning permission is necessary for new constructions, and to obtain this you may be compelled to undertake a study of the effects of the project on the local environment;

(d)   regional investment incentives are available for investment in high unemployment areas (details of these are available from the French regional action board, DATAR, which has an office in London). DATAR's role is to encourage regional economic development. Firms investing in certain depressed regions qualify for a cash grant based upon the number of workers employed, and there are Enterprise Zones in which newly established businesses pay no corporation tax for the first ten years of operation.

DATAR gives (substantial) cash grants for investments in certain designated development areas. Extensions to existing businesses in these areas also attract subsidy (up to 20 per cent of the capital cost in some cases). Grants of up to 50 per cent are available for staff and instructor training. Further incentives include: tax exemptions; grants for the payment of employee relocation expenses; and subsidised rents on local authority owned factory buildings.

France has traditionally welcomed good quality foreign investment, and regional officials will be pleased to advise on appropriate locations, detail the grants available, and generally help investing companies to obtain central government approval for intended projects.

DATAR
1 Avenue Charles-Floquet
75007 Paris
010 33 1 47 83 61 20

and

113 Park Lane
London W1Y 4AY
071-493 5021

French businesses

These can be sole traders, partnerships or limited companies. All new enterprises must register with the French Companies and Commercial Register.

Partnerships

The commonest French partnership is the SNC (*Société en nom collectif*) which is the standard non-limited liability form. As in Britain, partners are jointly and severally liable for the business's debts.[1] The partnership is allowed to trade under the name of one of the partners, provided the name is followed by the words *et Cie*. Annual accounts must be filed with the local Commercial Registry, but are not available for public inspection. Other forms of French partnership are as follows.

1.   The SP (*Société en participation*). This has a senior partner without limited liability plus sleeping partners whose liability is limited but whose identities are not made known to the public. If sleeping partners' names are disclosed the individuals concerned lose their limited liability.
2.   The SCS (*Société en commandité simple*). Here the senior partner has unlimited liability, but the partnership as a whole can issue shares to outsiders. Thereafter, however, shareholders need the permission of all partners before they can sell their shares. A variation on the SCS exists whereby shares are freely transferable. This is called an SCA (*Société en commandité par actions*).

---

[1] This means that each member has unlimited liability for all debts incurred by all other partners on behalf of the firm. If some partners have no assets when the partnership is terminated, the partnership's creditors may claim from the remaining partners the full amounts they are owed.

Branches and joint ventures

No special arrangements apply to the establishment in France of branches of other companies. However, branches are taxed as if they were independent companies, regardless of their actual legal form. There are no restrictions on joint ventures.

French companies

There are two main types of French company:

1. the *Société anonyme* (SA), which is a joint stock company able to sell shares to the general public in a manner roughly comparable to a public limited company (PLC) in the UK;
2. the *Société à responsabilité limitée* (SARL) which is broadly comparable to a UK limited company. A SARL needs between two and 50 shareholders. It is not allowed to obtain a quotation on the French stock exchange or to sell shares to the general public. Share transfer is by stamp duty of about 5 per cent of the value of the transaction.

An SA must have at least seven shareholders, and minimum share capital requirements apply. The board of a French SA is compelled by law either to have:

- three to 12 directors who own company shares (although these directors need not be French nationals – or even live in France); or

- a supervisory board to which a lower level executive committee reports (rather similar to the situation of an *Aktiengesellschaft* (AG) in Germany, see Chapter 10).

If a French company has more than 50 employees its workers elect a committee, two representatives of which are legally entitled to attend all meetings of its board of directors. Any firm with more than ten workers must allow employees to elect representatives who are legally entitled to demand monthly meetings with management. It is important to note that (as in Germany) French companies are less inclined to raise money via share issues than their UK counterparts. In consequence, hostile takeovers are far less common than in Britain (although benign mergers and takeovers occur continuously). Even companies with substantial share capitals tend to be family owned or to place their shares with institutional investors which effectively guarantee not to sell them to unwelcome outsiders.

Firms with more than 100 employees are statutorily required to operate a profit sharing scheme. Companies are legally obliged to negotiate employee terms and conditions on an annual basis. All SAs and larger SARLs require statutory audits.

Taxation

Companies, limited partnerships and branches of foreign firms are liable to Corporation Tax at (currently) 40 per cent, regardless of their level of profits. VAT is 18.6 per cent standard rate, 25 per cent for luxuries. Certain necessities bear negligible VAT (as little as 2 per cent for some items).

Chapter 10

Germany: Powerhouse of the European Community

Germany is the UK's second biggest export market which, prior to unification, took $7^1/_2$ per cent of all exports leaving this country. At the time of writing, however, Britain's trade with Germany shows a substantial deficit, and (depressingly) the major UK export to that country is oil and petroleum products rather than manufactured goods. Nevertheless, Germany takes a wide range of British manufactures, many of which are supplied by small UK firms. Indeed, one third of British exports to Germany comprise various categories of machinery and transport equipment, and many diverse niche markets are served.

Germany is perhaps the most competitive market to break into in the entire world: everyone wants a stake in the continuing prosperity of the German economy, and German buyers of foreign products are spoiled for choice. British goods, therefore, must be attractively priced and of high quality if they are to succeed in the German market.

What Germany is

The German nation is extremely populous. It covers West and East Germany (these two states were created in 1945 but have recently rejoined), plus large numbers of people in Poland (the borders of which were extended into the previous German state immediately after the Second World War), Hungary, Czechoslovakia, Switzerland and the USSR.

Before reunification, nearly all the UK's trade with Germany was with the Federal Republic (West Germany), which for administrative purposes is divided into 11 regions. The most important of these economically is North Rhine Westphalia, which has a population of about 16 million. Other large regions are Bavaria (population 11 million), Baden-Württemburg (9 million) and Lower Saxony (7 million).

Banking, finance and financial services (including a rapidly expanding insurance industry) are centred on Frankfurt. Heavy industry is found mainly in the Ruhr; electronics and information technology businesses tend to be located in Baden-Württemburg. Germany is a country that manufactures goods rather than providing services and, while its service sector has expanded, the rate of growth of service industries has been lower than the

179

corresponding rate in other EC countries. One reason for this, perhaps, is that in Germany service industries (especially financial services) are controlled far more closely than elsewhere.

Reasons for selling to Germany

There are several good reasons why UK firms should focus their attention on the German market.

(a)   German economic growth – while slower today than previously – is seemingly unstoppable. The country is politically stable, has low inflation, sound industrial relations, and may well be destined for a second economic miracle as German businesses extend into the new markets currently opening up in eastern Germany and beyond.

(b)   The continuing strength of the Deutschmark relative to sterling reduces the import prices of British goods. Germans are affluent and have plenty of money to spend on consumer (and other) products. Overall, imports into Germany are expanding at about 5 per cent annually, but at substantially higher rates for manufactures and finished consumer goods.

(c)   Over 70 per cent of Germany's exports consist of motor vehicles (20 per cent), machinery, office equipment, machine tools and other manufactured items. Accordingly, German industry itself needs continuous supplies of input materials and components that can originate abroad. UK small businesses (ie employing less than 200 workers) already export more to West Germany than to any other country.

(d)   Increasingly, German business involvement with Hungary, Czecho-slovakia, Poland and the USSR creates opportunities for the re-export of UK products to these countries via German firms.

(e)   Your business will operate under exactly the same conditions and regulations as, and compete on equal terms with, local German firms. West Germany does not discriminate against foreign companies.

(f)   Trains, lorries and ships leave for Germany *every* day, so there are few groupage problems (see Chapter 5) attached to sending goods to that country. Also, Germany has already abolished quota restrictions on internal lorry movements by foreign firms. Hence, UK vehicles have free access to German *autobahnen* for the distribution of products.

(g)   Many German business people speak English, and most are quite willing to correspond in English when it is convenient to do so.

(h)   West Germany is the world's largest venue for international trade fairs. A presence in Germany enables you to exhibit at relevant fairs easily and at short notice, and hence to promote your products in many international markets.

(i)   You can establish a German subsidiary at will, using the same procedures as German nationals. There are no restrictions on how much equity you may hold in the subsidiary, and its directors need not be German citizens or residents of the country.

(j)   Compared to other EC countries, Germany has a relatively large number of small businesses serving niche markets, particularly for technically sophisticated goods. Hence there is a wide variety of demands for specialised inputs into these smaller firms that can be met by competent British firms.

What the Germans want from British goods

UK products will appeal to German consumers if they:

- project a stereotypical British image;
- are robust, functional and of high quality;
- are stocked locally by a German supplier;
- carry officially recognised German 'tested for safety' marks (see below);
- are stylish and attractively designed;
- are delivered *on time* (a major problem with British goods in the past);
- are price competitive in local currency terms.

German customers expect the same sorts of credit terms and prompt payment discounts as are usual in the UK. Funds are freely transferable from Germany to Britain, and payment can be made in any currency desired (US dollars, for example).

Note that Germany's population is ageing more rapidly than in any other EC country, so products which appeal to middle-aged consumers stand a better than average chance of longer-term success. This could change by virtue of the current influx of (young) East Germans and German speaking refugees from the Soviet Union, but the effects will not be felt for some time.

Actually, an ageing population could cause German industry to become even more efficient than it already is, since labour shortages may force still further the computerised automation of production processes. German workers are among the highest paid in the world and take the longest holidays. It follows that robotics and other labour saving devices are in heavy demand.

Germans value education in its own right, and there is compulsory education for all citizens up to a high level, regardless of their occupation. This makes for intelligent and discerning consumers who are not easily misled by misrepresentative advertisements. And many Germans speak foreign languages, especially English and French.

Technical standards

Until product standards are fully harmonised across the EC (see Chapter 2) German technical specification requirements continue to apply to imported British goods. These come in two forms: general consumer protection laws and industry specific *Deutsche Industrie Normen* (DIN) standards set by professional and other bodies.

There are laws which affect technical and scientific equipment, engineering products, machines, tools, domestic appliances, sports and children's products, and many other categories of goods. Essentially these laws require that products are safe and comply with 'recognised rules of technology' at the time they are supplied.[1]

DIN standards, however, are not legally binding, although the saleability of goods which fail to adhere to them is greatly reduced (virtually impossible in certain cases). They are established by industry trade associations and published by the Federal Government in a catalogue. Examples of DIN accreditation bodies are the German associations of electrical engineers (the VDE), mechanical engineers (VDI) and gas engineers (DVGW). More than 25,000 DIN standards currently exist.

Nevertheless, Germany has always welcomed UK goods and no unfair product standard barriers have ever been erected against British products.

Pre-shipment testing

It may be possible to have your goods tested against German standards here in the UK. Otherwise you must send them to a German test centre or pay a representative of the latter to visit your premises and test the goods *in situ*. Detailed advice on UK/German product standard comparisons are available from the British Standards Institution (see Chapter 2) or direct from:

German Standards (DIN)
Pergamon Orbit Information Ltd
Achilles House
Western Avenue
London W3 0UA
081-992 3456

[1.] For the UK version of these laws (which are incorporated into the 1987 Consumer Protection Act) see Chapter 10 of my book *Small Business Survival*, Pitman/Natwest, 1989.

Transporting goods to Germany

Germany has highly developed road, rail and water transport systems. Goods may be sent via the Channel Tunnel (see Chapter 5), by ferry and then by road or rail from the French coast, or by sea to the north of the country. Duisburg in North Rhine Westphalia has Europe's largest inland port which serves a hinterland (including the Ruhr) that contains a quarter of the country's population. In the past the bulk of imports into Germany have entered through the north of the country (notably through the ports of Hamburg and Bremen), although this is altering rapidly as southern transport access facilities continue to improve.

There is a ferry service from Harwich to Hamburg, but this involves a 24-hour sea journey and (currently) does not run every day. Many firms use short cross-channel ferry routes to France, followed by a relatively tedious road journey; or they opt for a longer ferry passage to one of the Belgian or Dutch ports and then use the fast motorway links into western Germany.

The German rail network is fast and efficient and has international services connecting to all other European countries. Apart from the Tunnel, direct rail services from the UK to Germany operate via Dover/Ostend and from Harwich to the Hook of Holland. Germany has an extensive system of road links with surrounding countries, including major international motorways from Belgium and France. The Belgian motorway connects at Aachen and goes towards Bonn, Cologne, Dusseldorf and surrounding industrial areas. Motorway entry from France is via Saarbrucken (a rather depressed German region bordering on France) leading to *autobahnen* that travel both north and south. Motorways built since 1945 invariably run from north to south in consequence of the partition of the country. Airfreight services are available to all parts of Germany. Freeport facilities are available in Hamburg, Bremen and Bremerhaven.[2]

Packaging

You only need to disclose the country of origin of your goods if German rather than English words are used on packages. Prepackaged consumer goods have to conform to certain labelling and package design requirements, and there are special regulations for foodstuffs, pharmaceuticals and textile products. Information on these constraints is available from the German Foreign Trade Information Office, the DTI and the Institute of Packaging (see Chapter 5).

[2.] A freeport is a designated area at a seaport where goods may be imported, worked on, altered in form and substance, repackaged and then re-exported without paying any import tax (the equivalent of VAT in EC countries, see Chapter 8) or excise duties. Inland 'freezones' offering similar facilities have been established in several EC countries, usually at or near airports.

German Foreign Trade Information Office
Postfach 10 80 07
D-5000 Cologne

Selling direct to retail outlets

The leading German department store groups (the top two of which account for nearly 10 per cent of total West German retail sales) have buying offices in London, which you can approach direct. The DTI should be able to help you identify central buying points relevant to your business within Germany. Buying groups exist for grocery stores, retail chains, hypermarket consortia and symbol groups (SPAR, for example) which operate in Germany in much the same way as in the UK.

Voluntary chains

These are associations of independent retailers that have established common buying and wholesaling facilities. A chain will advertise regionally or nationally on behalf of the entire group. Buying officers for voluntary chains are in a position to place extremely large orders, but demand large discounts in return. Chains exist for hardware, textiles, footware, foodstuffs and many other categories of goods. The largest chains purchase on behalf of 20,000 to 30,000 retail outlets. For information on these and on buyers from hypermarkets (see below) contact:

British Chamber of Commerce in Germany
Secretariat
Heumarkt 14
D–5000 Cologne 1
010 49 221 234284

The German Chamber of Commerce in the UK may also be able to give you some initial leads.

German Chamber of Commerce and Industry in the UK
12–13 Suffolk Street
London SW1Y 4HG
071-930 7231

Hypermarkets

German hypermarkets tend to be extremely large (5000 square metres of floor space at least) and – while they rely primarily on self-service – sell a wide range of goods, including expensive consumer durables. Hypermarkets are found in urban areas and depend heavily on car users for their clientele. More than 10 per cent of all West German retail sales occur through hypermarkets.

German hypermarkets typically belong to a chain rather than being individually owned. Chains can control up to 40 units, normally concentrated in one or two particular regions. A couple of the chains are British owned.

Direct mail selling

Mail order transactions account for a continuously increasing proportion of German sales, as indeed they do in all other developed western countries. Many of the German firms that control the mail order business are small companies although the bulk of mail order selling is done through larger concerns. Nearly 4000 German firms are involved exclusively in mail order.

The big mail order companies operate their own product testing system and through it provide goods with government approved 'tested for safety' marks – GS (*Geprufte Sicherheit*) marks. These are not legally necessary, but it is unlikely that your output will be accepted by German mail order consumers if it does not carry the GS logo.

National direct mail expenditures split approximately evenly between consumer and business-to-business DM activity. Eighty per cent of the aggregate bank and insurance company advertising spend is on DM, and the medium is expanding rapidly in other areas (eg more than one third of all German advertising of machine tools and electrical equipment is through direct marketing). Mail order catalogue companies have extensive coverage of the German market.

All this creates problems for the UK business wanting to sell by DM to Germany. The Germans have come to expect high standards in DM presentation and if yours does not match the local equivalent it will not be acceptable. Equally, the creation of the Single Market opens up new opportunities for German competitors to target your own customers using DM.

German sales promotions law forbids anything that constitutes an 'over inducement to buy'. This can embrace many free premiums and 'attention grabbers' commonplace in DM materials transmitted in the UK. Moreover, free samples can be declared illegal if the promoted product has been on the market for a significant period.

Agents

Commercial agents work on commission, under their own names, and enjoy a number of legal protections (see below). Commissions are negotiable, but you can expect to pay 15 to 25 per cent of the final selling price. Agents will arrange deals with customers on your behalf; will organise the warehousing of your products; and will attend to the provision of local after-sales service. They have detailed knowledge of German distribution systems, of buying organisations (chain stores, hypermarkets, franchise companies, etc) and of the nuances of German consumer behaviour. Note, however, that German agents invariably carry the outputs of competing client businesses.

Commission agents are immensely important in Germany – for domestic selling as well as for imported goods (especially manufactured products). Most German agents are small businesses rather than individuals acting alone. German agents generally prefer being allowed the discretion to decide final selling prices themselves, having regard to all relevant circumstances.

German agency laws and regulations

The essential features of German agency law are as follows:

(a)   If you terminate an agency agreement without good cause you have to pay the agent substantial compensation. This will be computed on the basis of past average annual commission or, if the agency agreement has been recently established, on expected commissions reasonably anticipated from the contract. In the latter case a court will look at the returns from similar agreements in related industries. Compensation of up to one year's commission, averaged over the previous five years, may be awarded – possibly more in special circumstances.

(b)   It is permissible to stipulate that English law will apply to the agency agreement, although it is unlikely that a German agent will accept this on account of the removal of legal protection that the inclusion of such a clause would involve.

(c)   Exclusive agency/distribution arrangements are allowed, subject to EC rules (see Chapter 6).

Agency networks

A special problem with choosing a German agent is the strong regional cultures within the country. Tastes, consumer perspectives and purchasing habits differ significantly between regions. You may need a separate agent in each area who is capable of understanding local consumer behaviour and of modifying your promotional methods and advertising messages to correspond to local needs. Alternatively, you may choose to concentrate all your efforts on a single region.

This problem applies to German businesses as much as to foreign firms. In response to the situation, German agents sometimes establish networks of independent agency businesses (termed associations of mutual interest) that collectively offer national coverage, but with just a single customer contact point. Details of German laws on agency and distribution are available (for a small fee) from the London office of the German Chamber of Industry and Commerce (see page 184). The German desk of the DTI also has a pamphlet on the subject.

Distributors

Distributors, who buy and sell as principals and who act as stockholders in their own right, are regarded in German law as independent intermediaries and are not entitled to the legal protections afforded to agents. Nevertheless, German courts have held that on termination of an agreement a distributor is entitled to compensation for his or her contributions to enhancing the supplier's image and to having built up the supplying firm's goodwill. It is standard practice in Germany for distributors to determine final selling prices. Distributors are less common in Germany than in most other EC countries. In Germany the term import agent usually means a distributor rather than an agent. German distributors are legally responsible for the safety of all the goods they sell.

Import tax

Domestic German producers have to pay VAT on their output. To protect internal producers against unfair foreign competition, imported goods are subject to a 'turnover tax' set at exactly the same level as German VAT (see page 193). This is levied on the basis of a product's CIF price (see Chapter 8). If the CIF invoice price is suspiciously low, or if it has been reduced by virtue of a large discount given by a wholesaler or sole distributer, the German authorities are empowered to deem that the consignment is actually of a higher value and to impose import tax on this higher notional amount.

Invoicing

As in other EC countries nowadays, FOB quotes (see Chapter 8) are not normally acceptable unless specifically requested by the customer. It is usual to quote Delivered Duty Paid. However, the long run strength of the Deutschmark relative to UK currency has caused many German buyers not to object to being invoiced in sterling as sterling currency depreciations regularly result in their needing to spend fewer Deutschmarks to buy the sterling required to settle UK suppliers' invoices. It is important to bear in mind that if you invoice in German currency you may need forward cover (see Chapter 8) to protect you against the risk of sterling depreciation.

Obtaining payment

Collection procedures in respect of German customers are straightforward.

Most import trade is financed through open account transactions, the remainder (about 20 per cent) through letters of credit and (for larger transactions) bills of exchange (see Chapter 8), upon which stamp duty is required at the time of payment. Germany, like France but unlike Britain, has a codified business law. Nevertheless, litigation is just as expensive in Germany as in the UK so hasty resort to the courts to collect outstanding debts is not to be recommended.

Advertising in Germany

German advertisements are generally more factual and less emotional than in other EC countries. At the time of writing a proposal is before the European Commission that will severely restrict the use of superlatives and/ or comparative claims incorporated into advertising messages (statements that a product is 'better', 'best' or 'superior', for example). This is *already* the case in Germany. So any such claims must be removed from all your advertising literature. If it is not, you could be sued under German law for damages claimed by the manufacturers/suppliers of the goods with which you are making a comparison. Moreover, in Germany, 'knocking copy' – whereby one firm publicly criticises its competitors' products – is not allowed.

Wherever rules exist, of course, organisations look for profitable ways in which they can be circumvented, and superlatives and implicit cross-brand comparisons do sometimes creep into German advertisements. Foreign small businesses unfamiliar with the nuances of German advertising legislation should, however, avoid these potential difficulties; so keep your promotional messages simple, accurate and informative.

Advertising agencies

The big Anglo-American agencies operate extensively in Germany. Additionally, numerous small agencies are scattered throughout the country. You can obtain details from:

Gesellschaft Werbeagenturen
Friedenstrasse 11
D–6000 Frankfurt am Main
010 49 611 235096

Establishing a permanent presence

Start-up procedures for new businesses are straightforward, and few restrictions are imposed except that (as in Britain) licences are needed for certain types of trade (passenger transport and the provision of financial services, for example). Exactly the same rules apply to German and foreign firms. Foreigners can purchase as much German property as they require.

Rental prices for commercial premises vary considerably around the country, and in prime inner-city areas are extremely high. German commercial estate agents are expensive by British standards, charging lessees anything up to 4 per cent of ten years' aggregate rent. A number of factors contribute to high rents, notably the Federal government's tight restrictions on suburban commercial property development, which causes developers to compete fiercely for inner-city sites. Out of town development is possible, but strict planning regulations apply and it can take years to steer an application through the system. Other influences on rental values include:

- planning laws designed to preserve the character of inner-city areas;

- general excess demand for all kinds of property;

- the large number of foreign firms seeking premises in Germany in preparation for the completion of the Single Market;

- the fact that much prime site property is owned by a handful of retail chains that are unwilling to sell. Also, the predominance of family firms in Germany has possibly led to an innate conservatism where the speculative sale of a business's property is concerned.

Of course, many companies are bound to relocate their premises in what used to be East Germany, where property prices are much lower than in the west.

Normally, the most tax efficient way of operating *in situ* in Germany is to establish a self-contained subsidiary – set up as a GmbH or KG, for example (see pages 190 and 191) – rather than as a branch of your own UK firm, since if you create a branch you will be bound to adhere to certain (quite complicated) accounting procedures that apply to transactions between branches of all German business.

Subsidiaries of foreign firms must declare themselves to the German Commercial Register before they commence trade – otherwise the subsidiary will not enjoy limited liability and your UK business can be held responsible for the subsidiary's debts.

Taxation of branches

A branch of a foreign firm must register with the local authority of the district in which it sets up, although this is only a formality. Thereafter, however, branches are taxed on the basis of (usually high) notional figures which the German authorities assume represent that proportion of the *parent company's* total profits deemed attributable to the branch's operations in Germany! In other words, if the German tax authorities believe that (say) three quarters of your aggregate group profits result from your presence in Germany they can tax your German branch on the value of that amount, regardless of the book profits the branch declares.

New start-ups – as opposed to market acquisitions of existing firms – are the norm in Germany in consequence of the low incidence of equity financing and hence the shortage of companies that can be taken over in this way. Leverage buyouts are uncommon in Germany.[3]

At present there are three types of limited liability legal structure available in Germany:

1.   The *Aktiengesellschaft* (AG), which is for big businesses and corresponds to a UK public company.
2.   The *Gesellschaft mit beschränkter Haftung* (GmbH), corresponding to a private limited company.
3.   The *Zweigniederlassung*, which is a registered branch of a foreign corporation.

An AG must have at least five founding members and a minimum of three directors. The maximum number of directors is linked to the value of the share capital of the company. Most companies are in fact GmbHs, which require just a single founding member and only half the minimum share capital (50 per cent of which must be paid up at inception) of a public AG. A solitary person can be the sole director and shareholder of a GmbH.

Forming a Company

The procedures for setting up a GmbH are straightforward, certainly more so than for forming a British company. Instead of a Memorandum and Articles of Association, the German GmbH has a simple charter that lists its major activities in outline terms (nowhere near as comprehensively as needed for the objects clause of a company in the UK). Larger GmbHs (size is measured by sales, value of net assets and number of employees) must publish annual audited accounts.

AGs need formal Articles of Association plus other legal documents, which must be filed with a local commercial court. The company's articles must contain an objects clause. Twenty-five per cent of an AG's share capital (which has to exceed a substantial minimum amount) needs to be fully paid up *before* registration of the company.

[3.] A leverage buyout is an acquisition financed by a loan made to a predator secured in effect against the assets of the target firm.

Boards of directors

By law, an AG must have two boards of directors: a *Vorstand* (management board) and an *Aufsichtsrat* (supervisory board). A GmbH is compelled to establish an *Aufsichtsrat* only if it employs more than 500 workers.

Members of the *Vorstand* are full-time executive directors who control particular functions within the firm (marketing, operations, personnel, etc). This board is responsible for strategic and tactical decision making and for the day-to-day running of the business.

The *Aufsichtsrat* comprises part-time non-executive directors. There is a chair plus other members, half of whom are elected by shareholders (and will normally be bankers, technical specialists, company lawyers and other managerial experts), while the other half are elected by the workforce. In the event of fundamental disagreement between the two sides, the casting vote rests with the chairperson who is always a shareholders' representative. The size of a company's *Aufsichtsrat* varies between three and 20 according to the value of the share capital of the business. *Aufsichtsrats* have the following functions:

- to ratify the *Vorstand's* strategic and tactical decisions (although an *Aufsichtsrat* is not involved in day-to-day executive management);
- to appoint and remove *Vorstand* members;
- to represent employees' views to senior management;
- to bring expert outside experience and knowledge to bear on important company decisions.

Partnerships

Partnerships are a popular form of business ownership in Germany, and the establishment of a partnership with a local resident is a useful and convenient way of entering the German market. In Germany, moreover, individual members of partnerships can easily acquire limited liability. The basic forms of German partnership are as follows:

(a) The KG (*Kommanditgesellschaft*). This consists of a collection of individuals whose personal liabilities for partnership debts are limited to the value of their investments in the partnership. Unlike in Britain, limited liability partners in German businesses play an active role in running their firms.

(b) The GmbH KG. This is a partnership between an individual and a private limited company. Sometimes the major shareholders of a GmbH enter into partnership – as individuals – with their own company! This enables profits resulting from the arrangement to be taxed at lower rates than otherwise would be the case, since corporation tax is avoided. Also there are no auditing or company disclosure requirements for this type of business.

(c)   The KGaA (*KG auf Aktien*). Here a KG partnership itself admits outside shareholders whose liability is limited to the extent of their investments.

Regional development grants

Any business – German or foreign – that establishes new plant or expands an existing operation in certain German regions is entitled to investment grants and subsidised state loans which could save up to 25 per cent of the initial cost of the investment. The highest grants are for new businesses in Berlin and in areas that border on Eastern Europe.

Incentives include government built factory space and other accommodation at low rentals, cash handouts, special tax reliefs, low cost electricity and subsidised use of research facilities in local colleges and universities. The variety of the subsidies available is so extensive that details can be extremely confusing, especially since separate and different schemes operate at federal, regional and local authority levels. It is thus possible to obtain multiple grants for the same operation. Each grant awarding body has discretion (usually) to vary the amounts awarded according to local needs and circumstances. Thus, grant levels are subject to negotiation with individual applicants. Cash grants for specific purchases of capital equipment and for research and development are also available. Initial advice on these matters is available from the German Chamber of Commerce and Industry (see page 184) or from:

The Federation of German Industry
Gustar-Heinemann
Upr 84–88
Postfach 510548
D–5000 Cologne 51
010 49 221 370800

There are no restrictions on foreign investment whatsoever, and profits can be repatriated to Britain without penalty or hindrance.

Employee participation in German firms

Worker participation in management is legally required. It is termed codetermination and operates through the *Aufsichtsrat* (see page 191), and through lower level Works Councils which are elected by employees in secret ballot and are compulsory for firms with more than five workers. A Works Council has a legal status and must be consulted about changes in wages, working conditions, holidays and sick pay, hiring and firing, and so on. Also a Works Council may bring an action against an employer in a national Labour Court, roughly equivalent to a UK Industrial Tribunal but with more extensive powers.

Unions are industry based, and unions determine who shall represent employee interests on supervisory boards. However, unions have no power to control Works Councils.

Taxation

Corporation tax in Germany is high – normally about 50 per cent. Tax on distributed profits is lower (currently about 35 per cent). Additionally there are business income taxes of 10 to 20 per cent which are payable to local authorities. (A special low rate of 9 per cent applies to Berlin.)

German firms have, therefore, an incentive to plough back their profits into new projects in order to minimise their liabilities for tax. And since the share market for German companies is restricted, the fact that they do this does not make them vulnerable to asset stripping or other unwelcome takeover attempts as sometimes happens in the UK.

Subsidiaries of other businesses pay the lower tax rate applicable to distributed profits, plus a further tax of 25 per cent on profits not remitted to the parent firm. All German companies have to pay annual taxes (currently about $1/2$ of one per cent on net assets exceeding a certain amount) on their net worth to both local and national government. VAT is 14 per cent, 7 per cent for food and passenger transport.

Chapter 11

Benelux

Belgium, Luxembourg and the Netherlands are among the most prosperous of all the Community nations, and arguably the countries best equipped and positioned to benefit from the Single Market.

Belgium

Belgium has a population of around 10 million (of whom about 1 million are foreigners) spread over 30,000 square kilometres (half the size of Wales). The country is divided by the language of its inhabitants. Dutch is the first language of the people in the north, French is spoken in the south, and German in a small part of the east of the nation. Goods need to be labelled in both French and Dutch.

Brussels, the nation's capital and the home of the administrative headquarters of the EC, is predominantly French speaking even though it is situated within northern (Flemish) territory. The latter has attracted a considerable amount of new industry. It has an efficient industrial infrastructure, ready access to sea ports and excellent inland communications. Britain is Belgium's fifth largest supplier of imported goods, after Germany, France, the Netherlands and Italy.

Belgium is a highly industrialised state, with substantial engineering, textiles, paper, footwear and agricultural equipment industries. Metalworking is particularly important, with three-quarters of that industry's output being exported to the rest of the EC. The country is a major provider of European horticultural products, which in turn has generated a number of service and supply industries specifically geared to the horticultural trade. There is also a major food processing industry which exports nearly 80 per cent of its output.

Characteristics of the market

Belgians are affluent so there are many opportunities for the export of quality consumer goods, especially automotive products, home furnishings, tableware, household appliances and cosmetics. Belgians on average spend more on household electrical appliances than consumers in any other EC country. The wide diversity of the Belgian economy, moreover, creates numerous markets for industrial items. Further export opportunities arise from Belgium's role as the administrative headquarters of the European Community, notably for the provision of management and other consultancy services.

English is widely spoken as a second language throughout Belgium (all national English daily and Sunday newspapers are available in main Belgian towns), and many Belgians watch British TV. Goods from the UK are easily transported to the country and are acceptable to Belgian consumers. There is evidence, however, that when purchasing significant consumer durables (washing machines, fridges or vacuum cleaners for example) Belgians are attracted to a 'Made in Belgium' label. Think twice, therefore, before committing yourself to a 'typically British' image and promotional messages if you are selling these types of goods.

The standard credit period is 60–90 days – even 120 days in some cases. Cash discounts of $2/3$ of one per cent are normally expected for prompt payment. Large firms (including importers) with annual turnovers exceeding a certain level are required to inform the Ministry of Economic Affairs about intended price increases at least two months before they happen (one month in certain industries). It is possible, however, for a company or (commonly) a trade association to agree with the Ministry that prices will not fluctuate beyond certain pre-specified limits, in which case notification of individual price increases is not necessary.

Advertising

Although it is acceptable to write to Belgian customers in English, advertisements in Belgian media must, of course, be in the local language – which creates problems for the exporter in view of the linguistic division of the state. Hence, the use of a local advertising agent is essential. Not surprisingly under the circumstances, there are a large number of Belgian advertising agencies. There are few restrictions on advertising other than for tobacco and pharmaceuticals, although poster advertising is strictly controlled. Details are available from:

Jury d'Ethique Publicitaire
Rue de Colonies 54
PO Box 13
1000 Brussels
Belgium
010 32 2 2190662

The association of Belgian advertising agencies is:

Chambre des Agences Conseils en Publicité
Avenue de Barbeau 28 (3rd Floor)
1160 Brussels
Belgium
010 32 2 6722387

A third of all advertising expenditures are devoted to consumer magazines. Newspapers and free sheets absorb a further third of the total advertising spend. Direct marketing is increasingly important as a means of selling goods.

Retailing is well organised and there are a number of central purchasing groups. Hypermarkets are common and attract a great deal of custom. Information on Belgian retail buying consortia is available from:

Association des Grandes Entreprises de Distribution
Rue de la Science 3
B–1040 Brussels
Belgium
010 32 2 5373060

Door-to-door selling is not allowed in Belgium without a government licence.

Major trade buyers

Belgium has a highly developed retail distribution system and there are a number of centralised buying agencies. Some of the more important of these are listed in the DTI pamphlet 'Marketing Consumer Goods in Belgium', which can be purchased from the DTI's Exports to Europe branch (see Chapter 2). Distributors enjoy a special status under Belgian law, which provides for minimum periods of notice of cancellation of 'indefinite' contracts and for compensation. If a contract is renewed more than twice it is automatically regarded as being of indefinite duration. The minimum permitted notice period (except in cases of serious breach of contract) is taken as the period necessary for the distributor to find a comparable alternative distributorship.

Agents

Most UK exporters appoint a single agent to cover the entire country. If no termination date is specified in an exclusive agency agreement, it may only be cancelled if there is serious misconduct by one of the parties. Otherwise 'reasonable' notice must be given and compensation is payable. The amount of compensation is subject to negotiation. Anyone who carries your stocks may, under Belgian law, claim to be your agent; no written agreement is required.

It is common in Belgium for the same firm to act as agent, importer and wholesaler.

Transporting goods to Belgium

Belgium is easily accessed via the Channel ports. Antwerp is Europe's second largest port; Liege is the third largest inland port in the Community. There is another large port at Ghent. There are numerous road and rail links to surrounding countries and beyond. The E motorway system provides direct links from Belgium to Düsseldorf, Cologne, Vienna, Hanover and Lyons.

Belgium lies at the crossroads of Europe. The main highways linking Paris and Hamburg, Lisbon and Stockholm, and Geneva and Amsterdam all intersect on Belgian soil. Brussels is the hub of the Belgian transport system. All UK airports provide scheduled airfreight services to Brussels, and there are many direct airfreight services to Antwerp and Liège. Trains run from London Victoria, via Dover, to Ostend and Brussels. Ferries operate from several UK ports to Ostend and (particularly) Zeebrugge.

Belgium has no freeports or free zones. However, there are liberal provisions for repackaging, sorting and for certain manufacturing operations within Belgian bonded warehouses.

Establishing a permanent presence in Belgium

Establishing a permanent presence in Belgium gives access to much of the European Community. Nearly two-thirds of the EC's population live within 200 miles of Brussels, and can easily be reached using fast and efficient road/rail networks. Also the major ports are linked to 1500 kilometres of inland canals. It is therefore an excellent Continental centre for the distribution of goods.

Subsidiaries may be companies, branches or partnerships with local nationals. Authorisation is only needed for businesses involved in banking, insurance and certain other financial services, and transport.

Belgian companies

The equivalent of a public limited liability (able to have its shares listed on the Belgian Stock Exchange) company is the *Société anonyme* (SA), which requires at least seven shareholders and three directors, none of whom need be EC nationals or even resident in Belgium. At least 20 per cent of the company's nominal capital must be paid into a bank prior to incorporation, and minimum capital requirements (which are subject to periodic altera-tion) apply.

Private limited companies are called *Société privée à responsabilité limitée* (SPRL). These also must have a minimum share capital, but only 60 per cent of the minimum for an SA. At least two shareholders and one director are required. Employee participation in management is compulsory for all firms with more than 100 workers. A peculiarity of Belgian companies is that they are required to place 5 per cent of each year's profits into a reserve until the value of the reserve is at least 10 per cent of issued capital. The purpose of the reserve is to provide security for creditors and thus it may not be distributed to shareholders until all debts are cleared and the company is finally wound up.

A wide range of government investment incentives is available for companies setting up or expanding in Belgian development areas and/or designated industry sectors. Incentives focus on tax exemptions, training grants to employers, and subsidies for firms that hire additional staff – especially if the new employees have been out of work for a long period.

Belgian Foreign Investment Services
rue de l'Industrie 10
1040 Brussels
Belgium
010 32 2 5126760

All companies – Belgian or foreign – require government permission to engage in certain activities, notably road transport, insurance, banking, the production or sale of food, and the operation of department stores.

Branches and partnerships

Partnerships, including limited partnerships, and limited liability co-operatives are also available. Branches of foreign companies are subject to the same laws as branches of domestic firms. Hence they must register with the Trade Register of Commerce and file certain documents, including (a) a copy of the Articles of Association of the parent firm, (b) a written statement signed by the parent company's board authorising the setting up of the branch, and (c) details of the powers delegated to the branch and the names and addresses of branch representatives. Specific accounting procedures must be followed by branches of other businesses. Chambers of Commerce will provide useful information on these matters.

Belgo-Luxembourg Chamber of Commerce in Great Britain
36 Piccadilly
London W1V 0PL
071-434 1815

Taxation

VAT is 19 per cent standard rate, varying from 6 per cent for foodstuffs to 33 per cent for certain luxury goods. The standard rate of corporation tax is 43 per cent. For low profit companies the rate is 30 per cent. High profit firms pay part of their corporation tax at 45 per cent.

Sources of useful information

Information and advice on doing business in Belgium are available from:

British Chamber of Commerce for Belgium and Luxembourg
30 Rue Joseph II
B–1040 Brussels
Belgium
010 32 2 2190788

Brussels Chamber of Commerce
Rue de Trevs 112
1004 Brussels
Belgium
010 32 2 5123030

Antwerp Chamber of Commerce
Markgravestraat 12
Antwerp
Belgium
010 32 3 2322219

Several UK banks (National Westminster, Barclays, Kleinwort Benson, Lloyds) operate directly in Belgium and will give advice on trade and local investment.

Luxembourg

Luxembourg is a tiny country covering just 3650 square kilometres (about the size of Dorset) with a population of about 350,000, of which around a quarter are of foreign nationality. From north to south Luxembourg is about 51 miles; from east to west, 35 miles. The main town is Luxembourg city, which is situated on the main railway lines running from Ostend and Amsterdam to Strasburg and Basle. Luxembourg's roads now link into the European E motorway system. The city has an airport that carries cargo as well as passenger flights, and there are direct airfreight services from Britain. Access to the Rhine is possible via the Moselle River canal network.

Luxembourg has three official languages: French, German and the indigenous language of Luxembourgish. French is normally used for commercial correspondence. There are four industries: steel, agriculture, banking and financial services, plus recently introduced computing technology and software development activities. Many opportunities exist for the supply of machinery, chemical products, transport equipment, foodstuffs and mineral products. The UK is Luxembourg's seventh largest supplier.

Characteristics of the market

Consumers in Luxembourg are extremely affluent – in per capita terms they are among the richest in the EC. Thus the market is ideal for the sale of high price, high quality consumer products. Although the market is itself small, most purchases made in Luxembourg are in fact made by residents of the adjoining countries of France, Germany and Belgium, who shop in Luxembourg because of its lower excise duties, VAT, and hence lower retail prices. Fifty per cent of all goods purchased in Luxembourg are imported; 90 per cent of consumer goods.

Government price controls on certain goods operate within the country. Maximum prices for basic consumption goods (bread, heating and petrol, for example) apply.

Advertising

Advertising in Luxembourg occurs through four radio and three TV channels and six daily newspapers which are printed in one or more of the official languages. Premium selling (see Chapter 4) is illegal.

Agents

Luxembourg has no special agency law. Disputes are resolved according to the general law of the country in which the agency agreement was signed.

Establishing a permanent presence in Luxembourg

All intending businesses must obtain a state licence prior to commencing trade. Applicants for licences must produce evidence of their good conduct, solvency and – for certain types of business – professional qualifications (eg, an educational diploma or a testimonial certifying the acquisition of practical experience, which may have to be as long as three years for some trades). For limited companies, these conditions must be met by the directors who are to run the business.

Every firm in Luxembourg is legally required to join the Luxembourg Chamber of Commerce, from which further information on Luxembourg company and other business procedures may be obtained.

Luxembourg Chamber of Commerce
7 rue Alcide de Gaspert
BP 1503
L–2981 Kirchberg
Luxembourg
010 352 435853

Forming a company in Luxembourg

The equivalent of the private company is the *Société à responsabilité limitée* (SARL). An organisation similar to a UK public company is called a *Société anonyme* (SA). Minimum capital requirements apply to the SA, for which at least 25 per cent of share capital must be paid up at the time of incorporation. Both the SA and the SARL must have at least two founding shareholders. An SA needs a minimum of three directors, for which there are no nationality or residence requirements. Employee participation is compulsory in firms with more than 150 workers.

Investment incentives are intended to encourage economic development in the south of the country and include:

* up to 25 per cent relief on corporation tax;
* cash grants of up to a maximum of 15 per cent of the cost of fixed assets;
* interest rate subsidies;
* bonuses for hiring young workers and/or ex-employees of certain industries.

Venture capital is sometimes available from government sources. Details of incentives are available from:

Luxembourg Ministry of the Economy
19 Boulevard Royal
Luxembourg City
Luxembourg
010 352 4794312

Partnerships

These may be general (*Société en nom collectif* [SENC]), with joint and several liability (see page 176), or limited. The latter can be either a 'simple' limited partnership (*Société en commandité simple* [SCS]) or one in which the limited partners are issued with shares (the *Société en commandité par actions* [SCA]). Both forms require partners with unlimited liability. All partnerships must be formed by deed. In contrast to the situation in Britain, Luxembourg partnerships do not have to terminate on the death, retirement or incapacity of a partner.

Joint ventures

Joint ventures can be established as limited liability co-operatives (*Société coopérative* [SC]) or merely through the existence of a contract. In the latter case two alternatives exist: the *Société en participation* and the *Association momentanée*. The SC is formed by a deed specifying its life, purpose, powers and how profits are to be appropriated. Seven or more shareholders are required and the business must be registered. Shares cannot be transferred to third parties.

An *Association momentanée* is formed to undertake a specific purpose without trading under a business name. Partners are jointly and severally liable to third parties. The same applies to the *Société en participation* which is a relationship between a local operator and those with an interest in the operation.

Branches

Branches of foreign companies must register with the Court of Commerce and deposit (a) copies of their parent organisation's documents of incorporation (Articles of Association, for example), (b) a statement by the parent company's board giving the branch power to act, and (c) a specification of the extent of the branch's authority. Copies of these documents must be certified by a public notary. Branches are obliged to publish their accounts annually, but these accounts need not be audited.

Taxation

VAT is 12 per cent standard rate (including luxuries); 6 per cent for necessities (3 per cent for certain items – medicines, for example). These are the lowest VAT rates in the entire EC. Corporations are taxed at the rate of 46.5 per cent.

The Netherlands

The Netherlands is a small country both in terms of its population (less than 15 million people) and geographic size (41,000 square kilometres, about one fifth the size of the UK). A large part of the Netherlands has been reclaimed from the sea. Half the population live in the west of the country where the principal cities – Amsterdam (population 1 million), Rotterdam (population 1 million) and the Hague (the nation's capital, which has a population of about 650,000) – are situated. Rotterdam is the world's largest port. Amsterdam also handles a large volume of sea traffic. The country is ideally located for trade with other EC countries, facing Britain on one side and having borders with Germany and Belgium on the other.

Major industries in the Netherlands include chemicals, paper manufacture and processing, mechanical engineering, electrical components, printing, energy, oil and petroleum products. There is also a small but profitable shipbuilding industry. Three-quarters of the country's exports and imports involve other EC nations and, although the Netherlands accounts for only 5 per cent of the Community's aggregate population, it is responsible for 10 per cent of the EC's total foreign trade. The bulk of the country's international transactions are with Germany.

Characteristics of the market

Dutch consumers are affluent and spend much of their money on consumer durables. They have, for example, the highest rate of ownership of stereo and personal electrical entertainment units in the entire EC. Accordingly, the Netherlands presents numerous opportunities for the sale of quality British products. Because the Dutch are internationally minded they are largely indifferent to the geographical origin of merchandise; rather, they look for reliability, novelty, style and the attractive presentation of goods. The key features of the Dutch market are as follows:

(a)   Population and economic activity are concentrated into a single industrialised area (the *Randstrad*) encompassing Rotterdam, Amsterdam, The Hague and Utrecht. The rest of the country is largely agricultural, although Dutch agriculture is itself highly mechanised and in consequence creates a significant demand for industrial agricultural goods.

(b)   The Dutch economy is extremely diverse, supplying an enormous range of manufactured products and services, especially financial services.

(c)   Dutch transport firms dominate the EC road haulage industry. About 40 per cent of international trucking within the Community is Dutch owned. In consequence, there are many demands for automotive and transport related products.

(d)   The annual rate of inflation in the Netherlands is usually very low, enabling local Dutch producers to keep down their materials and other input costs and hence their output prices. Matching the price of a locally produced product can be a major problem for exporters to this country.

(e)   High living standards and wage costs during the post Second World War years have led to extensive automation of industry and great economy in the use of labour. In consequence, Dutch manufactures are of excellent quality and produced to a high level of precision. The Dutch expect the same standards in imported goods.

(f)   Consumers spend a high proportion of their incomes on home furniture, white goods and household equipment. The Netherlands is a major market for sports and leisure goods: over a quarter of the adult population belong to a sporting or recreational club, particularly for football, golf, hockey and tennis.

(g)   Dutch business is well organised and highly efficient and expects its suppliers to be the same. Products have to be of sound quality, attractively presented and (most important) delivered on time.

(h)   Dutch customers will expect the same payment terms as are available from local suppliers and (most important) to settle transactions on open account (see Chapter 8).

The Netherlands has been described as the distribution centre of Europe and, as such, has highly sophisticated warehousing (including bonded warehousing) and physical distribution systems. There are no freeports or free zones in the Netherlands, but arrangements for bonded warehousing are extremely liberal – goods can be labelled, repacked, repaired, blended and processed while under bond. Moreover, bonded goods can be moved around the country and kept for several years without paying duty. A good account of these arrangements is contained in the BOTB *Netherlands Country Profile* that can be purchased from the DTI.

The Dutch are and always have been absolutely determined to obtain maximum benefit from the Single Market. They are innovative, expansionist, multilingual, internationally minded and arguably the best equipped people to take advantage of the Community as it liberalises its trade. A recent survey of the UK and its four nearest EC partners, (France, Germany, the Netherlands and Belgium) rated the Netherlands as (easily) the highest ranking of the five countries in several critical areas, including:[1]

- its transport system;
- the quality and relevance (for new technology) of its higher education system;
- the population's mastery of foreign languages;
- acceptability of the country's products in other EC markets;
- low rental values of offices and industrial sites;
- standard of living;
- rate of return on investment;
- industrial relations.

A formidable list! Note that Britain itself is already one of the Netherlands' most important export markets and that fierce competition from Dutch companies selling to the UK is sure to develop on completion of the Single Market. In particular the quality of Dutch banking, insurance and other financial services is high, and financial service providers will compete aggressively in Britain as soon as these sectors are opened up to Continental EC companies.

Reasons for doing business in the Netherlands

There are several sound reasons why British firms should focus their efforts on the Dutch market, including the following:

- Most of the population can speak English.
- Dutch lifestyles, attitudes, perspectives and business methods are essentially similar to those in the UK.
- Many Dutch people watch British television, listen to UK radio stations, and are in consequence culturally acclimatised to British products.
- Advertising messages and images created and used in the UK travel easily to the Netherlands.

[1.] For details see P Gibbs, *Doing Business in the European Community*, Kogan Page, 1990.

- There are excellent transport and communications systems in the Netherlands; travelling to the Netherlands from other countries is easy too.

Agents

Agency law is governed by the Dutch Civil Code, which sets out detailed regulations on agency contracts. An important feature of Dutch agency law is that if an agent is appointed to act in a given area, in the absence of evidence to the contrary, a court will assume that the agent has exclusive rights to represent the company. Termination of a Dutch agency agreement is difficult and can be extremely expensive.

Advertising

Advertising is growing rapidly in the Netherlands, particularly in relation to direct marketing, which absorbs over 40 per cent of the total advertising spend. Newspaper and magazine advertising takes another 45 per cent of all advertising expenditure.

The Dutch list broking market is well developed and a large number of precise and carefully targeted lists can be bought. Details are available from the Dutch Direct Marketing Institute:

Direct Marketing Instituut Nederland
Weerdestein 96
1083 Amsterdam
The Netherlands
010 31 20 429595

There are many general restrictions on how directly marketed products may be advertised, plus particular rules for the advertising of certain items (notably confectionery, consumer credit, property and financial services). Responsibility for these matters rests with:

De Stichting Reclame Code
Westermarkt 2
1016 DK Amsterdam
The Netherlands
010 31 20 257690/721

The Dutch equivalent of the UK Institute of Practitioners in Advertising (see Chapter 3) is:

Nederlandse Vereniging van Erikende
Reclame-Advies
A J Ernstraat 169
Buitenweldert
Amsterdam
The Netherlands
010 31 20 221944

There is a central government buying office. Its address is:

Central Government Buying Office
Het Rijksinkoopbureau
Rechterland 1
Postbus 10200
8000 GE Zwolle
The Netherlands

A useful list of major Dutch supermarket buying chains, cash and carry operations, hypermarkets, etc is contained in the BOTB booklet *Marketing Consumer Goods in the Netherlands*, which is available from the DTI.

Door-to-door selling requires registration with the local Chamber of Commerce.

Transporting goods to the Netherlands

There are Ro-Ro ferry links (see Chapter 5) between the main UK ports and the Hook of Holland, and the country is readily accessed from the Belgian ports of Ostend and Zeebrugge. The Netherlands has an excellent motor-way system linking the main business centres of Rotterdam, Amsterdam, Arnhem and Utrecht (in the east of the country), and Groningen in the north. Rail services connect the Hook of Holland to Britain and the rest of Europe. Most airfreight goes to Amsterdam or Rotterdam, although several other domestic airports take cargo flights on an *ad hoc* basis.

Movement from the Netherlands to nearby countries is easy, and is to become still easier following the *Schengen* agreement (see Chapter 1).

Establishing a permanent presence in the Netherlands

All new businesses (including sole traderships) are required to register with the Trade Register of the Chamber of Commerce of the area in which they are situated. Agents authorised by foreign principals to operate on their behalf and branches of foreign businesses must also register. Chambers of

Commerce are an important element of the Dutch business scene. The major chambers are at:

Amsterdam
Koningin Wilhelminaplein 13
010 31 20 172882

The Hague
Alexander Gogelweg 16
010 31 70 614101

Rotterdam
Coolsingel 58
010 31 10 145022

There is also the Netherlands-British Chamber of Commerce, which will issue preliminary advice to British and Dutch companies wishing to set up in or trade between the two countries.

Netherlands-British Chamber of Commerce
The Dutch House
307–308 High Holborn
London WC1V 7LS
071-405 1358

and

Holland Trade House
Bezuidenhoutseweg 181
2594 AH The Hague
The Netherlands
010 31 70 478881

Forming a company in the Netherlands

The commonest form of limited liability organisation is the *Naamloze Vennootschap* (NV), which has a minimum capital requirement and needs at least two founding shareholders and a minimum of three directors. Shareholders and directors do not have to be resident in the Netherlands or EC citizens.

There is another kind of limited liability organisation, the *Besloten Vennootschap* (BV) which, although it enjoys limited liability, cannot issue share certificates. Also, transfer of ownership of stakes in a BV is restricted. There is no Dutch equivalent to the UK Registrar of Companies. Rather, companies are registered with the local Chamber of Commerce, of which there are 26 regional organisations. Dutch Chambers of Commerce are statutory bodies to which every registered company must annually contribute a small fee, based on the value of the company's capital.

Company accounting requirements in the Netherlands are significantly less onerous than in Britain, although obligations are increasing in consequence of various EC Directives. Currently, the extent of the information depends on the size of the company (measured in terms either of annual turnover, value of assets or number of employees). For small companies the only requirement is to produce an annual balance sheet with accompanying notes.

Because of the country's popularity as a business centre there are lengthy delays in completing the formalities needed to register a company (up to three months on occasion). However, Dutch law permits companies to trade during the period of formation. All the commitments assumed by the business in this period are then automatically passed on to the fully formed company. If anything goes wrong the debts incurred prior to final formation are the personal responsibility of the company's promoters.

Tax relief is available for the construction of new buildings and for the installation of fixed assets and machinery in certain regions.

For information on Dutch investment incentives contact:

Netherlands Ministry of Economic Affairs
Bezuidenhoutseweg 30
The Hague
The Netherlands
010 31 70 798911

Employee representation in company decision making is legally required in firms with more than 35 workers.

Partnerships

In a Dutch general partnership (*Vennootschap onder firma*) each member is jointly and severally liable (see page 176) for all partnership debts. The partnership must be formed by written contract, a copy of which has to be registered with the local Chamber of Commerce. Two forms of limited partnership are available:

1. The *Maatschap* in which each active partner is only liable to the extent of his or her personal investment in the partnership. This form is sometimes used by professionals such as lawyers or accountants.
2. The *Commanditaire Vennootschap* which has at least one member with unlimited liability. Partners with limited liability must not participate in the management of the business and their names must not appear in the name of the firm.

Branches of foreign firms

These must provide to the Trade Register details of their parent company and the purpose for which the branch exists. A branch is not regarded as a separate legal entity, and the parent company is deemed liable for its debts. Nevertheless, local branch managers can be held personally liable (without limit) for local tax obligations. Branches do not have to publish accounts.

Joint ventures

There are no special rules relating to joint ventures, which can take any legal form.

Taxation

VAT is 18.5 per cent basic rate; 6 per cent for essentials. Corporation tax is 40 per cent on the first tranche of a company's profits (currently the first Fl. 250,000), falling to 35 per cent thereafter. In other words, Dutch companies have an incentive to make and declare high profits. Another notable feature of the Dutch tax system is the high rate of tax (currently 6 per cent) on the transfer of real estate.

For taxation purposes, profit is computed as the difference in the net worth of the business at the start and end of a trading period, allowing for certain pre-specified capital injections and withdrawals.

Chapter 12

Italy

Italy is a large country with a population of around 58 million, spread over 301,000 square kilometres (about one third larger than the UK). Northern Italy is highly industrialised; the south (including Sardinia and Sicily) relies heavily on agriculture. The south of the peninsula, Sardinia and Sicily are collectively known as the Mezzogiorno.

Italy's major cities are Milan (population 4 million), Turin and Piedmont in the north, Venice in the north east, Rome and Florence. Genoa and Naples are also important centres of population and industrial/commercial activity. Nearly a third of Italy's industry and a fifth of the country's banking services are to be found around Milan and Lombardy. A wide range of industries is located in this region, particularly steel, machine tools, footwear, chemicals and automotive products. Lombardy is a prosperous area; per capita incomes there have recently overtaken those of the south east of England.

Post-war Italy has been a success. In terms of gross domestic product it is behind France and Germany but – starting from a low base – has equalled and now overtaken Britain. Income per head of population first exceeded that of the UK in 1984.

Reasons for doing business in Italy

The advantages of doing business in Italy include the following.

(a) It is one of the largest markets in Europe, offering export opportunities over the entire range of industrial and consumer products.
(b) Many Italian business people have a working knowledge of English.
(c) The Italian economy is expanding and is poised to achieve greatly increased living standards in future years.
(d) Italian consumers continue to be impressed by a 'Made in Britain' label, associating UK products with style and up-market sophistication, especially *vis-à-vis* fashion clothing, alcoholic drinks, furniture and DIY items.

Characteristics of the market

Italy's mountainous geography causes communications and transport difficulties that in the past led to regional divisions that persist (in their social and
cultural aspects) to the present day.

The city of Milan is the industrial and commercial powerhouse of Italy.
Local manufacturing covers a wide range of industries, with particular
strengths in steelmaking, motor vehicles, clothing, confectionery, and the
production of machine tools. Venice is another major manufacturing centre.
It hosts numerous small enterprises, focusing on footwear, textiles, furniture and ceramics.

An important feature of the Italian consumer market is that Italians
currently spend less on household equipment and appliances than do
consumers in many other EC countries, and expenditure in this area is sure
to increase as Italian prosperity advances. Accordingly, export opportunities for furniture, white goods, carpets, table utensils and (especially)
home electrical appliances will arise. Italian banking and other financial
services (including credit cards) are not as well developed as in comparable
Community countries so there is scope for rapid expansion of these
industries. The DTI lists the following as representing the major opportunities for UK exports to Italy: telecommunications, computer software,
aerospace products, foodstuffs, medical equipment, industrial automation
equipment, high-technology industrial materials (eg carbon fibre, industrial
ceramics), clothing, textiles and chemical products.

A negative feature of Italian business is that industrial buyers tend to be
slow payers. Long payment terms (anything up to seven months) are
common in domestic trading, and exporters need to match these terms if
they are to compete effectively. On the consumer side, Italians do much
business in cash. There are far fewer credit card transactions in Italy than in
most other EC states.

Product standards

There are perhaps more regulations concerning product standards in Italy
than anywhere else in the EC and, until these are harmonised on a
Community-wide basis, it is necessary to check extremely carefully whether
particular items meet Italian standards. Product standards extend to
labelling and packaging, and apply nationwide. Procedures for checking UK
goods against foreign product standards are discussed in Chapter 2.

Advertising

Legislation passed in 1988 has led to a boom in advertising within Italy, and today Italians are bombarded with advertisements. It is thus essential for exporters to advertise their products extensively in order to keep up with local competition. A notable feature of the Italian advertising scene is the use of television by quite small businesses to advertise their products. This is because of the existence of over 350 local TV channels, all of which carry (extremely cheap) advertising. There are, moreover, about 4000 local commercial radio stations, and Italy has many local newspapers and magazines. There is also a highly developed trade and technical press, with over 2000 specialised titles.

About 20 per cent of the total national advertising spend goes to newspapers, and about the same to magazines. TV takes half of all advertising expenditures. There are few restrictions on advertising, except for advertisements on the three state owned TV channels where control is extensive. Details of all restrictions are available from the Italian advertising association:

Associazione Italiana delle Agenzie di Pubblicità a Servizio Completo
Via Larga 19
I–20122 Milan
010 39 2 802086

and/or from the national control body:

SACIS
Via Tomacelli 139
Rome
010 39 6 396841

Trade fairs (see Chapter 4) are an important promotional medium in Italy. There are at least 400 trade fairs annually, of which nearly a quarter are held in Milan.

Locating major buyers

The last ten years have seen a rash of mergers and takeovers in the Italian retailing sector resulting in large chains of supermarkets, chain stores and multiples, served by perhaps no more than 1000 centralised buying organisations nationwide. Chambers of Commerce are good sources of information about these buying groups. The British Chamber of Commerce in Italy is a good initial contact.

British Chamber of Commerce in Italy
Via Agnella 8
I–20124 Milan
010 39 2 876981

Otherwise try the Italian desk of the DTI (see Chapter 2).

Agents

Most agents are located in the north of the country and operate nationally, although the size and diversity of the country have caused many of them to appoint local representatives in the various regions. Italian agency law is governed by the Italian Civil Code plus government regulations that (by Presidential decree) are legally binding. An agency contract for a specified predetermined period will automatically end on the expiry of that period and no claim for compensation can be made. Contracts that do not state a termination date are subject to periods of notice which vary according to how long the agreement has been in force, and the agent is entitled to compensation for loss of business. The value of compensation payable is ultimately determined by the courts, depending on the circumstances of the particular situation. The value of agency commissions earned over the 12 months prior to the termination of the agreement is a frequently used rule of thumb.

Getting goods to Italy

There are major sea ports at Genoa (Italy's third largest city) and Naples, both of which support industrial hinterlands. Genoa is in fact one of Europe's largest ports. There are substantial container ports at Livorno, La Spezia, Trieste, Venice and Palermo.

Italy has an extensive rail system with direct international services to Boulogne, Paris and Brussels. The main railfreight route is to Rome via Calais/Paris/Turin/Genoa. Journeys take about a day and a half. Major high speed developments are being implemented on the lines between Turin, Venice, Milan and Florence. The long distance of Italy from Britain means that the Channel Tunnel should be an attractive means of transporting goods to that country (see Chapter 5).

European Community road traffic normally enters Italy through France, although access via Switzerland, Austria and Yugoslavia is also possible. Turin, Milan and the rest of northern Italy can be reached directly from central France or by following the Mediterranean coastal autoroute from Marseilles through Cannes, Nice and Monaco. There are motorway links between all principal Italian cities. Many northern motorways are subject to tolls, although the south is virtually toll free.

Road traffic to Italy must pass over or through the Alps. The high Alpine passes are, of course, frequently closed during winter, but road communications continue through the St Bernard and Mont Blanc tunnels. Italian main roads have not in the past been as suitable for fast moving heavy goods traffic as in France or Germany, although the situation is rapidly improving. Airfreight services operate from Heathrow to Milan, Pisa (for Florence), Rome, Turin and Venice; from Gatwick to Geneva, Bologna and Naples; and from Birmingham and Manchester to Milan. The principal airports are Rome, Milan and Turin. These act as the main distribution centres for internal airfreight to numerous other Italian cities.

Establishing a permanent presence

Foreign investment in Italy is allowed without restriction in all fields, although special authorisation is required for banking and insurance. At the time of writing, however, there continue to be technical (though not substantive) restrictions on the repatriation of profits arising from certain types of foreign investment. Businesses concerned with the production of goods and services which require investment in capital equipment over an extended period (rather than temporary or 'speculative' investment) are classed as 'productive' and can repatriate profits at will and in any quantity. Other firms *could* face restrictions, not withstanding the fact that repatriation of capital and accrued income on liquidation is always allowed. Planning permission is required for the establishment of (large) new businesses above a certain size. All Italian businesses are legally required to join their local Chamber of Commerce.

Subsidiaries may operate as companies, partnerships or as joint ventures with local firms. Large companies normally adopt the *Società per Azioni* (SpA) form of organisation. This requires a minimum of two founding shareholders, one director, plus a substantial share capital – all of which must be paid up when the company is first incorporated. Shareholders and directors need not be EC citizens or residents.

A smaller business could become a *Società a Responsabilità Limitata* (SrL). Less share capital is needed for this; otherwise the formation procedure is the same as for an SpA. Company formation is a legalistic process that takes between four and six weeks. The company's Articles of Association must be witnessed by a local public notary and deposited with the regional Commercial Registry and the local Chamber of Commerce. Documents are then inspected by the local Commercial Court and tax office.

Investment incentives are regionally determined, and include:

- reductions in corporation tax for the first ten years of operation (cuts of up to 50 per cent for the area south of Rome);
- exemptions from local business taxes and from capital gains tax;
- cash grants and low cost loans, especially for small businesses.

Partnerships

These require at least two partners but there is no legal maximum. There are three main types:

1. The general partnership (*Società in nome collectivo* [Snc]) with unlimited joint and several liability.
2. Partnerships containing members with limited liability (*Società in accomandita semplice* [Sas]).
3. The incorporated partnership (*Società in accomandita per azioni* [SapA]), which has a share capital like a company but which contains some members whose liability has no limit. An SapA is subject to the same laws as Italian companies.

Partnerships must, under the Italian Civil Code, be formed by written deed specifying partners' contributions, duties and share in the firm's profits, and duration of the partnership. This deed must be filed with the local Registrar of Business Enterprises within 30 days of the partnership's formation, and fees (roughly equal to the cost of forming a company) are payable. It takes about a month to process the necessary documents.

Branches and joint ventures

Branches of foreign corporations must register with the local Register of Business Enterprises. Note, however, that all the tax problems described in Chapter 7 apply to Italian branch offices. The branch must register its parent company's Certification of Incorporation and most recent annual report and accounts. Names and addresses of appointed branch managers must be specified. Sole traders may set up and operate without restriction, but also have to register with the Registrar of Business Enterprises.

Joint ventures can occur through partnerships, joint subsidiaries, or *Associazioni in Partecipazione*. The latter are governed by the Italian Civil Code, which requires the existence of an agreement regarding the division of profits and/or payment of fees to participants. One party agrees to give to another a share in the revenues from an operation or *ad hoc* project in return for a specified contribution or financial investment.

Taxation

The standard rate of VAT is 18 per cent. Food and drink, books and medical equipment are charged at 2 per cent; luxury goods at 38 per cent. For agricultural products, hotel and restaurant services the rate is 9 per cent. Companies are liable to corporation tax at 36 per cent plus local income tax at 16 per cent. Numerous tax concessions apply to businesses starting up in the Mezzogiorno. And many other investment incentives are available in the region. It is important to note that southern industrial development incentives apply not only to firms that actually locate in the south, but also to any business – wherever it is located – that directly or indirectly contributes to the economic development of the area.

Chapter 13

Doing Business in Spain

Spain – through its extensive tourist industry – is perhaps the EC country best known to Britons; yet it has in the past presented a difficult market for UK firms. Today, however, it is an increasingly attractive nation to which to sell. The country's previous high import duties and extensive system of quotas are being abolished and, despite many years of post-war economic stagnation, entry to the European Community has created much new investment (with concomitant demands for imports of industrial goods) in many fields.

It is Spanish government policy to encourage high technology manufacturing, electronics and software engineering, telecommunications, and other technically advanced industries. Hence, there are many opportunities for the sale of precision manufactures, components and electrical equipment of all kinds. And as the Spanish economy catches up with the more prosperous members of the EC there will be numerous openings for the sale of domestic white goods, foreign foodstuffs, fashion clothing, do-it-yourself items, household and motor car gadgets, and all the other adjuncts to an increasingly affluent society.

At the time of writing Britain has the fifth largest share of Spanish imports, behind the USA, Germany, France and Italy. Unfortunately, other countries seem to be increasing their high technology exports to Spain at the expense of the UK.

Characteristics of the market

Spain is geographically the largest country in the Community, covering 504,750 square kilometres, and has a population of about 40 million. The effective market is substantially enlarged by the many millions of foreign tourists who visit Spain.

The country divides into 50 provinces which are in turn split into municipalities. Central government is based in Madrid, the nation's capital. Branches of the various government ministries are located in the provinces. Catalonia in the north east is Spain's most prosperous region, with extensive trading, cultural and transport connections with the south of France. The regional capital is the port of Barcelona, which has a freeport zone and supports a wide range of industries. Tarragona is the second biggest port in the region and itself supports an industrial hinterland. Valencia (in the south of the country) is another important industrial centre, as is the river port of Seville. Madrid is the main centre for banking, insurance and general financial services. English is widely spoken as a second language among the business community.

Spain controls the Balearic Islands and the Canaries. The Balearics comprise Majorca, Minorca, Ibiza, Formentera and Cabrera, plus six smaller islands. The Canaries consist of seven islands, of which Tenerife and Grand Canary are the most important.

The country joined the European Community in 1986 and is still in its transitional period. Accordingly, not all the liberalisations required by EC membership apply to Spain immediately – although the pace at which the Spanish economy is being opened up and developed is constantly increasing. Existing restrictions on all major aspects of importing and foreign exchange should disappear shortly.

Opportunities provided by the Spanish market

Apart from the size and recent expansion of the Spanish market, Spain offers the following advantages to British exporters:

(a) The country's relative economic decline in the post-war period meant an inadequacy of manufacturing capacity for both consumer and producer goods. Spain's manufacturing capability is growing rapidly, but there will be shortfalls in domestic output for several years to come.

(b) Branded UK goods (whisky, expensive clothing, foodstuffs, etc) still carry a quality image in the Spanish market.

(c) Spanish industry is extremely diverse, creating a wide range of business opportunities.

(d) The country has extensive links with Spanish speaking Latin America and hence offers possibilities for through trade with these countries. (Many customers in Latin America purchase imports from Spain that they would not consider buying from other nations.)

(e) British and other EC firms can now do business in the Spanish Canary Islands on equal terms with Spanish companies. The Canaries, with a (high income) population of nearly 2 million people, are a lucrative market for luxury goods.

(f) Low wages and other low input costs have led to an influx of American and Japanese companies to the Spanish mainland in order to use it as a point of access to the remainder of the Community. These firms have invested heavily in Spanish operations, creating in consequence further demands for industrial products, for office and data processing equipment, and so on.

(g)   Spain is poised to become one of Europe's leading motor manufac-
      turers. This will generate numerous opportunities for the supply of
      automotive equipment and component parts.

(h)   Successive Spanish governments have been, and continue to be,
      committed to reducing personal taxation, hence stimulating the
      demand for consumer products.

(i)   The country has a wide-ranging government aid programme for
      modernising traditional industries, generating numerous oppor-
      tunities for the export to Spain of high technology capital goods.

Consumer spending

Consumer spending is rising by about 3 or 4 per cent annually. Demand is
especially strong for automotive products, home entertainment items,
fashion clothing, do-it-yourself goods, and all types of household goods
(notably furniture, carpets, white goods, household utensils and fittings).

At present there are fewer cars per thousand head of population in Spain
than in many other EC countries. Hence there is great potential for the
expansion of the automotive industries. The biggest Spanish consumer
markets are in Madrid (which has a population approaching 3.5 million),
Barcelona (population 1.8 million) and Bilbao.

The difficulties involved

German, French and Italian businesses are determined to increase their
shares of the Spanish market, as indeed are many non-EC companies in the
US, Korea and Japan. Competition will be ruthless, and only the fittest will
survive. Overall the UK normally has a trade deficit with Spain in relation to
manufactured items, and Spanish firms will attack the UK market ferociously as it opens up to free competition from EC businesses.

To date, UK exporters to Spain have done well in areas where there was
little domestic competition, but the number of instances where this is the
case is sure to diminish in the future. Also, the orientation of Spanish
industry is increasingly towards complex, 'state of the art' manufacturing
methods; the supply of imported inputs involved in this is dominated by
technologically sophisticated companies in Germany, France and Japan.
Only the most advanced, reliable and top quality industrial products can
succeed in this environment. Concurrently, there will be greatly intensified
competition in the consumer goods field, particularly from local indigenous
firms.

Selling to Spain

Correspondence with Spanish customers needs to be in Spanish, unless the
acceptability of English has been previously agreed. Prices should be quoted

in Spanish pesetas and, wherever possible, specify Delivered Duty Paid (see Chapter 8). Standard correspondence may be undertaken using proforma letters specially translated into Spanish for this purpose (see Chapter 3).

Advertising is developing rapidly in Spain, with half the total spend going to newspapers and magazines. There is a liberal approach to advertising, although advertisements for financial products and pharmaceuticals require special permission from the state authorities. The top ten Spanish advertising agencies are foreign owned, although there are about 1250 small local agencies scattered around the country – including 300 or so based in Madrid. The trade association for Spanish advertising agencies is:

Asociacion General de Empresas de Publicidad
Gran Via 57
Madrid
010 34 1 2499458

Direct marketing to Spain

Catalogue selling, off-the-page responses to newspaper advertisements, loose inserts in magazines and telephone selling are well established in Spain for the marketing of low price non-perishable items. The Spanish direct marketing industry is growing rapidly. Lists of direct marketing agencies with interests in Spain can be obtained from the UK and European Direct Marketing Associations (see Chapter 4) and within Spain from:

Asociacion de Venta Directa
Avenida de Roma 101
E 29 Barcelona
010 34 3 2590948

Using a Spanish agent

In the past the Spanish import trade has not been as well developed as in other EC countries (although the situation is rapidly changing). Thus there are few Spanish central buying organisations with offices in the UK than is the case with other large European nations. Information on Spanish buying offices that do have a UK office can be obtained from the Spanish desk of the DTI (see Chapter 2).

Spain's distribution system is diverse and fragmented, so it is perhaps more important to have expert local agents and distributors in this country than elsewhere in the EC. Agents are normally based in big cities (notably Barcelona, Bilbao and Madrid) and operate nationally through networks and branch office systems.

A feature of the Spanish market is the extent to which its regions differ culturally, attitudinally and in terms of economic structure and wealth. It follows that you may need several agents to cover the entire market effectively. Agency finding procedures are discussed in Chapter 6.

Spanish agency law
This is embodied in the Spanish Civil Code, but only covers individual people who act as commercial representatives and not firms or companies that work as agents. The law states that the agent's terms of engagement must be agreed in advance by the principal and individual representative and that the representative operate strictly within these parameters.

At the time of writing, public sector contracts can only be given to foreign companies through a Spanish based agent, although this will have to change as Spain assumes its obligations as a full member of the EC.

Distributors
In Spain a distributor is regarded as an independent business selling the goods of a third party in its own name and on its own account. If a distribution contract is properly terminated (eg through the expiry of the pre-specified duration of the agreement, or in consequence of the distributor's breach of one of the terms of the contract) the distributor will not be entitled to any compensation – even if the distributor has invested in property, staff or other resources necessary to execute the distributorship. To avoid disputes concerning what exactly is covered by the contract it is advisable to have it confirmed as a public deed with a Spanish notary.

Transporting goods to Spain

Spain shares a common border with France and should benefit as the latter's excellent high speed railway system is extended towards other countries. Motorway traffic enters Spain from France via the E network which has direct links from Toulouse/Nimes/Montpellier to Barcelona and from Biarritz to Bilbao. Within the country there are motorways connecting Barcelona, Bilbao and Madrid. You are free to use your own lorry to deliver to Spanish customers without the need for a permit or to pay any special vehicle taxes. However, until EC road transport is completely liberalised (see Chapter 5) the vehicle driver will require a signed and dated document giving details of the journey, your own address and that of the customer, the nature of your business, how far the lorry is to travel within Spain, and where it crossed and is to cross the frontier. Tolls are payable on certain Spanish motorways.

The cost of rail freight from the UK to Spain should fall significantly in consequence of the Channel Tunnel (see Chapter 5). Otherwise goods enter

Spain by air or sea. There are regular airfreight services from Heathrow and Gatwick to Madrid, Barcelona, Bilbao, Malaga, and to the Canaries and Balearics. Irregular services operate from Manchester and Glasgow to these destinations and from London to Valencia, Alicante, Almeria, Gerona and Santiago.

There are freeport facilities in Barcelona in the east of the country and Vigo in the south. In the Canary Islands there are freeports at Las Palmas and Santa Cruz de Tenerife. Apart from these freeports there are equivalent inland free industrial zones near Barcelona, Bilbao, Vigo and Cadiz, where goods can be sorted, subjected to industrial operations that change their nature, packaged and stored up to six years. Bonded warehousing is available for periods not exceeding five years.

Bilbao in the north west has extensive container facilities. It is Spain's largest port in terms of annual throughput, and a major inlet/outlet for the country's European trade. Bilbao is an important industrial centre in its own right and a major centre for the provision of financial services. The north west has two other major ports: Vigo and La Coruna. Vigo has freeport facilities. There are twice weekly ferry services from Plymouth to Santanda (on the Spanish north coast west of Bilbao).

Although under EC rules it is not necessary to provide a Certificate of Origin for goods manufactured in any other EC state, this does not always apply to the Canary Islands (which have a special arrangement with the EC negotiated by Spain on their behalf).

Obtaining payment

Spanish firms expect local suppliers to give trade credit of (at least) 30 to 60 day's duration (longer for major capital expenditures) and you need to match these terms to be competitive in this market.

Although open account payment for imports is increasingly common in Spain, requests for settlement using letters of credit (see Chapter 8) are more acceptable to Spanish customers than to buyers in most other EC countries. This is because of Spain's late accession to the Community and the fact that its pre-accession import licensing and documentation procedures (which are still in the process of being abolished) were extremely complicated. Payments could only be made through authorised banks, and import licences stipulating the precise terms of the contract were required. Letters of credit were useful as a means of assuring exporters that import licences had been obtained, since credits would only be issued by Spanish/UK banks once the necessary documentation was complete.

The Spanish authorities are rapidly dismantling the elaborate import and exchange control regulations imposed during the Franco years, but it will be some time before the process is fully concluded. Accordingly, you should always check the licence/exchange control situation relating to your firm's products before doing business in Spain. Your bank or the Spanish desk of the DTI will assist you in this respect.

Debt collecting
Collecting debts through the Spanish courts is complex, costly and can take several years. Expert legal advice is needed on these matters.

Establishing a permanent presence

There are no restrictions on foreign investment in Spain and profits and capital may be fully repatriated. However, it is still necessary to register foreign investments with the Spanish Department of Foreign Transactions (DFT), including branches and majority holdings in Spanish businesses by foreign firms. This is merely a formality in normal circumstances, although more complex registration procedures apply to the registration of foreign operations in banking, telecommunications and air transport.

In the past the DFT was concerned with monitoring and controlling the activities of foreign firms. It was intimately involved with exchange control authorisation and the licensing of foreign companies to work in various fields. Today, however, its role is mainly the collection and analysis of statistical information.

Forming a company

While there are several forms of corporate legal entity available in Spain, the commonest is the *Sociedad Anonima* (SA). There is no minimum capital requirement, but there have to be at least three directors and three founding shareholders. The Spanish equivalent of a private company is the *Sociedad de Responsabilidad Limitada (SL)*, which can have just a single director and shareholder. Employee participation in management is compulsory in firms employing at least 500 workers. It is not possible to purchase Spanish companies 'off-the-shelf' as happens in the UK.

Investment incentives are organised regionally through the Spanish Ministry of Industry. Levels of support differ between regions. However, all regions offer tax exemptions, cash grants and loans for new developments. Details are available from:

Spanish Ministry of Industry
Paseo de la Castellana 160
Madrid
Spain
010 341 458 8010

Partnerships

A general partnership is known as a *Sociedad Regular Colectiva* (SRC). Liability for such a business's debts is unlimited, and each partner may be held entirely responsible for the debts of the firm. Partners have the legal right to participate in the management of the business, but cannot transfer their partnership rights to third parties without the consent of all other partners. A partnership can operate under the names of all the partners or just some of them. In the latter case the words *y Compania* (& Co) must be added to the business name used.

Limited partnerships are allowed and are a popular form of business organisation. The liability of some of the partners for the firm's debts is restricted to the amount of their contributions to the business. Such a partnership is called a *Sociedad en Comandita* (SC). Partners with limited liability cannot take part in managing the business and their names must not appear in the firm's title, which must include the words *Sociedad en Comandita*. At least one member of a limited partnership must have unlimited liability.

A third option is the partnership limited by shares (*Sociedad Comanditaria por Acciones*) which is a sort of limited partnership in which the financial contributions of the limited partners are divided into shares in the business. This and the previously mentioned forms of Spanish partnership must be evidenced by a written agreement deposited with the Commercial Registry. The agreement must contain details of partners, their contributions and authority to act on behalf of the firm, the duration of the partnership, and the returns to each partner.

Registering a partnership can be expensive: it costs about 3 per cent of the business's registered capital plus 2 per cent tax on each partner's contributions.

Joint ventures

These can be developed as associations of enterprises (*asociacións de empresas*) or as a contract of joint accounts (*cuentas en participación*). The former may be established with or without an independent legal identity.

(a) *With independent legal identity*. Here a separate business (*Sociedad de empresas*) is created by at least three members, which can be SAs, SLs (see above) or individual persons. No participant can hold more than a one-third share in the business. Unlike other Spanish companies, joint venture companies constituted in this way pay negligible company formation tax.

(b)   *Without independent legal identity*. This type of venture exists to promote the common interests of the participants in some way. It does not pay any tax in its own right. Rather, profits are shared by the members of the arrangement who then include these profits in their own tax returns (even if the profits are temporarily retained within the joint venture itself). Such a venture requires prior approval from the Ministry of Commerce and must be evidenced by a written agreement specifying each participant's financial contribution and profit share. There are three varieties of this organisational form:

1.   *Agrupaciones de empresas* which are loose collaboration agreements between enterprises to further a common interest;
2.   *Uniones temporales de empresas*, ie agreements to undertake specific *ad hoc* projects;
3.   *Cesiones de unidades de obras*, which are subcontracting arrangements.

Contracts of joint accounts comprise businesses conducted by one party (the promoter) on behalf of several other parties. Profits are distributed to the members according to a predetermined formula. The arrangement is useful for Spanish businesses which undertake collective assignments for a number of foreign firms (establishing joint warehousing or distribution facilities, for instance).

Joint ventures without legal identity are common in Spain because the resulting organisation can trade without a common name, can be set up by word of mouth and, most important, enjoy substantial tax advantages. Information about these matters is available from:

The Spanish Chamber of Commerce
5 Cavendish Square
London W1M 0DP
071-637 9061

Branches

Foreign branches are not regarded as entities independent of parent companies, which are held liable for their branches' debts. They must register with the Spanish Commercial Registry and supply copies of the parent company's incorporation documents, in Spanish and certified by a public notary, and a statement by its board authorising the branch to act. Other formalities include (a) a declaration by a UK based Spanish consul that the parent company actually exists, and (b) the need to obtain a certificate from a Spanish bank saying the branch has sufficient funds to cover its initial expenses. The extent of the parent company's financial interest in any Spanish company and/or other relationships with Spanish firms must be declared. A branch will be taxed as if it were a company. Despite these formalities, branches can be established quickly and with little further bureaucratic control.

Taxation

The basic rate for VAT is 12 per cent, with a range of 6 per cent for essential items to 33 per cent for luxury goods. Corporation tax is 35 per cent. All businesses must obtain a licence from the local authority. This is in fact a tax, payable in lump sums twice yearly. Information (in English) on tax, investment incentives and other fiscal and legal matters can be obtained from:

The Ministry of Economy and Finance
Dirección General de Incentivós
Económicas Regionales
Paseo de la Castellana 147
28046 Madrid
010 34 1 5710271

Local contacts

1. Spanish Chambers of Commerce. These are well established in Spain, and a useful source of information to local businesses. The addresses of the major Chambers are as follows:

   Barcelona
   Ample 11
   010 34 3 3023366

   Madrid
   Plaza de la Independencia 1
   010 34 1 2321011

   Bilbao
   Rodriquez Arias 6
   010 34 4 4238546

2. British Chambers of Commerce in Spain

   Madrid
   Marques de Valdeiglasias 3
   E–28004 Madrid 4
   010 34 1 5219622

Barcelona
Paseo de Gracia II
08007 Barcelona
010 34 3 3173120

Bilbao
Alameda de Mazarredo 5
48001 Bilbao
010 34 4 4238605

Valencia
Pl. Rodrigo Botet 6
46002 Valencia
010 34 6 3512284

The Canaries
Edificio Cataluna 3, Piso
Calle Luis Moroto 35007
PO Box 2020
Las Palmas
Gran Canaria
010 34 28 262508

3.   **British Diplomatic Posts**
      British Embassy in Spain
      Calle de Fernando el Santo 16
      Madrid 4
      010 34 1 419 0200/1528

4.   **British Consulates-General**

      Barcelona
      Edificio Torre de Barcelona
      Avenida Diagonal
      Apartado de Correos 1211
      Barcelona 36
      010 34 3 3222151

      Bilbao
      Alameda Urquijo 2, 8 planta
      Bilbao 8
      010 34 4 415 7600/7711

Chapter 14

The Smaller EC Markets: Ireland and Denmark

Although lacking the size and depth of larger EC markets, Ireland and Denmark offer many opportunities to British firms. A major advantage is that English is spoken as the first language of most Irish people, and as the second by the majority of Danes. Also, business attitudes, methods and perspectives in Ireland and Denmark are essentially similar to those in the UK.

The Republic of Ireland

The Irish Republic is a small country with a population of around $3^1/_2$ million, of which over 1 million live in Dublin. Nevertheless, Ireland is an important market for UK goods.

Characteristics of the market

Ireland has a younger population than the rest of The European Community: about half the country's residents are under 25. Historical propensities for the population to shift towards the larger Irish cities have intensified in recent years, notably in Dublin, Waterford, Wexford and Cork. This growing urbanisation of the Irish creates fresh opportunities for the supply to that country of city dwellers' consumer goods. The Republic's government boasts that its young labour force is well educated, mobile, internationally orientated and possesses many high technology skills.

Advantages of doing business in the Irish Republic

The majority of Irish citizens speak English as their first language and share many sporting, cultural and other interests with the UK. A great number of Irish residents watch British television, and advertising messages travel easily from Britain to the Republic. Problems occasionally arise in relation

Selling To Europe*

to consumer resistance to British goods following downturns in political relationships between the two countries, but there is little evidence to suggest that these have been significant. A major advantage for UK firms is that British and Irish business laws, methods and systems are essentially the same. Indeed, many companies already operate in both countries. Other reasons for doing business in the Irish Republic include the following:

- Irish consumers are already familiar with UK goods.

- Ease of travel to and within Ireland.

- Ability to communicate instantly with customers either by telephone or face to face.

- The country's 1989–93 National Economic Development Plan commits the country to a low tax policy intended to stimulate economic growth and increase incomes, employment, and hence the demand for imported goods.

- Similarity of Irish and UK debt collecting procedures and the relative ease with which outstanding balances may be collected (trade terms are normally based on end of the month settlement).

- Although Ireland has one of the lower per capita income levels of EC nations, spending on household goods is high, particularly on electrical appliances. And the market for consumer goods overall is expanding rapidly.

Agents

A single agent is usually sufficient to cover the entire Republic, which has no special laws on agency. Contracts signed in Ireland are governed by normal commercial law. This is essentially similar to the commercial law of Britain. A contract signed in the UK will be deemed subject to UK contract law.

Advertising

Newspapers attract about a third of all the Republic's advertising expenditures. Radio is important (state as well as private radio stations carry commercials), as are outdoor advertising and magazines. There are few legal controls over advertising, although there are codes of practice similar to those currently operating in the UK. Details of these codes are available from:

Advertising Standards Authority for Ireland
IPC House
35/39 Shelbourne Road
Dublin 4
Republic of Ireland
010 353 1 608766

For names and addresses of possible local agents contact:

Institute of Advertising Practitioners in Ireland
35 Upper Fitzwilliam Street
Dublin 2
Republic of Ireland
010 353 1 765991

Association of Advertisers in Ireland
44 Lower Lesson Street
Dublin 2
Republic of Ireland
010 353 1 761016

Direct marketing in Ireland

The Irish direct marketing industry is developing rapidly, and increasingly precise and sophisticated DM analyses of Irish consumers are being produced. For example, there are now databases covering all professionally qualified Irish personnel, active investors in the Republic's quoted companies, Irish people who regularly travel abroad, and so on. Each street in the Republic has been classified with respect to household value and type into standard socio-economic groupings. (Details of this research are published periodically in *Direct Marketing International*, see Chapter 4.) Lists of Irish DM agencies are available from:

The Irish Direct Marketing Association
Connaught House
44 Upper Mount Street
Dublin 2
Republic of Ireland
010 353 1 785798

Irish lists
The publisher of the Irish Republic's Yellow Pages offers for sale numerous

standard and customised lists of Irish firms categorised according to type of business and geographical location. It also provides telemarketing services, copy/design consultancy for promotional literature and facilities for handling mail. For details contact:

Golden Pages Direct Marketing
Waterloo Road
Dublin 4
Republic of Ireland
010 353 1 608488

There are several other major list providers. For details of how to locate them, see Chapter 4.

Transporting goods to Ireland

Direct airfreight services to Dublin operate from numerous UK airports. There are flights to Cork from London, Birmingham, Manchester and Plymouth. Shannon is serviced from Gatwick and Heathrow.

The major ports are at Dublin, Cork, Limerick, Waterford and Wexford (which is increasingly important for Ro-Ro ferry traffic). Additional ferry services operate from Liverpool and Holyhead to Dublin and Dun Laoghaire, from Fishguard and Pembroke to Rosslare, and from Stranraer and Cairnryan to Larne. All these ports support industrial hinterlands. Other important industrial centres are located at Galway, Dundalk, Drogheda and Sligo.

Documentation of consignments to the Republic requires a couple of (straightforward) declarations regarding discounts, quantity rebates where applicable, value of items and packaging charges. These regulations are explained in the DTI booklet *Hints to Exporters: Ireland* which can be purchased from the DTI (see Chapter 2).

Many small towns and industrial estates in Ireland cannot be reached by train, although express rail services link the major cities.

Establishing a permanent presence in Ireland

Foreign firms can set up Irish subsidiaries as companies, as branches, or as partnerships with local residents.

Irish companies

Irish company law is essentially the same as that of the UK, with private and public limited liability companies. Numerous investment incentives apply, details of which are available from the Irish Industrial Development Authority.

Irish Industrial Development Authority
Lansdowne House
Dublin 4
Republic of Ireland
010 353 1 656633

Partnerships

Irish partnership law was determined by the 1890 and 1907 Partnership Acts of the Westminster Parliament, when Ireland was controlled by Britain. These Acts have continued to apply within the Republic. Partnerships (and sole traders) must register their business names with the authorities.

Branches of foreign companies

These must file the incorporation documents and annual accounts of the parent firm with the Irish Registrar of Companies. Branches are assumed to carry the legal identity of the foreign parent.

Joint ventures

There are no formal rules on the formation of joint ventures.

Taxation

Corporation tax is levied on a sliding scale rising to 43 per cent. VAT is 25 per cent standard rate; 10 per cent for trade services. Food and children's clothing are zero rated.

Sources of business information

The Irish office of the accountancy firm Ernst and Young has produced a useful booklet, *Doing Business in the Irish Republic*, which covers the main aspects of Irish business methods. This can be purchased from:

Ernst and Young
Stephen Court
18–21 St Stephens Green
Dublin 2
Republic of Ireland
010 353 1 760151

For detailed advice and information contact the Irish Chamber of Commerce or the Commercial Section of the Irish Embassy.

Irish Chamber of Commerce
7 Clare Street
Dublin 2
Republic of Ireland
010 353 1 686633

Embassy of the Irish Republic
14 Three Kings Yard
Davies Street
London W1Y 2EH
071-629 8200

Denmark

Denmark is the gateway to Scandinavia, so a permanent presence in the country provides a useful springboard for through trade to Norway and Sweden as well as the northern regions of the EC. The country has a substantial population (5 million) of high income consumers, some of whom are among the most affluent in the world. Denmark has long trading associations with the United Kingdom, and British goods and business methods are accepted and widely known. Once, Britain was Denmark's primary trading partner. Today, however, Denmark takes most of its imports from Sweden and Germany, with Britain in third place.

The country comprises that part of the Jutland peninsula which does not belong to Germany, plus about 500 islands between the Danish mainland and the south of Sweden. Two of the islands, Funen and Zealand, are more important economically than the rest. The capital, Copenhagen (population 1.4 million) is sited on Zealand. It is the country's commercial centre, has a freeport, and is the hub of Denmark's rail, air and shipping systems.

Other important industrial centres are the Jutland harbour town of Aarhus (population 200,000) which has important engineering, brewing and foodstuffs processing industries; Odense in Funen (population 140,000) which is another port with engineering, shipbuilding, textile, food and electrical equipment industries; Aalborg (population 115,000); and Esbjerg (population 75,000).

Although Denmark covers Greenland and the Faroe Islands (both of which enjoy home rule), most export possibilities for UK small businesses lie within Denmark itself.

Characteristics of the market

The Danish market has the following characteristics:

(a) Population is heavily concentrated in a few areas, notably around Copenhagen and other Zealand cities.

(b) Although Denmark was for many years an agricultural society, it now has a strong and expanding industrial base. Agriculture itself has been transformed into a highly efficient mechanised industry.

(c) There is minimal government intervention or involvement in industry; this means there are few centralised state owned buying units.

(d) Denmark relies heavily on the import of raw materials. It has hardly any mineral resources.

(e) The Danish mechanical engineering industry has grown rapidly in recent years, especially in the manufacture of diesel engines. This has created numerous opportunities for the supply of precision instruments, machine tools and related products.

(f) Manufacturing capacity in Jutland is increasing at an extremely high rate.

(g) Small firms dominate the economy: more than half the industrial workforce is employed in companies with fewer than 200 people. This creates numerous niche markets for British businesses.

(h) Locally produced items are stylishly designed, robust and generally of high overall quality. Imported goods need to possess equivalent properties in order to compete. Danes are sometimes accused of inordinate nationalism in deliberately selecting locally produced items in preference to imports.

Reasons for doing business in Denmark

Many Danes speak English, and Danish culture and national perspectives are essentially similar to those of the UK. The country produces a range of industrial goods, notably engineering products, cement, bricks and lime, components for motor vessels, textiles, and (increasingly) electrical and electronic equipment. This creates export opportunities for many varieties of capital goods and household industrial equipment. Danish consumers are affluent, and spend their money on quality products. There are demands for furniture and other household goods, and for electrical appliances.

Denmark has fast and efficient transport networks, and Danish marketing and distribution systems are basically the same as those found in the UK.

Advertising

The diversity of Danish industry (and hence of the occupational groups within it), in conjunction with the relatively small scale of each field of operations, means that there are few trade and technical publications in Denmark, because only a few industries or occupations are big enough to make their production financially worthwhile. Consequently, daily newspapers carry a wide range of advertisements, including many business-to-business advertisements only relevant to a particular industry or profession.

Ignoring television, half of all Danish advertising goes on direct marketing. A third is spent on newspapers, and 15 per cent on freesheets and magazines. Television advertising was illegal before 1989, and is only now beginning to have an impact on the Danish advertising scene. There are restrictions on the advertising of certain products, notably alcohol, tobacco and pharmaceuticals, and on sales promotions that include lotteries. Advertisements that target children and/or use child models are strictly controlled. Business associations that could be defined as representing 'economic interest groups' are not allowed to advertise on TV. Details of controls are available from:

Consumer Ombudsman
Bredgade 31
DK-1260 Copenhagen
Denmark
010 45 1 138711

There is also a trade association of Danish advertising agencies:

Danske Reklamebureaurers
Brancheforening
Snaregade 12
DK-1205 Copenhagen K
Denmark
010 45 1 134444

Exhibiting in Denmark

Most Danish trade fairs take place in centres near Copenhagen airport, although there are small trade fair centres in Herning and Fredericia in Jutland. Goods sent to Denmark for inclusion in exhibitions are free of all duties and restrictions, provided they are sent via the Danish Exhibition Centre.

> Danish Exhibition Centre
> Bella Center
> Center Boulevard
> DK-2300 Copenhagen S
> Denmark
> 010 45 1 518811

Agents

The concentration of industry and population into a few areas and the relatively small size of the country mean that it is usually possible to cover all of Denmark using just one agent (although separate agents will be needed for sales to Greenland and/or the Faroe Islands). There is no consolidated agency law in Denmark; each agreement is subject to negotiation between the parties. An agency agreement may be cancelled without notice and the only compensation the agent may claim is an appropriate sum relating to a demonstrable entitlement to continuation of the agreement. The amount of compensation is determined by the courts. But Danish agency law is being revised in line with EC draft Directives that provide for minimum periods of notice, compensation for the agent's loss of 'goodwill', etc (see Chapter 6).

The trade association of Danish import agents (see page 241) produces a standard form of contract for use by its members. This provides for terminal compensation to be payable to an agent on the basis of one to one and a half years' commission averaged over the last five years. You need not agree to such a clause appearing in the agency contract.

Transporting goods to Denmark

Jutland links directly to the main European road and rail systems, most of which converge in Germany north of Hamburg. The distance of Denmark from Britain plus the geographical complexity of its islands mean that airfreight is an attractive option where that country is concerned. The main airports are at Copenhagen and Aarhus. Copenhagen airport is the fifth largest in Europe, and there are 11 other civil airports. Airfreight traffic is expanding rapidly.

There are direct daily flights to Copenhagen from Heathrow, Gatwick, Manchester and Glasgow. Sea and rail services operate via Harwich to the Hook of Holland and thence to Copenhagen with a journey time of about 24 hours. Direct sea links operate between Harwich and Newcastle in the UK and Esbjerg and Copenhagen in Denmark. Roads within Denmark are of high quality, and there is an extensive internal railway system.

Establishing a permanent presence in Denmark

All businesses other than sole traders must register with either the Registrar of Companies or, if they are unlimited liability organisations, the Registrar of Commerce. No licence is required for normal trading purposes, and there is no obligation to join a Chamber of Commerce.

Sole traders do not need authorisation to trade, but may elect to register with the Registrar of Commerce in order to protect a business name.

Setting up a Danish company

Danish joint stock companies are called *Aktieselskab* (AS). They have a minimum of three founding shareholders, of which a majority must be EC citizens or Danish residents. Likewise, at least half of a company's directors must reside in Denmark or be citizens of the EC. Minimum capital requirements apply, and capital must be fully paid up within a year of incorporation. The equivalent of a UK company's Memorandum of Association is necessary, including an objects clause.[1] Permission to change the company's objects must be obtained from the Danish Ministry of Industry, although this is only a formality.

The nearest thing to a Danish private company is the *Anpartsselskber* (ApS) which does not issue share certificates as such, but whose subscribers enjoy limited liability. There is a minimum capital requirement. An ApS can have just a single shareholder and, if it is a small firm, one director.

Directors, managers, auditors or founding shareholders who deliberately or negligently inflict losses on a company are personally liable for the damage they cause. A decision on whether to invoke the laws that enable a company to claim such compensation is taken either by a company general meeting or by shareholders who hold at least 10 per cent of the company's shares.

[1.] A company's objects clause is a statement of the purposes for which it exists. As in the UK, contracts entered into by a Danish company that are not covered by its objects clause are *ultra vires* and hence not legally enforceable.

The Danish government has encouraged (by tax incentives and grants) the relocation of businesses away from the Copenhagen area, particularly towards the Jutland towns of Aarhus and Aalborg, where labour and other inputs are cheaper than in Copenhagen. Investment incentives available to Danish companies include:

- subsidies for hiring employees who have worked less than six months during the last three years;

- grants for technical development and for exporting from Denmark;

- up to 25 per cent of the cost of new buildings in depressed regions, plus a maximum of 20 per cent of machinery costs;

- loans at subsidised rates of interest.

For further information contact:

Danish Ministry of Industry
12 Slotholmsgade
DK-1216 Copenhagen K
Denmark
010 45 1 121197

Companies with more than 35 workers must have employee representatives on their boards of directors. The number of such representatives depends on how many people the firm employs.

Branches

A branch (*filial*) of a foreign company must include its parent company's name and nationality in its trading title and have Danish residents as managers. Notice of establishment of a branch must be sent to the Danish Registrar of Companies prior to the branch commencing business. A copy of the parent company's most recent annual report and accounts must also be filed.

Partnerships

General partnerships (*Interessentskab* [IS]) have unlimited joint and several liability (see page 176) for business debts. Income tax is payable by each partner, and not by the firm as a whole. Denmark has no equivalent to the UK Partnership Act, so a written agreement is essential. Limited companies can be members of an IS, thus effectively creating limited liability for some of its members.

A limited partnership (*Kommanditselskab* [KS]) contains at least one partner (which may be a company) whose liability is limited to the extent of that partner's investment in the business. It must have at least one unlimited liability member. Limited partners take no part in the management of the firm. The name of the business must state that it is a limited partnership.

Limited partnership companies (*Kommanditaktieselskabs*) are limited partnerships in which the capital contributed by limited partners is distributed as shares. It is regarded in Danish law as essentially the same as a joint stock company.

Itinerant selling by foreigners

Non-residents are not allowed to engage in 'itinerant selling' (ie selling door to door), even if they are doing this through a branch or subsidiary of an EC business.

Taxation

Company profits are taxed at 50 per cent. VAT is currently 22 per cent. Additional sales taxes apply to alcoholic drinks, confectionery, certain foodstuffs and home entertainment items. Certain goods are exempt from VAT, principally products relating to sports, education, health services, travel, insurance, real estate and social services.

Useful contacts

There is an organisation of Danish business people interested in advancing Danish–British trade:

The Denmark British Import Union
Borsbygningen
DK–1217 Copenhagen K
Denmark
010 45 1 136349

The same address houses the national Danish Chamber of Commerce and *Danmarks Agentforening*, the association of Danish commercial agents.
Some Danish purchasers of imports operate through:

Association of Purchasing Agents
Danske Indkobschefers Landsforening
Charlottenlundvej 26
2900 Hellerup
Denmark

Copenhagen has its own Chamber of Commerce at the following address:

Copenhagen Chamber of Commerce
DK-1217 Copenhagen K
Denmark
010 45 1 155320

The only Danish bank currently operating in the UK and providing extensive import/export services to companies trading with Denmark is:

Privatbanken Limited
107 Cheapside
London EC2V 6DA
071-726 6000

Chapter 15

The Developing Markets: Portugal and Greece

Portugal and Greece are the less industrially developed members of the European Community, yet both are committed to industrialisation, to expanding their Community trade, and to total involvement with the Single Market. They have much to gain from a prosperous and united Europe.

Portugal

Portugal has a population of 10 million, concentrated along the coast mainly around Lisbon in the south (population 1 million) and Oporto (population 750,000) in the north. Other important industrial centres are Setubal (fish canning, automotive products, metallurgy and cement); Coimbra (food products, textiles, chemicals); and Aveiro (wood products, footwear, engines).

The demand for imports in Portugal is varied and fast changing. Currently, there is particular interest in metal working machinery, food processing equipment, textile machinery, and agricultural and materials handling equipment. Portugal is not a rich country, and it has experienced exceptionally high unemployment levels in recent years. Output per employee is lower in Portugal than in any other Community state – especially in agriculture. Nevertheless, the country has substantial reserves of mineral resources, and there is much new investment, some of it stimulated by large government grants (see page 246).

Portugal joined the Community in 1986 and is still in its transitional period, hence there remain a number of exchange and other controls regulating trade with that country. Information about these controls can be obtained from UK banks, the DTI, and from:

The Banco Totta e Açores
68 Cannon Street
London EC4N 6AQ
071-236 1515

Characteristics of the market

A quarter of Portugal's workforce is engaged in agriculture, and its industries are on the whole labour intensive and low technology. Industry is concentrated in the north of the country, particularly around the city of Oporto. The main industries are textiles, paper manufacture, woodwork, ceramics, footwear, engineering and pharmaceuticals.

The Portuguese economy is bound to improve in consequence of its involvement with the Single Market and, as it does, so too will opportunities for the export to Portugal of manufacturing equipment (including agricultural equipment) and consumer goods. There are heavy demands for the computing, telecommunications and information technology hardware necessary to update business systems, especially in the financial services field.

Delays in the settlement of invoices can be longer in Portugal than in most other EC states. The standard payment period is 90 days. Credit is important in Portugal and suppliers compete fiercely by offering attractive credit terms.

Letters of credit and bills of exchange (see Chapter 8) are still widely used in Portugal so Portuguese customers are less likely to feel insulted by a demand for this means of payment than customers in certain other EC states.

Advertising

Development of the Portuguese economy plus the country's accession to the European Community has led to an explosion in the nation's advertising industry, although most of the main advertising agencies are subsidiaries of foreign firms. Television is the most important advertising medium. There are few restrictions on Portuguese advertising except for tobacco, alcohol and pharmaceuticals. Details are available from:

The Portuguese Association of Advertising Agencies
Rua Rodrigo da Fonseca 20–4
4 DTO
1000 Lisbon
Portugal
010 351 19 656518

In the past the Portuguese have lacked confidence in mail order selling, but this is changing. Unsolicited delivery of goods to Portuguese customers is illegal.

Agents

Most exporters use a single agent for the entire country. No special agency laws apply. Agency agreements follow the normal law of contract. It is a trade custom, however, that agents be given six months' notice of intention to terminate the contract. Most agents are located in Lisbon and Oporto.

Transporting goods to Portugal

Northern Portugal can be accessed via the Atlantic coast road from La Coruna in Spain and through major roads from Madrid and Seville. The road journey from a channel port to Lisbon (1200 miles) takes about four days. Road transport to and within Portugal is not at present as easy as for most other EC states. The same applies to rail services.

Many consignments reach Portugal by sea or air to Lisbon, Oporto or Faro (in the south of the country). Ninety per cent of Portugal's external trade is by sea. There are large seaports at Lisbon and Oporto, and there is a further industrial seaport at Sines.

Establishing a permanent presence in Portugal

All new businesses must register with the Portuguese Commercial Register and join and contribute financially to an appropriate employers' association. Subsidiaries of foreign firms can be companies, branches, partnerships or limited partnerships.

Portuguese companies

The *Sociedades por Quotas de Responsabilidade Limitada* (SRL) resembles a UK private company, while the *Sociedade Anómina de Responsabilidade Limitada* (SARL) is roughly equivalent to the British PLC. Minimum capital requirements apply, and at least two founding shareholders are needed. The capital of a limited company is divided into quotas (which need not be of the same amount) and each member may apply only for one quota. Transfer of a quota or part of a quota must be evidenced by deed. Companies have to file a copy of their Memorandum and Articles of Association with the Portuguese Commercial Registrar. A notable feature of Portuguese company law is that the auditors of a public company are part and parcel of its management system. Portuguese employment protection law is stringent: periodic pay rises and promotion are legally guaranteed and it is extremely difficult to dismiss workers. There is no national retirement age and an employee must be declared medically unfit by a doctor before his or her retirement can be imposed compulsorily.

Partnerships and branches

The basic forms of Portuguese partnership are the general partnership (*Sociedade em nome colectivo*), which has unlimited joint and several liability, and the limited partnership (*Sociedade em comandita*) which has to have at least one general partner without limited liability.

A branch of a foreign company is called a *Surcursal*, and must register with the Commercial Registrar and obtain formal permission to use its desired trading title. The parent company must formally declare that the branch may act on its behalf, and is required to deposit with the Registrar copies of its UK Articles of Association and annual accounts.

Investment incentives

The Portuguese government offers a variety of financial and tax based investment incentives that are available to foreigners and local residents alike. These include:

- cash grants of up to one-third of the cost of new industrial plant and equipment for the manufacturing, mining and quarrying industries;

- modernisation grants;

- grants for new job creation (up to 15 per cent of the wage of a newly employed worker);

- interest rate subsidies for projects connected with the tourist industry;

- training subsidies (financed from the European Social Fund) of up to 55 per cent of the cost of training programmes.

As Portugal is a recent entrant to the European Community, its tax, investment and company procedures remain complicated. For details of these matters contact:

Instituto do Investimento Estrangeiro
(Foreign Investment Institute)
Avenida da Liberdade 258
1200 Lisbon
Portugal
010 351 19 14712

This body must also approve joint venture arrangements, although this is nothing more than a formality in normal circumstances.

A useful guide to Portugese company and other procedures is the Touche Ross publication, *Tax and Investment Profile: Portugal*, available from:

Touche Ross International
Hill House
1 Little New Street
London EC4A 3TR
071-353 8011

Taxation

VAT is 17 per cent standard rate, ranging between 8 per cent for necessities and 30 per cent for certain luxury goods. Corporation tax is 36.5 per cent; 25 per cent for subsidiaries of foreign businesses (even less – 15 or 20 per cent – for foreign firms bringing new technologies into Portugal).

Useful contacts

Important Chambers of Commerce are located at the following addresses:

The Portuguese Chamber of Commerce and Industry
  in the United Kingdom
New Bond Street House
1–5 New Bond Street
London W1Y 9PE
071-493 9973

The British-Portuguese Chamber of Commerce
Rua de Estrella 8
P–1200 Lisbon
Portugal
010 351 19 661586

Lisbon Chamber of Commerce
Rua de Santo Antao 88
P–1000 Lisbon
Portugal
010 351 19 327289

Oporto Chamber of Commerce
Palacio da Bolsa
Oporto
Portugal
010 351 29 24497

Greece

Greece, like Portugal, is a relative newcomer to the European Community and as such is being allowed a transitional period in which to abolish trade and exchange controls. Accordingly, you may experience more bureaucratic red tape when doing business in Greece than in most other Community nations. You will probably need the advice of your bank to deal with Greek exchange controls over foreign transactions.

The country covers a geographical area of 130,000 square kilometres, similar in extent to that of England, yet it has a population of less than 10 million. Forty per cent of the population live in Athens or Salonika. About 20 per cent of Greece consists of islands. Over half of all Greek industry is concentrated around Athens (population 3 million), which has steelworks, refineries, shipyards, electrical industries, and textile and chemical plants.

Agriculture is crucial to the Greek economy, employing over a quarter of the labour force and accounting for a fifth of the country's exports. Manufacturing accounts for only about 20 per cent of gross domestic product. Automation of farming is not as developed in Greece as elsewhere in the Community, so numerous opportunities for the sale to Greece of mechanised farm equipment are sure to develop. Otherwise, Greece's major industries include mining, shipbuilding, footwear, cement, metallurgy, petrochemicals and textiles. Industrial activity is concentrated in Athens, Salonika, Patras, Volos and Larissa.

Most of Greece's trade is with Germany and Italy. France is also an important trading partner. Britain provides less than 5 per cent of Greece's imports.

Characteristics of the market

Currently Greece is one of the less prosperous members of the EC, although living standards are improving continuously. At present, therefore, the demand for household furnishings, fashion clothing, white goods, automotive products, and so on, is low compared to most other Community nations. Nevertheless, demand for such items is poised to increase as consumer incomes rise. It is quite acceptable to use English for business correspondence with Greek customers as English is widely spoken as a second language among the Greek business community.

Greece is bordered by Albania, Yugoslavia, Bulgaria and Turkey so there are numerous possibilities for through trade, particularly as these countries liberalise their economic and political regimes.

Advertising

Advertising has not in the past been as important in Greece as in most other

European countries, although this is rapidly changing. Advertising is today one of the country's fastest growing industries, for which there are two trade associations:

The Greek Advertisers' Association
46 Venizelou Avenue
GR–10564 Athens
Greece
010 30 1 9584383

Greek Association of Advertising Agencies
12 Ravine Street
GR–11521 Athens
Greece
010 30 1 7726990

Agents

Agents are usually based in Athens or Salonika. There are commission agents, and distributors who act as principals in import transactions but who then require exclusive dealership contracts (see Chapter 6). Greek business is characterised by a multiplicity of small family firms, so that use of a local distributor is normally essential when selling to the Greek market. Some Greek importers act for foreign firms both as exclusive distributors *and* as commission agents.

Greek commission agents have to be licensed by their local Chambers of Commerce. Applications must be sponsored by three referees, and candidates must demonstrate their financial solvency and a certain minimum level of education and/or experience of agency work. It is possible to insert a clause into the agency contract stating that UK law will apply in the event of disagreement, but if this is not done Greek law will automatically govern the agreement. No mandatory legal rules apply to Greek agency contracts, but custom and practice in that country normally require that the agreement provide for at least six months' notice of intention to terminate the contract and for compensation of one year's average commission earnings to be given to the agent as compensation. If you arbitrarily terminate the agreement for any reason other than expiry of a fixed term contract or the agent's proven breach of contract, compensation will be payable under normal Greek commercial law. Three months' average commission is typically awarded by Greek courts in these cases.

Transporting goods to Greece

There are no direct road links to Greece which do not require leaving EC territory and entering Albania or Bulgaria. Train services (to Athens) pass through Yugoslavia. Also, Greece is a long way from the UK so it is normally cost effective to transport goods by air or sea.

The most important Greek port is located at Piraeus, which has a limited freeport facility. Otherwise there are ports at Athens, Salonika, Patras, Heraklion (Crete), Volos and Kavella, all of which support industrial hinterlands. Direct airfreight services operate from London to Salonika and Athens, and there are transfer air services from Birmingham, Glasgow, Liverpool and Manchester.

All goods must carry on their packaging, in Greek, the name and address of the importer, the general type of contents, and the weight and volume of the goods.

Establishing a permanent presence in Greece

Greek company law and procedures are different from those of most other EC members. For example, a public company can have quota holders rather than shareowners able to transfer shares freely on the open market. Subsidiaries may be companies or branches. In either case the business must be registered with the Prefecture of the district where it is to be located.

Greek companies

The *Anonymous Eteria* (AE) is the Greek version of the public limited company. It requires at least five founding shareholders (who need not be EC nationals or residents), three directors and a minimum share capital that is fully paid up at the time of incorporation. The *Eteria Periorismenis Efthinis* (EPS) roughly corresponds to a UK private company. This has a minimum capital requirement and needs at least two shareholders and one director.

For investment grant purposes the country is divided into incentive zones each offering its own particular set of subsidies. Grants are available to assist the purchase of new machinery and for the introduction of advanced manufacturing technology. For details contact:

Greek Ministry of National Economy
Syntagma Square
GR–19563 Athens
Greece
010 30 1 323931

Currently, foreign investments have to be registered with the Ministry of National Economy. As Greece is a relative newcomer to the EC, and still in its transition period, exchange controls are not due for abolition as quickly as elsewhere, so there could still be problems with repatriating profits from Greek subsidiaries for the next couple of years. Soon, however, the situation will be liberalised to conform to the free trade provisions of the Greek version of the Single European Act.

Partnerships

A Greek general partnership (*Omorythmi Eteria* [OE]) has partners with unlimited joint and several liability. Limited partnerships (*Eterorythmi Eteria* [EE]) are available, although as least one member must have unlimited liability for all the business's debts.

Joint ventures

Joint ventures (*Kinopraxia*) have to be evidenced in writing, with a copy of the agreement being filed with the local tax authorities prior to commencement of operations.

Branches

Branches of foreign companies (*Ipokatastima Xenias Eteria*) can be established by filing with the Ministry of Commerce (a) the Articles of Association and other details of the parent company, (b) the names and addresses of local managers, and (c) a declaration from a UK Chamber of Commerce that the parent company actually exists. The balance sheet and other final accounts of the parent company must be deposited with the Greek Ministry of Commerce each year.

Taxation

Corporation tax is 46 per cent, or 40 per cent for manufacturing and certain other types of business. VAT is 16 per cent standard rate; 6 per cent for basic consumer goods; 36 per cent for luxuries.

Sources of information

An extensive listing of Greek importers and major manufacturers can be found in *The Financial Directory of Greek Companies* published by:

ICAP SA
64 Vas Sofias Avenue
GR–11528 Athens
Greece
010 30 1 7248837

Other useful publications include:

Who's Who in Greek Industry
Compu-Type Ltd
26 Kallirois Street
GR–11743 Athens
Greece

The Directory of Greek Commercial Agents
Association of Greek Commercial Agents
15 Voulis Street
GR–10563 Athens
Greece

Help for UK businesses wishing to sell in Greece is available from:

British Embassy in Greece
1 Ploutarchou Street
GR–10675 Athens
Greece
010 30 1 7236211

The British-Hellenic Chamber of Commerce
25 Vas Sofias Avenue
GR–10674 Athens
010 30 1 7210361/0493

Index

acceptance credits, 153
accepting bank, 162
ACP 90, 96
Active Exporting Scheme, 30
Advertisers Annual, 53–4
advertising:
  Belgian, 195
  Danish, 236
  Italian, 212
advertising, misleading, 59
  Portuguese, 243
  Republic of Ireland, 230
  Spanish, 221
advertising agencies, 51
Advertising Association, 60–61
advertising in Europe, 45
Advertising Standards Authority
  for Ireland, 231
advising bank, 155
after-sales service, 116
AG, German, 190
agency, advertising, 53
agency, research, 32
agency contracts, 115
agency law, 117
  Danish, 237
  Dutch, 206
  German, 186
  Italian, 214
  Spanish, 222
agent:
  distribution, 113
  finding a distribution, 118
  French, 171
  German, 186

Spanish, 221
airfreight, 93
airfreight rates, 96
Airstream Europe, 72
air waybill, 96
Aktiengesellschaft (AG), 190
Aktieselskab, 238
ALEC, 50
Anonymous Eteria, 249
Anpartsselskber, 238
arbitration clauses, 161
Articles 85 and 86 of the Treaty of
  Rome, 135
articulated lorries, 89
Aslib Information Resources
  Centre, 24
asociacións de empresas, 225
assignment of intellectual property
  rights, 132
Association momentanée, 202
Association Nationale du
  Marketing-Recherche, 168
Association of British Chambers of
  Commerce, 30
Association of British Factors, 157
Aufsichtsrat (supervisory board),
  191
avalised bill of exchange, 153
average, in cargo insurance, 161

back to back credits, 161
Banco Totta e Açores, 242
BC-Net, 130
Belgian companies, 197

Belgian Foreign Investment
  Services, 198
Belgian Post Office, 70
Belgium, 194
Belgo-Luxembourg Chamber of
  Commerce, 199
Benn's Media Directory, 55
Besloten Vennootschap, 208
bill of exchange, 152
bill of exchange, clean, 162
bill of lading, 99
  claused, 162
  stale, 163
  transhipment, 163
block exemption, 137
block exemption, franchising, 134
block exemptions, 136
body copy, advertisement, 46
branch, Italian, 216
branch, tax, 123
branches, EC, 123
branches, taxation of in Germany,
  189
branches and joint ventures, in
  France, 177
branding for EC markets, 61
British Airports Authority, 94
British Chamber of Commerce in
  Germany, 184
British Direct Marketing
  Association, 65
British Exporters' Association, 110
British Export Houses
  Association, 110
British Exports (Kompass Ltd), 17
British Institute of Management,
  20
British International Freight
  Association, 82
British List Brokers' Association,
  69
British Rate and Data (*BRAD*), 55
British Standards Institution, 38
British Telecom, 66

British Telecom Translation
  Bureau, 49
broker, French, 174
brokers, 113
budgets, advertising, 55
Business Co-operation Centre
  (BCC), 129
buyer credits, 149
Buyer Credit Scheme, 148

campaign strategy, 53
cargo insurance, 146
Carnets, 76, 105
Cassis de Dijon case, 36
CEN, 37
CENELEC, 37
centre of gravity of a market, 120
Channel Tunnel, 83
Chartered Institute of Marketing,
  20
Chartered Institute of Patent
  Agents, 62
*Choosing and Using Management
  Consultants*, 44
CIF, 146
Civil Aviation Authority, 97
claused transport documents, 155
clean collection, 162
CMR note, 93
co-determination, 192
collecting bank, 162
comfort letters, 138
Comité Européen de
  Normalisation, 37
Comité Européen de
  Normalisation Electro-
  technique, 37
commercial agent, French, 171
Commercial Register, German,
  189
commission agents, Greek, 248
commissionaires, 172
Commission of the European
  Community, 160
commitment fees, 159

companies:
  Danish joint stock, 238
  Dutch, 208
  French, 177
company formation, 124
company law, harmonisation of
  EC, 126
competition, EC laws on, 135
compiled lists, 70
comprehensive ECGD policies,
  147
concerted practice, 137
concessionaires, 172
Confederation of British Industry,
  39
confirmed letter of credit, 155
confirming houses, 110
consensus interest rates, 162
consolidation services, 81
consultants, use of, 41
containers, 102
Contract Airmail Packet Service,
  71
contract manufacturing, 129
contract of joint accounts, 225
contract of sale, 141
Copenhagen Chamber of
  Commerce, 241
copyright, 62
Cornhill Publications Ltd, 107
Corporate Location Europe, 121
Cost and Freight, 146
Cost, Insurance and Freight, 146
costs, distribution, 111
counter credits, 161
country desks, DTI, 21
courier services, 98
credit control, 143
credit insurance, private, 149
Croner's Europe, 23
Cross-Frontier Broadcasting
  Directive, 60
currency accounts, 142
customisation, 45
customs declarations, 105

customs numbers, 18
customs planning, 160

dangerous goods, transport of, 97
Danish import agents, 237
Danish Ministry of Industry, 239
Danske Indkobschefers
  Landsforening, 241
Dartford International Ferry
  Terminal, 91
data freight receipts, 100
DATAR, 175–6
deed of protest, 153
default bonds, 163
deferred payment credit, 162
del credere agent, 113
Delivered Duty Paid, 104
Delivered Duty Paid (DPP) price,
  145
demographic data, EC, 35
demurrage charges, 162
Denmark, 230, 234
Denmark British Import Union,
  240
Denmark, exhibiting in, 237
Department of Transport
  International Road Freight
  Office, 92
department store groups, German,
  184
Deutsche Industrie Normen (DIN)
  standards, 184
Dieppe Port Authority, 170
Directives on advertising, EC, 59
direct mail, 65
direct mail distribution, private, 73
Direct Mail Producers'
  Association, 65
direct marketing, 64
  Dutch, 206
Direct Marketing International,
  65, 69, 231
*Directory of Management
  Consultants in the UK*, 43
Direct Response magazine, 65

distribution agents, 113
distribution channels, 109
distribution systems, Spanish, 221
distributors, 112, 187
  Belgian, 196
  French, 172
  German, 187
  Spanish, 222
documentary collections, 152
documentation, 103
  advice on, 105
dominant positions, abuses of, 136
double taxation, 124
DTI, 17
DTI, research help from, 27
DTI Competition Policy Division, 139
DTI Country Desks, 21
DTI Exports to Europe Branch, 29
DTI Industrial Property and Copyright Division, 63
DTI regional and satellite offices, 28
DTI Service Card, 32
Dun and Bradstreet Ltd, 22

ECGD, 146–8
ECU, 151–2
EDI, 107
EEIGs, 127–8
Electronic Data Interchange (EDI), 107
Ernst and Young, 233
ESOMAR, 35
Eteria Periorismenis Efthinis, 249
Euro information centres, 19
Euromonitor Publications Limited, 69
Euro pallet, 102
Europartnership scheme, 130
European Commission (London office), 40
European companies, 126
European consumers, 25
European Court of Justice, 139

European Direct Marketing Association, 65
European Directory of Management Consultants, 42
European Directory of Marketing Information Services, 69
European Economic Interest Groups, 127
European public sector, researching, 38
Europ Production, 17
Euro Tunnel Ltd, 83
evaluation of the effectiveness of EC advertising, 61
excess, in cargo insurance, 147
excessive taxation, 160
Excluded Sectors Directive, 39
exclusive dealerships, 138
exclusive distribution, 137
exclusive licences, 132
exhibiting in Europe, 73–4
Export Credits Guarantee Department, 147
export houses, 110
Export Initiative, DTI, 41
Export Intelligence Service, 29
Export Market Information Library, 17–18
Export Marketing Research Scheme, 30
Export Network, 32
Export Opportunities Ltd, 32
export pricing, 144
extended reservation of title clauses, 144
Ex Works, 145

factoring, 156
Fairs and Promotions Branch of DTI, 75
fax, 0800, 67
Federation of German Industry, 192
ferry services, 89–91
ferry transport, advantages of, 91

field trips, 26
finance without recourse, 162
Financial Directory of Greek Companies, 250
FOB Airport, 145
Forfaiting, 158
forward exchange, 150
France, 164
    advertising in, 168
    direct marketing to, 169
    transporting goods to, 170
franchises and excesses, 147
franchising, 139
Franco-British Chamber of Commerce, 168, 174
Free Alongside Ship, 146
Free Carrier, 146
Free on Board, 145
freeport, 183
freezones, 183
freight forwarders, 81
Freightliner services, 84
Freight Transport Association, 92
French Association of Advertising Agents, 169
French businesses, 176
French Chamber of Commerce, 168
French Commercial Court, 171
French language, use of, 166
French market, researching, 167

general average, 161
Geprufte Sicherheit marks, 185
German Chamber of Commerce and Industry, 184
German Data Protection Act, 70
German Foreign Trade Information Office, 184
Germany, 179
    advertising in, 188
    corporation tax in, 193
    lists in, 70
    transporting goods to, 183
Gesellschaft Werbeagenturen, 188

GmbH, 190
GmbH & Co. KG, 191
Greece, 247
Greek Advertisers' Association, 249
Greek companies, 249
Greek company law, 249
Greek Ministry of National Economy, 249
Green Cards, 92
groupage, 81
GS logo, 185

Harmonised Commodity Coding System, 18
Heathrow Airport, 94
HERMES, 84
HM Customs and Excise, 19, 105
Hollis Europe, 53
hub and spoke system of the Channel Tunnel, 85
hypermarkets, German, 184

ICA, 161
ICC, 155
IDG, 95
igloos, 95
Incoterms, 145
indemnities, 155
information gathering agencies, 22
inner directed consumers, 26
Institute of Directors, 20
Institute of Freight Forwarders, 82
Institute of Linguists, 49
Institute of Management Consultants, 44
Institute of Packaging, 101
Institute of Patent Agents, 133
Institute of Physical Distribution Management, 101
Institute of Practitioners in Advertising, 53
Institute of Sales Promotions, 78
Institute of Trade Mark Agents, 63
Institute of Translation and

Interpreting, 48–9
insurance, 146
intellectual property, 62
Intercontainer, 84–5
Interessentskab (IS), 239
International 0800, 67
International Chamber of
    Commerce, 156
interpreters, 51
invoice, export, 104
Inward Mission Scheme, 31
Ireland, 230
    direct marketing in, 231
Irish Chamber of Commerce, 234
Irish Direct Marketing
    Association, 231
Irish Industrial Development
    Authority, 233
irrevocable letters of credit, 155
Italy, 211
    British Chamber of Commerce
        in, 213
    product standards in, 212

joint and several liability, 176
Joint ownership ventures, 128

KG auf Aktien, 192
know-how licensing, 132
Kommanditaktieselskab, 240
Kommanditgesellschaft, 191
Kompass directories, 22

Law Society, 118
laws on advertising, 59
LCIA, 161
LCL groupage, 99
letters of credit, 154–6
leverage buyout, 190
licensing, 131
lifestyles, European consumer, 25
liner services, 99
Lines of Credit, ECGD, 149
list broking, 71
list broking, Dutch, 206

lists, Irish, 231
local manufacture, 129
logistics, 109
lorry, using your own for
    European delivery, 92
L'Union des Groupements
    d'Achats Publics, 164
Luxembourg, 199
Luxembourg Chamber of
    Commerce, 201
Luxembourg Ministry of the
    Economy, 202
Lyons, 170

mail despatch services, 71
mailing lists, European, 68
Management Consultancies
    Association, 43, 161
Market Information Enquiry
    Service, 29
market research, 15
Market Research Society, 36, 168
Marketing, 69
Marketing Week, 69
market segmentation, 24
M-Bags, 72
media, choice of, 54
merchants, export, 110
Mezzogiorno, 211, 217
Minor Agreements, 136
Mohr, Nicholas, 91

Naamloze Vennootschap, 208
negative clearance, 138
Negotiated procedures in EC
    public sector tendering, 39
negotiating bank, 162
Netherlands, 203
Netherlands-British Chamber of
    Commerce, 208
Netherlands Ministry of Economic
    Affairs, 209
new approach to technical
    standards, 37

New Products from Britain (NPB)
    service, 78
Normandy, 170
notary public, 153
Notice on Minor Agreements, 137

objects clause, 238
Office of Fair Trading, 140
Official Journal of the EC, 19,
    39–40
open account, 142
open cover, 147
open tendering, 139
opposition procedure, 138
option contracts, 150
outer directed consumers, 26
Overseas Press and Media
    Association, 55
overseas seminars, 75

packaging, 100
packaging for air transport, 97
palletisation, 102
Paper Industries Research
    Association, 101
parcel post, 80
particular average, 161
partnership:
    French, 176
    German, 191
    Portugese, 245
    Spanish, 225
Patent Office, 62
patents, 62
paying bank, 162
payment by cheque, 142
performance bonds, 163
Pergamon Orbit Information Ltd,
    182
piggy-backing, 134
piggyback transport, 83
PIRA, 101
P & O Ferrymasters, 90
Port of Paris Authority, 170
Portugal, 243

Portuguese Association of
    Advertising Agents, 243
Portuguese Commercial Register,
    244
Portuguese companies, 244
Precision Marketing, 69
prejudice morale et commercial,
    172
premium offers, in Germany, 78
Price Waterhouse Ltd, 22
Printflow, 71
Product Data Store, 18
product standards, researching
    national, 36
professional advisers, using, 41
Profile Information, 30–31
protesting unpaid bills, 153
public sector contracts, 38

rail transport, 83
Railfreight Distribution, 84
Randstrad, 203
RD Trainferry, 84
red clause credit, 163
Reed Information Services, 54
remitting bank, 163
reply paid services, 72
research, desk and field, 15
research, syndicated, 36
research agencies, UK based, 33
researchers, local, 33
reservation of title, 143
responder lists, 70
restricted tendering, 39
restrictive agreement, 137
retail audits, European, 34
retail buying consortia, Belgian,
    196
revolving credit, 163
Ricks, D, 47
road haulage, European, 89
Road Haulage Association, 93
road hauliers, 93
Roll-on Roll-off (Ro-Ro) ferries,
    89

Romalpa clause, 143
Royal Mail Guide to Business Efficiency, 37
Royal Mail International, 71
Royal Mail International Sales, 72

SAD, 104
sales literature, drafting EC, 68
sales promotion, 77
sales promotions laws, 78
satellite broadcasts, 59
Schengen agreement, 11
Science Reference Library, 62
seafreight, 98
seafreight charges, 99
segmenting European markets, 24
short form bill of lading, 99
shuttle services, 83
sight (draft) bill of exchange, 152
Single Administrative Document (SAD), 104
sister companies, 127
SITPRO, 105–6
sleeping partners, 176
Small Firms Service, DTI, 42
Sociedad Anonima (SA), 224
Sociedade Anónima de Responsabilidade Limitada (SARL), 244
Sociedad em comandita, 245
Sociedad regular Colectiva (SRC), 225
Società a Responsabilità Limitata, 215
Società per Azioni, 215
Société anonyme (SA), 177, 198
Société à responsabilité limitée (SARL), 201
Société co-opérative, 202
Société en nom collectif, 202
Société en participation, 202
Société privée à responsabilité limitée, 198
sole licence, 132
Spain, 218

direct marketing in, 221
Spanish Chamber of Commerce, 226
Spanish Commercial Registry, 226
Spanish Department of Foreign Transactions, 224
Spanish Ministry of Industry, 224
SPEARHEAD, 27, 31
specific ECGD policies, 147
Speedbird, 98
standard shipping note (SSN), 99
standby credit, 163
Status Report Service, 119
stores promotions, 75
subsidiaries, local EC, 122
subsidiary businesses, 122
superlatives, use of in advertising, 59
supplies contracts, 38
swap body containers, 83
SWIFT, 142
Swiftair, 72

TARIC, 18
Tariff Classification, HM Customs, 19
Technical Help for Exporters, 37
technical specifications, German, 182
technical standards, 36
telemarketing, European, 67
telemarketing agencies, 67
telephone responses from EC customers, 66
tendering procedures, 39
Tenders Electronic Daily, 40
tenor bill, 152
terms of sale, 104
TFPL Publishing, 43
Timber Packaging and Pallet Confederation, 102
total order cycle, 111
Trade Indemnity PLC, 150
trade marks, 62
Tradeway system, 135

transferable credits, 163
translation problems, 47
translation services, 48
transport, 80
transport cost analysis, 82
Transports Internationaux Routiers (TIR), 90
Treaty of Rome, 135–6

Uniform Rules for Collection, 154
unit load devices, 95
usance bill, 152

Vacher's European Companion and Consultants' Register, 43

VAT, 159
Venture Consort project, 130
Vorstand, 191
Voyageur, Représentant, Placier, 173
VRP *multicarte*, 173

warehouses, location of, 120
Willings Press Guide, 54
works contracts, 38

Zweigniederlassung, 190